D1230798

OUTDOOR LIFE

THE ULTIMATE SURVIVAL MANUAL

OUTDOOR LIFE
THE ULTIMATE SURVIVAL MANUAL

Richard Johnson
and the Editors of ***Outdoor Life***
with **Brad Fenson** and **Robert F. James**

weldon**owen**

Contents

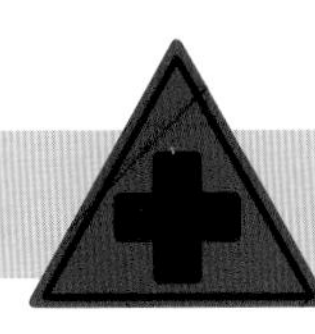

ESSENTIALS

WILDERNESS

DISASTER

URBAN

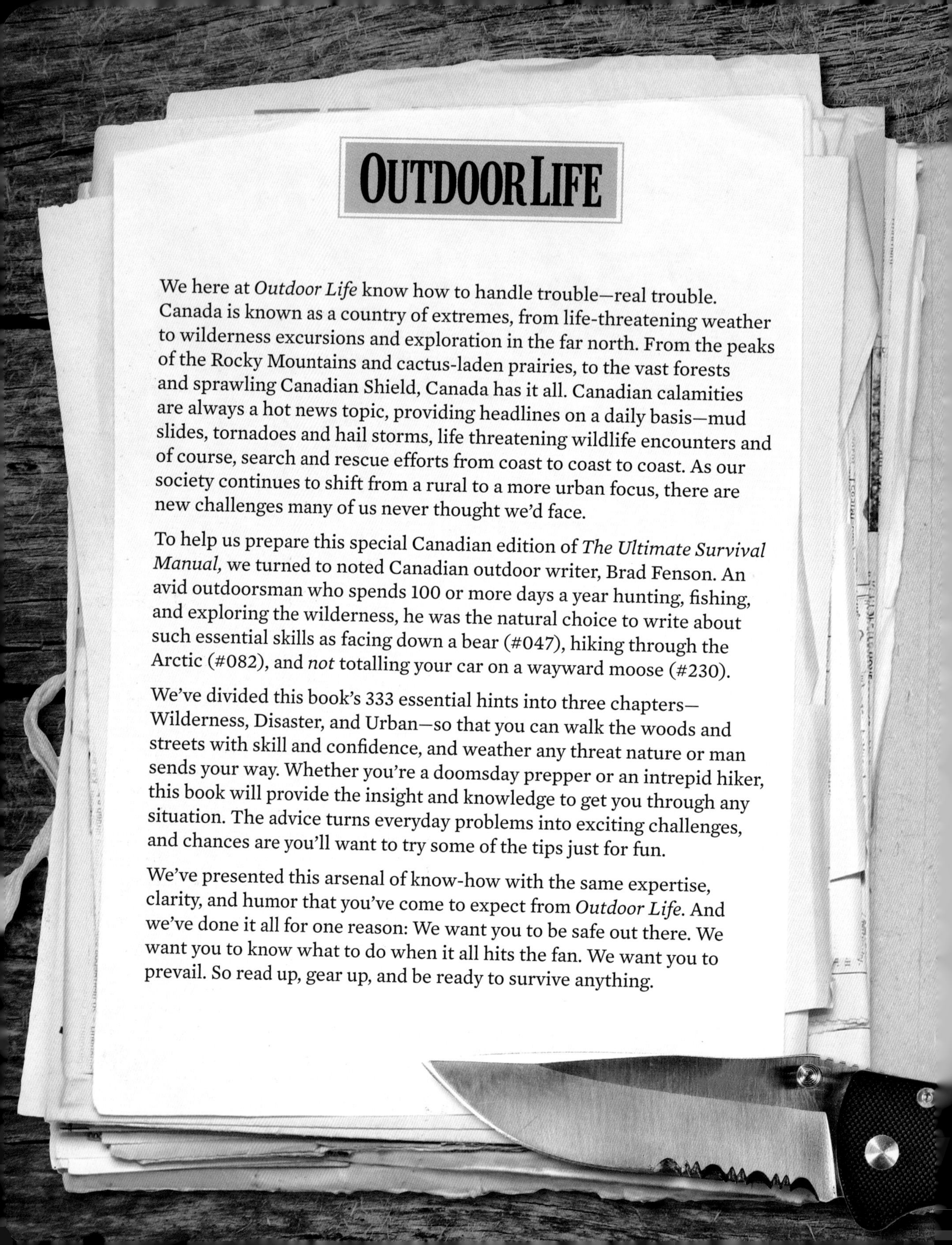
OUTDOOR LIFE

We here at *Outdoor Life* know how to handle trouble—real trouble. Canada is known as a country of extremes, from life-threatening weather to wilderness excursions and exploration in the far north. From the peaks of the Rocky Mountains and cactus-laden prairies, to the vast forests and sprawling Canadian Shield, Canada has it all. Canadian calamities are always a hot news topic, providing headlines on a daily basis—mud slides, tornadoes and hail storms, life threatening wildlife encounters and of course, search and rescue efforts from coast to coast to coast. As our society continues to shift from a rural to a more urban focus, there are new challenges many of us never thought we'd face.

To help us prepare this special Canadian edition of *The Ultimate Survival Manual,* we turned to noted Canadian outdoor writer, Brad Fenson. An avid outdoorsman who spends 100 or more days a year hunting, fishing, and exploring the wilderness, he was the natural choice to write about such essential skills as facing down a bear (#047), hiking through the Arctic (#082), and *not* totalling your car on a wayward moose (#230).

We've divided this book's 333 essential hints into three chapters—Wilderness, Disaster, and Urban—so that you can walk the woods and streets with skill and confidence, and weather any threat nature or man sends your way. Whether you're a doomsday prepper or an intrepid hiker, this book will provide the insight and knowledge to get you through any situation. The advice turns everyday problems into exciting challenges, and chances are you'll want to try some of the tips just for fun.

We've presented this arsenal of know-how with the same expertise, clarity, and humor that you've come to expect from *Outdoor Life*. And we've done it all for one reason: We want you to be safe out there. We want you to know what to do when it all hits the fan. We want you to prevail. So read up, gear up, and be ready to survive anything.

Dear Reader,

Great news! You're reading this book, and that means you must be alive. Which means you're following my **NUMBER ONE RULE** for survival: Stay alive. So far, so good. I can tell you're going to be a good student.

RULE NUMBER TWO Attitude trumps everything else. If your brain's not in the game, the rest of you will suffer for it. Survival is mental—and I'm not talking about your education, I'm talking about your mind-set. As important as it is to know proper survival techniques, if your attitude stinks, you're probably not going to make it. Eliminate the word "quit" from your vocabulary. QUIT is a four-letter word, and around here we don't talk like that (unless a bear is gnawing on us).

RULE NUMBER THREE Don't take avoidable risks. Always look for the safest path, and pace yourself to prevent injuries. Do the things you want to do—but be smart about how you do them.

RULE NUMBER FOUR Live with integrity—and a big part of that is caring about others. Find ways to help people through rough spots. Lift those who need lifting; someday you'll need lifting, too.

RULE NUMBER FIVE Continually work to better your situation, especially if it's dodgy. Even small improvements to comfort or security will improve your spirits. And possibly save your bacon.

MY PHILOSOPHY IN A NUTSHELL To give yourself the best chance for survival, fill your head with accurate information, fill your hands with skill, and fill your life with experience. Let wisdom be your guide and common sense your pattern.

Take care out there,

SURVIVAL STRATEGIES

KNOW WHAT'S HAPPENING Problems arise when you don't pay attention. If you're cognizant of your surroundings, you can respond appropriately.

PRIORITIZE Once you know what kind of fix you're in, decide what your most pressing need is. If your buddy has a bullet in his leg, your most pressing need isn't hunting dinner.

DEVISE A PLAN Now that you know what needs to be done first (and next, and then next), decide how to attack the problem. Weigh your options, then make smart decisions that will give you the desired result.

GO TO WORK The time has come for the rubber to meet the road. As you work on resolving each challenge, continually assess the situation. Decide if what you're doing is working, or if you need to change strategies.

Remember, you're trying to survive—a worthy goal if ever there was one. Give it your all and good luck!

ESSENTIALS

001 CHECKLIST Assemble an At-Home Survival Kit

Outdoor adventurers know not to venture into the wild without the necessary survival gear. But what about when you're at home? Or out running errands? No matter where you are, you should always have certain survival essentials at hand. And while there's no such thing as a universal "bug-out bag" (called a "BOB" for short), you can assemble a variety of kits for every situation.

Start off by putting together the items below to create a fully stocked at-home kit that can meet the needs of you and your family in a disaster scenario. Store it someplace accessible so that you're always at the ready.

- ☐ Nonperishable food (a three-day supply for each person)
- ☐ Small stove with propane or other fuel
- ☐ Kitchen accessories and cooking utensils
- ☐ Can opener
- ☐ Three-day supply of water (3.75 litres per person, per day)
- ☐ Water-purification tablets
- ☐ Bleach (add to water to make a mild disinfectant, or use 16 drops per 3.75 litres to purify water)
- ☐ Portable, battery-powered radio or television and extra batteries
- ☐ Flashlight and extra batteries
- ☐ Battery-operated, hand-cranked, or solar-powered cell-phone charger
- ☐ Tools, such as a wrench for shutting off utilities, a screwdriver, and a hammer
- ☐ First-aid kit and manual
- ☐ Sanitation and hygiene items, such as soap, moist towelettes, toilet paper, and towels
- ☐ Items for infants, such as formula, diapers, bottles, and pacifiers
- ☐ Signal mirror and whistle
- ☐ Extra clothing for each person, including a jacket, coat, long pants, and long-sleeved shirt
- ☐ Hat, mittens, scarf, or other climate-specific clothing for each person
- ☐ Sturdy hiking or athletic shoes and socks
- ☐ Sleeping bag or warm blanket for each person
- ☐ Special-needs items, such as prescription medications, eyeglasses, contact-lens solution, and hearing-aid batteries
- ☐ Photocopies of credit and identification cards
- ☐ Cash and coins in small denominations
- ☐ Plastic bags in various sizes
- ☐ Ground cloth or tarp
- ☐ Powdered, chlorinated lime to treat waste and discourage insects
- ☐ Strike-anywhere matches in a waterproof container

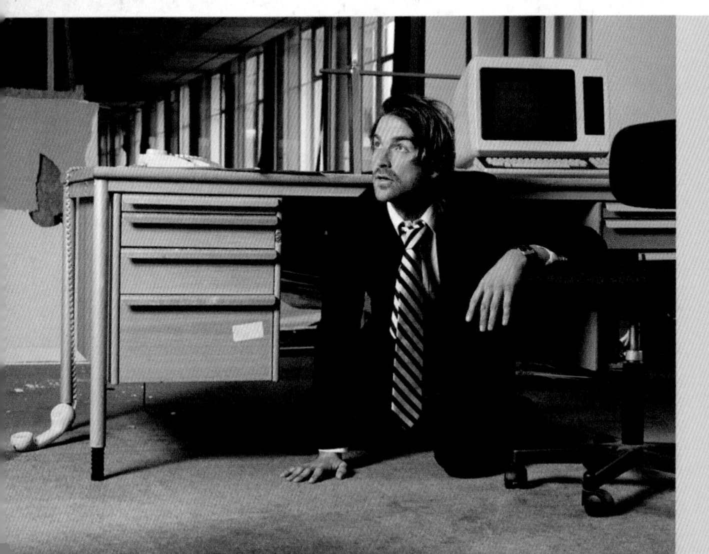

002 Stock an Office BOB

Disaster can strike at any time, including when you're at work. That's why it's smart to keep a BOB in your office or under your desk. It should include a set of rugged clothes (because scaling a wall in a suit is rarely a good idea), athletic shoes and socks (have you ever tried running in heels?), and a few food items and bottles of water. Toss everything in a single grab-and-go tote so you can evacuate efficiently, and then stash it in a drawer and forget about it. You'll be thankful to have it should your work environment ever become truly unpleasant.

003 CHECKLIST
Gear Up with a To-Go BOB

If you have to grab one bag and run because the world is caving in, that bag had better contain what you need for short-term survival. And since most of us evacuate in our cars, it's a good idea to keep this bag in your trunk, along with crucial road-safety items.

- [ ] Energy bars, trail mix, and a couple of separately packaged, ready-to-eat meals
- [ ] Several bottles of water, a filter, and water-purification tablets
- [ ] Tent and sleeping bag
- [ ] Fire striker and basic lighter, plus tinder cubes
- [ ] One entire change of clothing (such as pants, shirt, socks, underwear, gloves, hat, windbreaker, and poncho)
- [ ] Flashlight and extra batteries
- [ ] Knife and spork
- [ ] Military-grade can opener
- [ ] Heavy cord, snare wire, and fishing lures
- [ ] Battery-operated radio
- [ ] Battery-operated, hand-cranked, or solar-powered cell-phone charger
- [ ] First-aid kit and manual
- [ ] Sanitation and hygiene items, such as toilet paper, soap, and a small towel
- [ ] Special needs items, such as medications, eyeglasses, contact-lens solutions, and hearing-aid batteries
- [ ] Signal mirror and whistle
- [ ] Any car-safety items, such as a spare tire, a tire iron, jumper cables, a windshield scraper, and hazard flares, plus any needed winter items (a small collapsible shovel, tire chains, and a bag of kitty litter)

004 CHECKLIST Pack for Surviving in the Wild

It's easy: Before you hit the trail, hit the store—and pick up all the supplies you need to stay safe out there.

- ☐ Lightweight tent, plus extra poles and stakes
- ☐ Ground cloth or tarp
- ☐ Sleeping bag, blanket, and pillow
- ☐ Sleeping pad
- ☐ Water filter
- ☐ Large water jug and a bucket
- ☐ Matchbook, conventional matches, and waterproof matches, plus a striker
- ☐ Food for the duration of your planned trip, plus extra
- ☐ Can opener
- ☐ Small stove with propane or other fuel
- ☐ Cooking utensils
- ☐ Containers for food storage
- ☐ Assorted plastic bags
- ☐ Twist ties
- ☐ Strips of duct tape folded with adhesive sides touching so you can pry them apart and use
- ☐ Printed guide to survival in the wilderness
- ☐ Needle and thread
- ☐ Safety pins
- ☐ String or fishing line and hooks
- ☐ Signal mirror and whistle
- ☐ Flashlight and head lamp with extra batteries
- ☐ Small compass
- ☐ Alcohol swabs and adhesive bandages
- ☐ Small fixed-blade knife
- ☐ Razor knife and cased razor blade

005 CHECKLIST
Make a Kit in a Can

You can pack a surprising amount of crucial gear in a very small container—even one as small as a mint tin—to create a highly portable BOB that fits in your backpack. Check military surplus stores for ideal containers (grenade canisters work nicely), and stock the following items:

- ☐ Small pen and paper
- ☐ First-aid instruction cards
- ☐ Duct tape
- ☐ Razor blades
- ☐ Wire saw
- ☐ Waterproof matches or fire starter
- ☐ Needle and thread
- ☐ Safety pins
- ☐ Water-purification tablets
- ☐ Zip ties
- ☐ Adhesive bandages
- ☐ Disinfectant wipes
- ☐ Micro compass
- ☐ Fishing kit (ten hooks, four split shot, two swivels, 7.6 meters of 9-kg test line)
- ☐ Folded one-page guide to edible plants in your area
- ☐ 0.5 sq m of aluminum foil
- ☐ Signal mirror
- ☐ Bouillon cubes
- ☐ Shoelaces
- ☐ Copper wire
- ☐ AA batteries
- ☐ Alcohol swabs
- ☐ Painkillers

006 CHECKLIST
Build a First-Aid Kit

If you're the type of person who's always asking for a bandage or an aspirin, it's time to get it together. Make a kit that includes the following:

- ☐ Aloe vera gel
- ☐ Scissors
- ☐ Nonadhesive dressing
- ☐ Medical tape
- ☐ Gauze roller bandages
- ☐ Anti-inflammatory drugs
- ☐ Antibacterial ointment
- ☐ Elastic roller bandages
- ☐ Surgical scrub brush
- ☐ Disinfectant towelettes
- ☐ Arm sling
- ☐ Splint material, such as an inflatable splint or a rigid splint made of wood, plastic, or other material
- ☐ Sterile compress
- ☐ Tweezers
- ☐ Selection of adhesive bandages, including butterfly bandages

007 STEP-BY-STEP Stop Bleeding

No one likes to see blood coming out of somebody's body—least of all his or her own. But don't just cover it up: It's pressure that stops the bleeding. Here's how to squeeze off the flow.

STEP ONE Find the source of the bleeding. Got multiple cuts? Then deal with the worst first.

STEP TWO Place a sterile compress directly over the wound and apply firm pressure. Don't be afraid to push hard. If the cut is on an extremity, place pressure on both sides of the limb so that it doesn't bend back and away from the pressure.

STEP THREE If the compress soaks through, don't remove it. Simply add another compress on top of the first and continue with the pressure. Keep stacking bandages until the bleeding has stopped.

STEP FOUR Remove the compresses and flush the wound with water to clean.

008 STEP-BY-STEP Disinfect a Wound

Knowing how to disinfect a wound can be critical. Even small cuts can become infected—especially when you're out in the wilderness, which is not renowned for its sterility. And when your body is fighting off an infection, it's diverting valuable resources away from your overall health, leaving you susceptible to other illnesses and complications.

STEP ONE Stop the bleeding and assess the injury. If the bleeding won't stop, or if the wound is deep and you can tell it'll need stitches, seek medical attention. If you're going to the hospital, don't bother with cleaning a severe wound. Leave it to a pro.

STEP TWO Flush the wound with clean water. There's no need to use hydrogen peroxide, as the burning sensation doesn't mean the wound is getting cleaner—it just plain smarts.

STEP THREE Thoroughly saturate the wound with a triple antibiotic ointment before applying a dressing to keep out dirt and debris.

009 Bandage a Wound

It takes 72 hours for skin to close up and become airtight. For small cuts and scrapes, just keep the area clean. For large cuts, you may need to do a bit more.

DON'T STITCH IT UP We've all seen our action heroes use a needle and thread. Unless you have sterile sutures, a suture needle, and a tool to get the hook through the skin, this option isn't happening. (Likewise, leave sterilizing and closing a wound with a hot knife blade to the stars on the big screen.)

BUTTERFLY IT The best way to close a wound is to apply sterile adhesive strips after disinfecting it. First, line up the edges of the cut. Then, starting in the center of the wound, place an adhesive strip's end on one side of the cut. As you lay the strip across the wound, push the wound's edges together. Apply these bandages in a crisscross pattern down the length of the cut to keep the sides in contact, then dress with a sterile wrap.

BE SUPER In a pinch, superglue can hold your skin closed—it worked for soldiers in the Vietnam War. Just make sure you coat only the outside edges of the cut, not in the cut itself.

010 ASSESS AND RESPOND Deal with Blood Loss

When you're in the outdoors, many objects you encounter will be pointed, jagged, or razor-sharp. Your tender human flesh doesn't stand a chance against a misdirected axe or an errant blade, and that doesn't even begin to take into account accidents involving sharp rocks, or a skin-shredding tumble on a trail. So it's little surprise that blood-loss injuries are the most common afflictions in outdoor situations. Since there's a whole world of possible damage you can do to yourself out there, here are four common categories of bleeding and what to do for each.

OOZE An abrasion or common scrape tears open capillaries, resulting in a slow trickle of blood from the wound. Infection is your biggest threat here.

- Disinfect the wound.
- Use moderate pressure to stop the bleeding.
- Keep the wound moist with aloe vera or antibiotic ointment until it heals.
- Cover it with a semipermeable dressing.
- Change the dressing daily and inspect the wound for infection, which might require professional treatment.

FLOW If dark red blood gushes steadily, a vein has been opened. You've got to clean the wound and stop the flow until you can get the victim to a hospital.

- Elevate the injury above the heart.
- Use tweezers to remove any debris that is lodged in the cut. Disinfect the wound.
- Apply direct pressure to the injury. You can apply pressure with bare hands at first, but then search for something to serve as a direct-pressure pad.
- After the bleeding stops, use tape or cloth strips to secure the dressing over the wound.

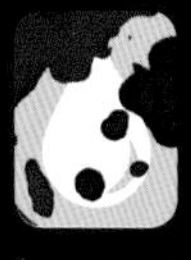

SPURT If bright red blood shoots from the wound, you have arterial bleeding, and it's highly dangerous. Forget disinfecting; just stop the bleeding.

- Elevate the injury above the heart.
- Aggressively apply pressure.
- If a wound on a limb won't stop bleeding, tie a tourniquet above the wound and tighten it until the blood stops flowing. But be warned that the use of a tourniquet can lead to the necessity for amputation. Use one only when you must.
- Call 911 or transport the victim to a medical facility immediately.

INTERNAL If someone has been in a high-speed automobile accident or if a sharp object hit near an organ, he or she may be bleeding on the inside.

- Monitor for hypovolemia (a state in which blood levels are drastically reduced). Shock, pallor, rapid breathing, confusion, and lack of urine are all signs.
- Incline the victim toward the injured side. This constrains the blood flow to the damaged area, and keeps the good side up and running.
- Stabilize the victim, treat for shock, and call 911 or transport the victim to a medical facility immediately.

011 STEP-BY-STEP Immobilize an Arm Injury

Boy, it sure is useful to have two working arms. But if you've injured one (with a fracture, a severe sprain, or an especially gnarly cut), you'll need to immobilize it for a while. Fashioning a sling is pretty straightforward, but it's a core bit of knowledge to have at your disposal; in particular, use this method if you're out in the wild and away from medical care.

STEP ONE Start with a square cloth approximately 1 m by 1 m. Lay the cloth out flat, then fold it once diagonally to make a triangle.

STEP TWO Slip the injured arm into the fold, and bring both ends up around the neck, slanting the forearm up slightly.

STEP THREE Tie the corners in a knot. Gravity will naturally pull the forearm back to parallel position.

STEP FOUR Use a belt to immobilize the arm against the body. Wrap it around the chest, above the forearm but away from the problematic zone. Cinch it closed but not too tightly, as circulation is key.

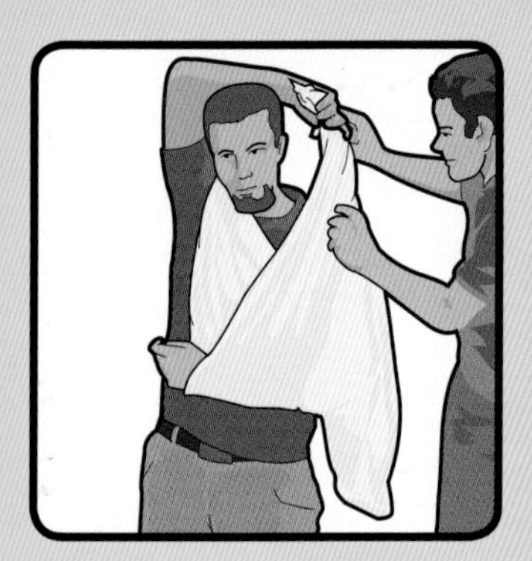

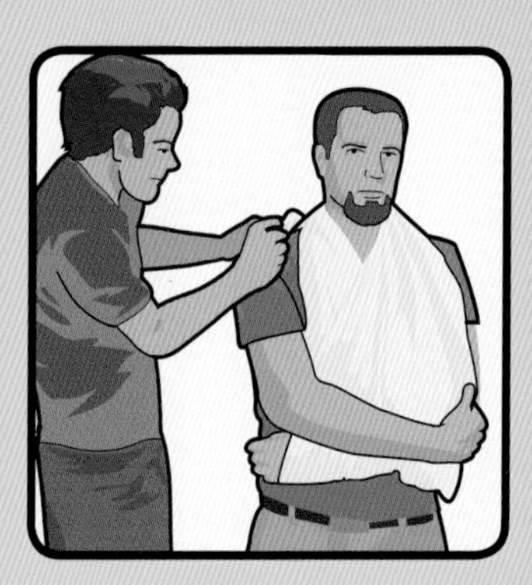

012 Fake a Sling

No sling? No problem. When it comes to immobilizing an arm, just about any kind of cloth or material can work, so look around. For instance, you can place a loop of rope or a belt loosely around the neck, slide the arm inside so that the wrist rests in the loop, knot or cinch the rope or belt in place, and there you go: The arm is unlikely to bounce and incur further injury.

But let's say you're out on a hike without any rope, and—on today of all days—you're sporting pants with an elastic waistband. Try unbuttoning a few buttons in the center of your shirt and putting your hand through the hole, or placing your hand under the strap of your backpack. A pair of pants also makes for an easy tie—just use the crotch of the jeans to support the arm, and knot the legs behind the neck. Sure, you may be the guy in the woods with your pants off, but if your arm's broken, you've got bigger problems to worry about.

013 Set a Bone

If you've ever heard the grim sound of a bone breaking, you know just how dire this situation can be. Getting to a hospital is always the best recourse, but if medical attention isn't readily available and blood isn't circulating to the limb, setting the bone might be the only way to save the arm or leg. Here's how to do it.

ASSESS THE BREAK Many breaks don't need setting, but a few, such as transverse, oblique, or impacted fractures, might. If the bone is protruding from the skin, don't try to set it. Just immobilize it.

CHECK FOR BLOOD FLOW Press on the skin below the fracture site. The skin should turn white and then quickly return to pink. Pale or bluish skin, numbness, tingling, or the lack of a pulse in the limb indicate a loss of circulation, and you'll need to set the bone.

PUT IT IN PLACE To reduce swelling, pain, and damage to tissues caused by lack of circulation, realign the limb into a normal resting position by pulling in opposite directions on both sides of the break.

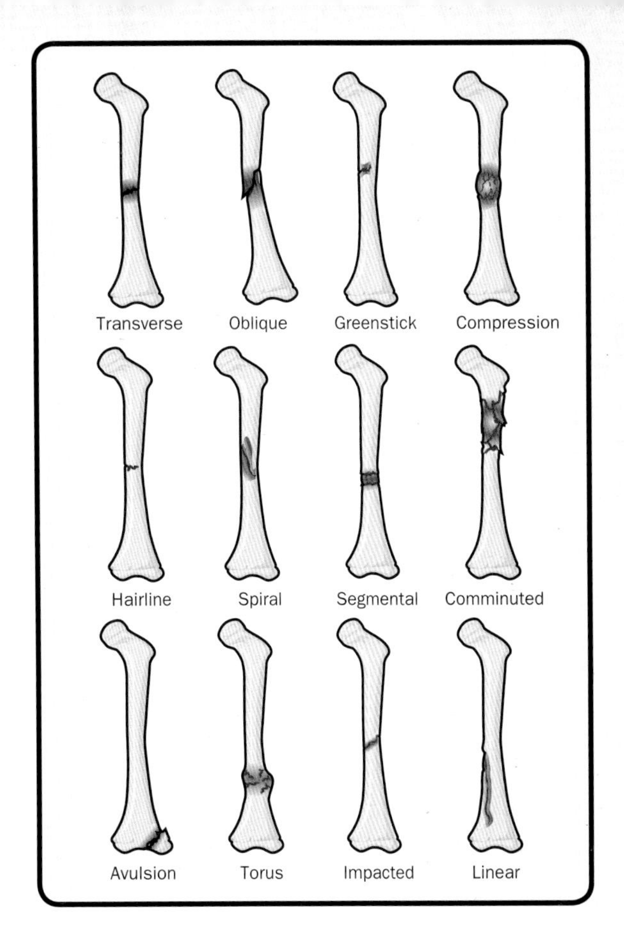

014 STEP-BY-STEP Make a Splint

If someone injures a leg in the wild, immobilization is key—but you still have to walk back to civilization, so staying still isn't an option. So craft a splint with a sleeping pad, cardboard, or other flexible material.

STEP ONE Stop any bleeding with direct pressure.

STEP TWO Check for a pulse below the fracture and look at the skin—if it's pale, circulation may be cut off and you may need to set the bone (see above).

STEP THREE Slide the unfolded splint material beneath the limb, and pad it for comfort and stability.

STEP FOUR Fold the splint around the leg, securing it with elastic, gauze, or other material. The splint should be just tight enough to prevent the bone from shifting, but not so tight that it impedes circulation. If the break involves a joint, secure the splint both above and below it for extra stability.

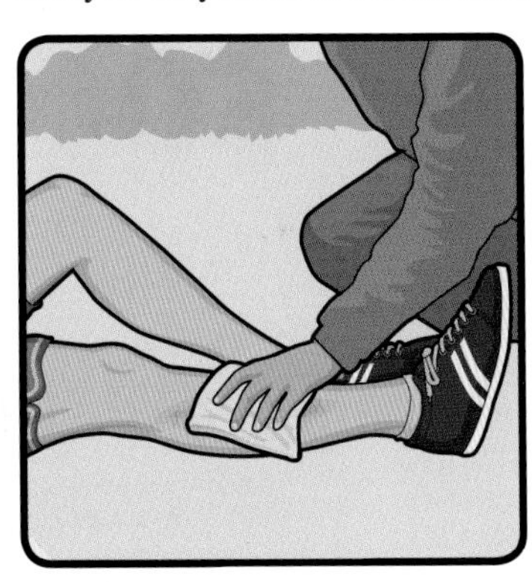

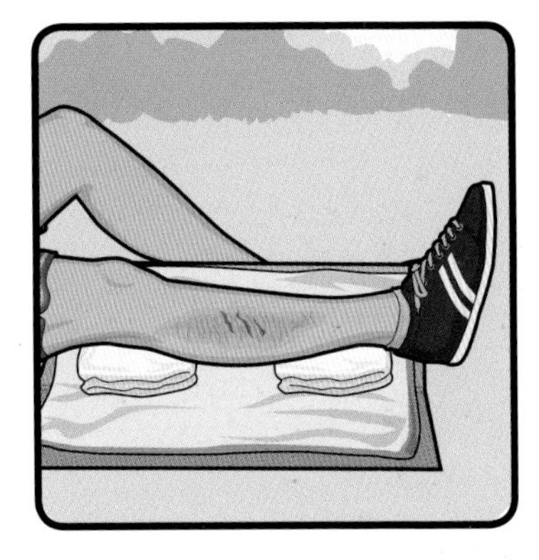

015 STEP-BY-STEP
Save with CPR

It's an absolute nightmare: Someone in your group loses his or her pulse and quits breathing, and it's up to you to get blood flowing to the heart and brain. The mere thought of this scenario should convince you to get trained in cardiopulmonary resuscitation (CPR). But if you're untrained, you can still help. Here's how.

STEP ONE Call 911. This is life or death, and you should get medics on the scene as soon as possible.

STEP TWO Place the heel of your hand in the middle of the victim's chest (just a bit above the bottom of the sternum) and stack your other hand on top of the first.

STEP THREE Begin compressions on the victim's chest, pushing 2 inches (5 cm) down. Keep your elbows locked, and for an adult victim, put your full weight over him or her—the more force, the better.

STEP FOUR Pump at a rate of 100 beats per minute, continuing until help arrives or the victim recovers. If other people are nearby, take turns performing compressions, as the effort will tire you easily.

STEP FIVE If you are certified in CPR, stop after 30 compressions and gently tip back the victim's head to open up the airway.

STEP SIX Again, only if you're certified, pinch the victim's nose. Seal your mouth over his or hers, and give two deep breaths. Keep repeating the entire process until help arrives or the victim recovers.

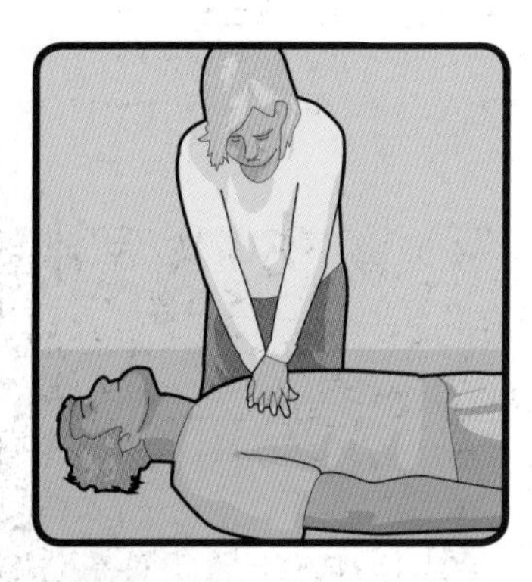

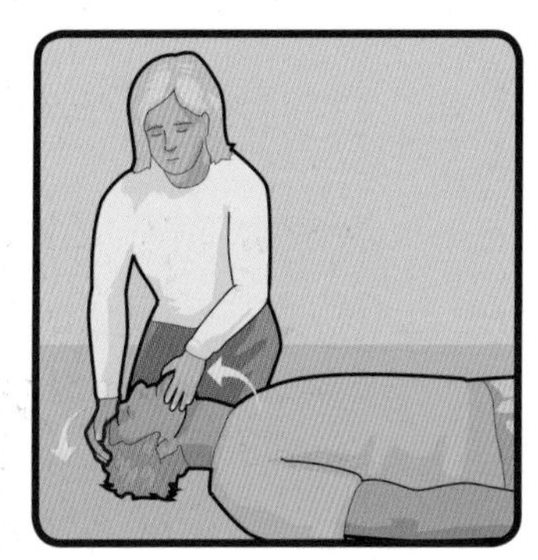

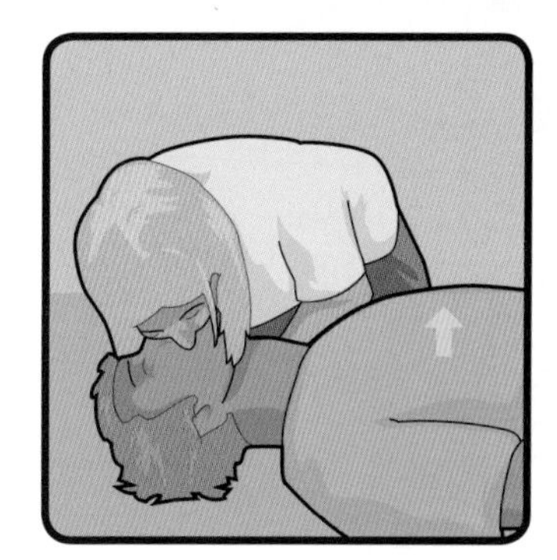

016 STEP-BY-STEP
Perform the Heimlich Maneuver

A choking victim can't tell you what's wrong or how to help him or her. Usually, people with a constricted airway will wrap their hands around their throat, but it's up to you to recognize the situation and act fast. Here's how to help if you're dealing with an adult.

STEP ONE Stand behind the victim and place one arm around the waist. Put your fist below the ribs but above the navel with your thumb against the stomach.

STEP TWO Wrap your other arm around the victim's waist and cover your fist with the palm of this hand.

STEP THREE Press your fist into the abdomen with quick, upward thrusts. Don't press on the rib cage, and try to keep the force in your hands, not your arms.

STEP FOUR Repeat the thrusts until the object is dislodged and the airway is cleared.

If you can't reach around the victim's waist, or if the victim is unconscious, move the person to a supine position on the floor and perform the maneuver while straddling the victim's legs or hips.

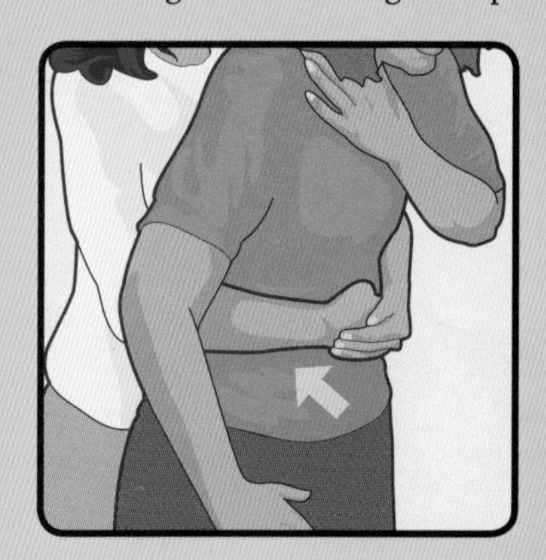

017 Identify and Treat Burns

To comprehend burns and their severity, first you have to understand skin: It's the body's largest organ, and it's made up of three layers of varying thicknesses. The severity of a burn depends on how deep into these layers it penetrates, and the treatment varies for each type of burn.

FIRST DEGREE Also known as superficial burns, these minor burns can be caused by anything from hot liquids to sun exposure. They heal on their own, but it's a good idea to remove any constraining jewelry or clothing and apply a cool compress or aloe vera gel. Anti-inflammatory drugs will hasten healing.

SECOND DEGREE Flame flashes, hot metals, and boiling liquids cause this burn, which usually penetrates the skin's second layer. You'll know if you've got one because blisters will form, and it takes longer than a few days to heal. Usually it's enough to flood the site with cool water and trim away any loose skin (but leave the blisters intact to prevent infection). A daily slather of aloe vera and a nonadhesive dressing are also recommended. The exception? If the burn is larger than 7.5 cm in diameter, or if the burn is on the victim's face, hands, feet, groin, or bottom, it's best to go to an emergency room for care.

THIRD DEGREE This full-thickness burn is very severe. It reaches through all three layers of the skin. In the event of a third-degree burn, treat the victim for shock and transport him or her to a hospital. Skin grafts are always required.

FOURTH DEGREE Another full-thickness burn, the fourth-degree burn damages structures below the skin, such as ligaments and tendons. These burns are bad news: They destroy nerves, so the victim won't feel anything. Amputation and permanent disability are likely, so your best bet is to evacuate the victim to a medical facility immediately.

018 STEP-BY-STEP Treat for Shock

During trauma, the circulatory system diverts the body's blood supply to vital internal organs. This redistribution of oxygen can ultimately lead to shock, which is fatal if not treated properly. Pain and fear both contribute to shock, compounding the danger from the injury.

STEP ONE Recognize the symptoms of shock, such as rapid pulse, gray or pale skin (especially around the lips), and cold, clammy skin on which the sweat doesn't evaporate. Other symptoms, such as gasping for air, nausea, and vomiting, can occur as the condition worsens.

STEP TWO Have the victim lie down, keeping his or her head low. Treat any outward injuries, such as bleeding.

STEP THREE Elevate the victim's feet slightly, carefully avoiding any injuries to the legs.

STEP FOUR Loosen restrictive clothing, such as belts—it'll help the victim breathe more freely.

STEP FIVE Keep the victim warm with blankets or coats.

STEP SIX Keep talking to focus the victim's mind, and reassure him or her that all will be well.

019 Handle Hypothermia

As I'm sure you remember from grade school, the ideal temperature for the human body is 37° C. If a person's temperature drops below 35° C, you've got a case of hypothermia on your hands. Symptoms range from mild chills to coma and even death, depending on how low that body temperature drops.

Treating hypothermia is simple and direct. Start by making sure you're warm and out of danger. If the environment is cold enough to cause hypothermia in the victim, then it's cold enough to put you at risk, too. Next up: Get the victim out of the cold and remove any wet clothing. You'll want to wrap him or her in blankets or coats and, if possible, place warm water bottles or chemical warmers in the armpits, groin, and stomach. A warm, sweet drink will help—just avoid the old adage about drinking warm booze, as alcohol is not your friend right now. Your next duty is to get your friend to a hospital as quickly as possible.

020 STEP-BY-STEP Treat Frostbite

Chances are you enjoy the use of your fingers and toes. If you'd like to keep them, and you frequently find yourself in very cold conditions, you'd better learn how to halt frostbite in its tracks.

STEP ONE Get out of the cold. If you'll be continuing to expose that frozen flesh to freezing temperatures, don't treat the frostbite until you've gotten to safety.

STEP TWO Remove any jewelry in case of swelling.

STEP THREE Put the affected area into a bath of body-temperature water. Refresh the water frequently as it cools to keep the water at a steady temperature.

STEP FOUR If water isn't available, use body heat to treat mild cases of frostbite. But don't position the victim near a heater or an open fire: If there's nerve damage, he or she may not feel tissue begin to burn.

STEP FIVE Dress the injury in sterile bandages, wrapping each affected digit individually.

021 Survive Heat Illnesses

There's heat, and then there's extreme heat—the kind that skyrockets your body temperature to 40° C, making you dizzy and hot to the touch, and even rendering you unconscious. Here are some of the warning signs of heat exhaustion and heatstroke.

HEAT EXHAUSTION The milder of the two heat-caused ailments, heat exhaustion occurs when the body's temperature gets too high. People affected with heat exhaustion experience dizziness, nausea, fatigue, heavy sweating, and clammy skin. The treatment is simple: Have the victim lie down in the shade, elevate his or her feet, and supply plenty of fluids.

HEATSTROKE If someone's body temperature reaches 40° C, that person needs immediate treatment for heatstroke, which can be deadly. Besides an alarming thermometer reading, the easiest signs to identify are hot, dry skin; headache; dizziness; and unconsciousness. To treat, elevate the victim's head and wrap him or her in a wet sheet. I'd also advise going to a hospital, as heatstroke can damage the kidneys, brain, and heart if it goes on for too long.

022 Defeat Dehydration

We humans can go a while without food, but water is a whole different story. Without a constant supply of drinkable H_2O, dehydration sets in quickly, along with low energy, poor judgment, and the eventual loss of the will to survive—not a good thing in my book.

DRINK ALL THE TIME Don't wait until you're thirsty to drink. Put yourself on a schedule and stick to it, and always have purified water on hand.

AVOID ASSUMPTIONS Little-known fact: Your risk of dehydration is just as high in the cold as it is in the heat. Every breath you take releases moisture into the dry air, and when it's cold, you're probably less thirsty, so your instinct to drink water is hampered.

CHECK THE ELEVATION We all know that activity in the heat leads to dehydration if we don't drink enough water. But it's worse at high elevation: The air is arid and thin, so you're breathing hard and sweating more.

REPLACE FLUIDS If you do start experiencing signs of dehydration, drink clear fluids, such as water, clear broths, and electrolyte-containing beverages.

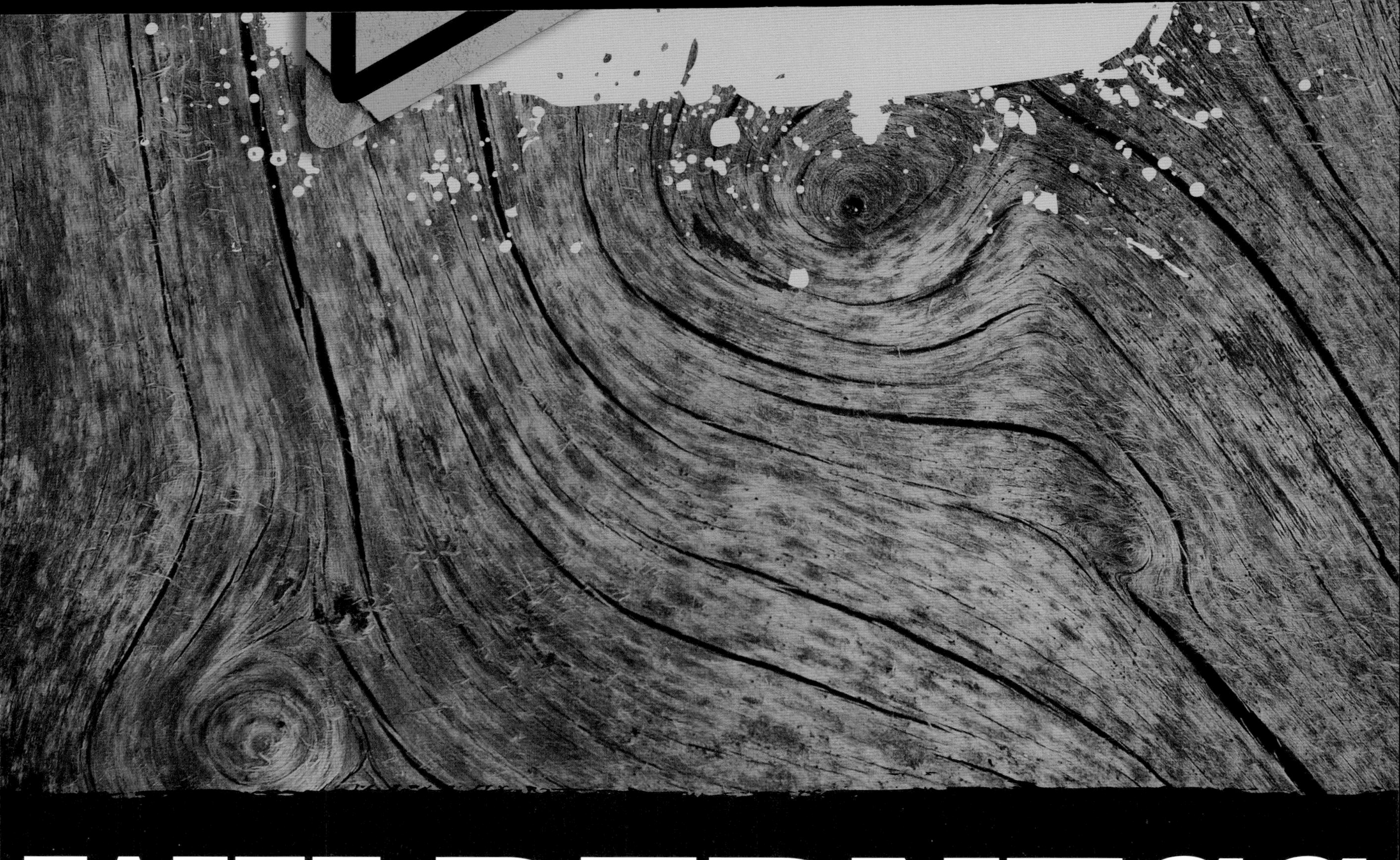

WILDERNESS

023 STEP-BY-STEP Avoid Getting Lost

Hey, we've all strayed off a trail or two, but losing your way when you're far from civilization is one of the foremost ways to wind up in deep trouble. Fortunately, getting lost is easily preventable.

STEP ONE Get a map of the area in which you'll be traveling, and study it before your trip.

STEP TWO Use the map and a compass or GPS while you're there, constantly staying aware of your position.

STEP THREE Keep a map in your mind, too. Imagine what the terrain would look like from a bird's-eye view and visualize your place in that terrain. Think of that little "You Are Here" arrow on the big map at the trailhead, and keep it updated in your mind.

STEP FOUR Take note of prominent topographical features and keep them in view as much as possible.

STEP FIVE Look back frequently and remember the landmarks behind you—especially if you'll be returning in that direction.

STEP SIX When venturing off the trails, use a compass or distant features like mountains or canyons to help you travel in straight lines.

STEP SEVEN Always make sure somebody responsible knows where you're going and when you're supposed to be coming back.

KNOW THE NUMBERS Lost and Found

$1,600 Cost per hour to operate a search-and-rescue helicopter.

100 Percentage of people who, without visual cues, will walk in a circle when lost.

3,000 Number of search-and-rescue operations conducted each year by the Mountain Rescue Association.

10 Percentage of those reported lost in the wilderness who are missing for over 24 hours.

2,000 Number of people who die in the Rocky Mountains each year.

58 Percentage of lost hikers who were hiking solo.

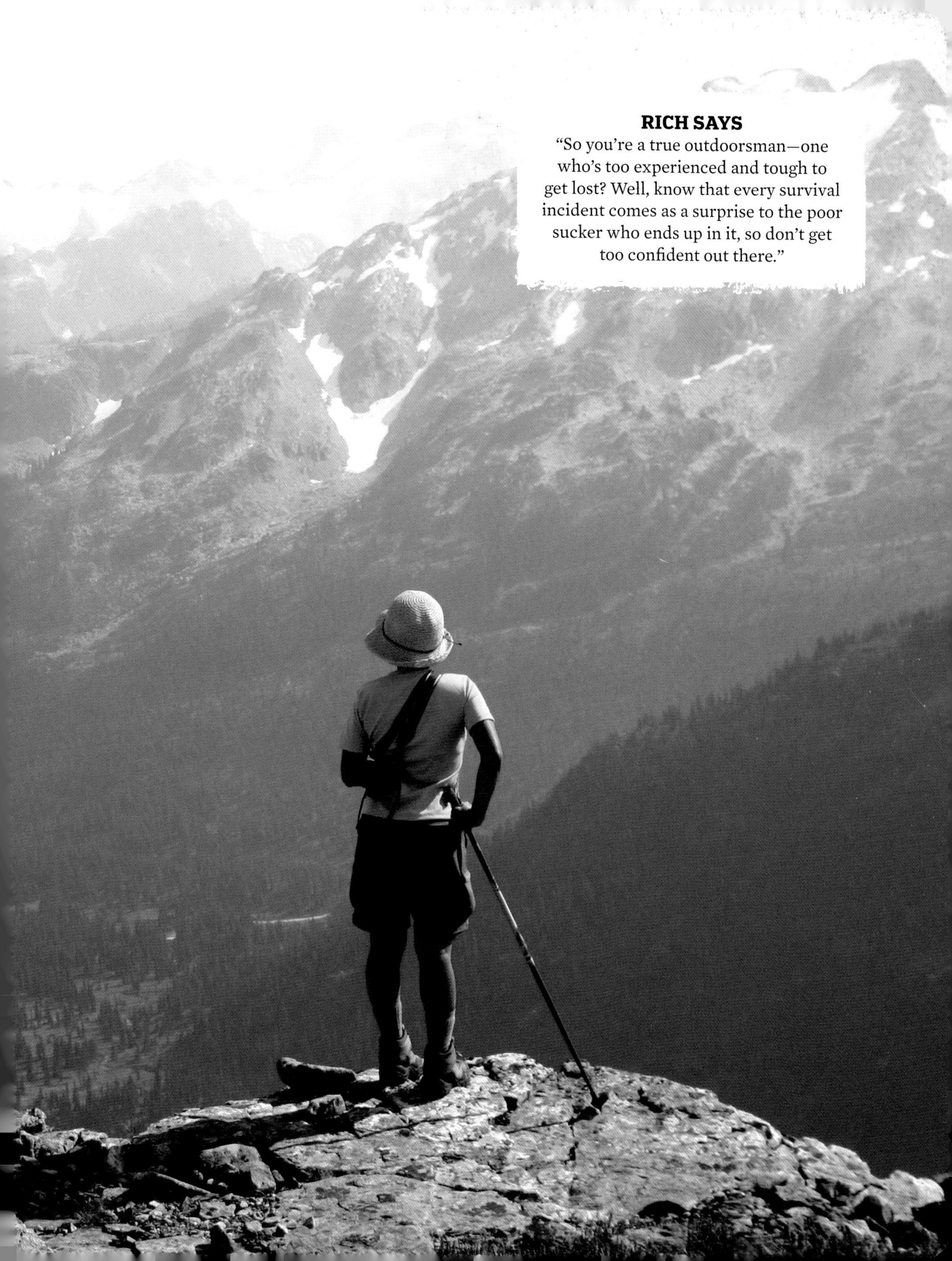

RICH SAYS

"So you're a true outdoorsman—one who's too experienced and tough to get lost? Well, know that every survival incident comes as a surprise to the poor sucker who ends up in it, so don't get too confident out there."

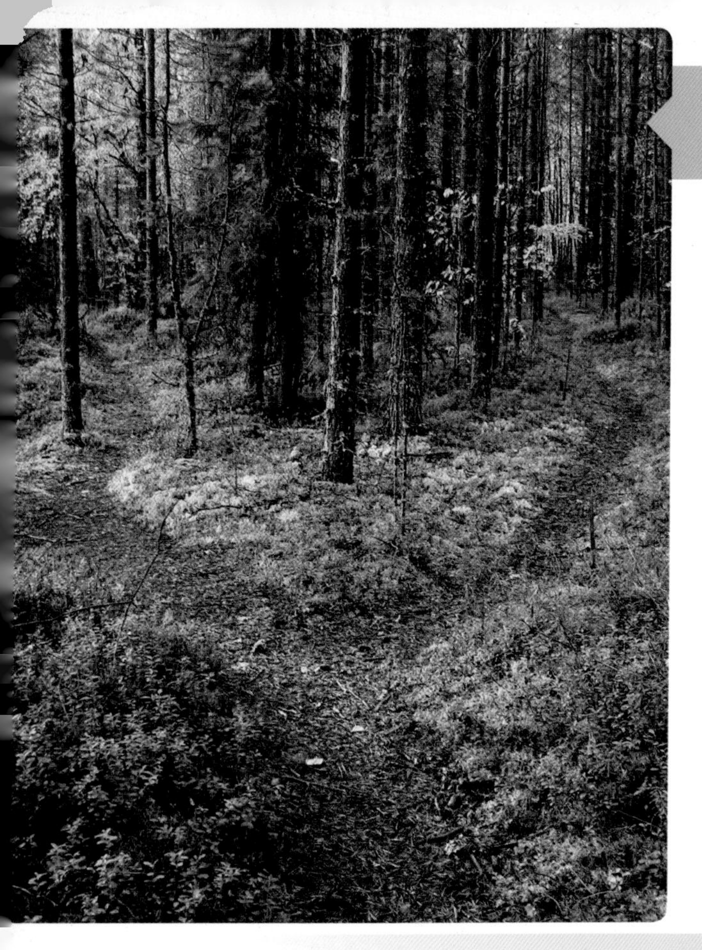

024 CHECKLIST Assess Your Situation

It's decision time: Do you stay or go? If you're stuck at a campsite or next to a failed vehicle, you can wait until help arrives—or you can try hiking back to civilization. Assuming you're healthy, here's your checklist for deciding whether to sit tight or get going.

STAY IF:

- ☐ The campsite or vehicle is intact. It's a ready-made shelter—leave it only as a last resort.
- ☐ Your camp or vehicle has ample food and water.
- ☐ You need to conserve energy because you lack supplies or are injured.
- ☐ The site or vehicle is visible to searchers.

HIKE OUT IF:

- ☐ You're certain nobody is looking for you.
- ☐ You're sure of which way to go and how long it will take to reach help.
- ☐ You've got a well-stocked wilderness survival kit that you can carry. If you don't, you shouldn't be in the wilderness in the first place, should you?

025 Measure Remaining Daylight

Setting up camp in the dark is no picnic. To help you decide whether you're better off continuing to hike or stopping to set up camp, estimate how much time is left until sundown. Hold your hand at arm's length with your fingers positioned horizontally between the horizon and the sun. The width of each finger between the sun and the horizon is roughly equal to 15 minutes before sunset.

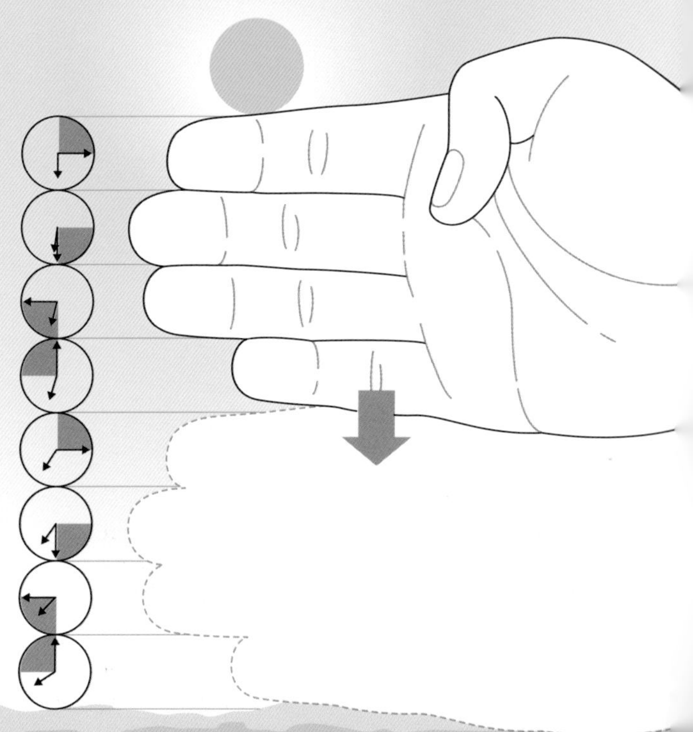

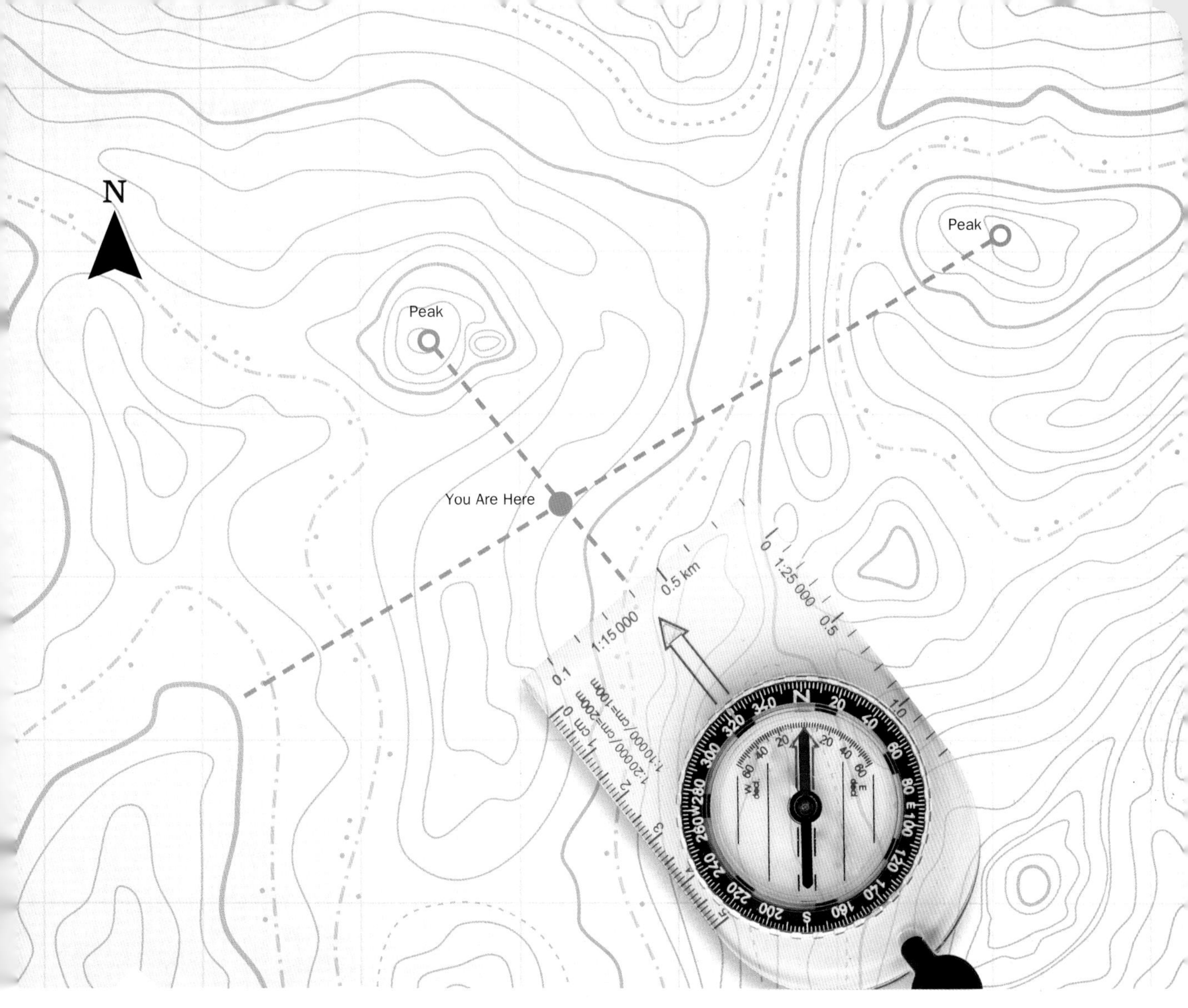

026 Find Yourself on a Map

First things first: To use a map and compass successfully, you have to figure out where you are on that map. Or to put it in outdoor geek terms, you need to triangulate a "fix" on your position.

KNOW WHICH WAY'S UP Maps are printed with north at the top. Using the compass, orient the map so it aligns with magnetic north.

FIND KEY LANDMARKS Once you have the map oriented, look around you for terrain features like a lake, river, or mountain peak. Identify the same features on the map.

PLOT A COURSE Looking up with your compass in hand, point the red arrow of the compass's base plate (this is called "shooting a bearing" in orienteering speak) at the visible terrain feature. If the compass shows a bearing of, say, 320 degrees, draw a line from that feature on the map at an angle of 140 degrees (320 minus 180). You are somewhere on that line, called a line of position (LOP).

LAY A FOUNDATION You don't know where you are on that line until you shoot another bearing, preferably at something between 60 and 120 degrees from the first one. When you draw the second LOP on the map, extend it so it crosses the first one. Where the two LOPs intersect is your "fix." That's where you are. Once you know your position, other decisions, such as which way to walk, become much easier.

027 Scout for Shelter

The fundamental purpose of shelter is to protect your body from the elements. When you're hunting for a prime shelter spot, look for one that does three things: keeps you dry, fends off the wind, and provides shade. Here are some location-scouting tips.

THINK ABOUT TOPOGRAPHY A rock overhang or cave can provide good protection. And you might want to avoid ridges (which tend to be windy) and low-lying land near water (where cold air hovers).

LOOK FOR THE MIDDLE Another good option is a level spot with good drainage on the middle one-third of a hill. These spots tend to have the most comfortable temperature and, if you're lucky, also block the wind.

CONSIDER CRITTERS Avoid dense brush where bugs live, and opt for sites that are off the ground or behind rock formations—they'll protect you from predators.

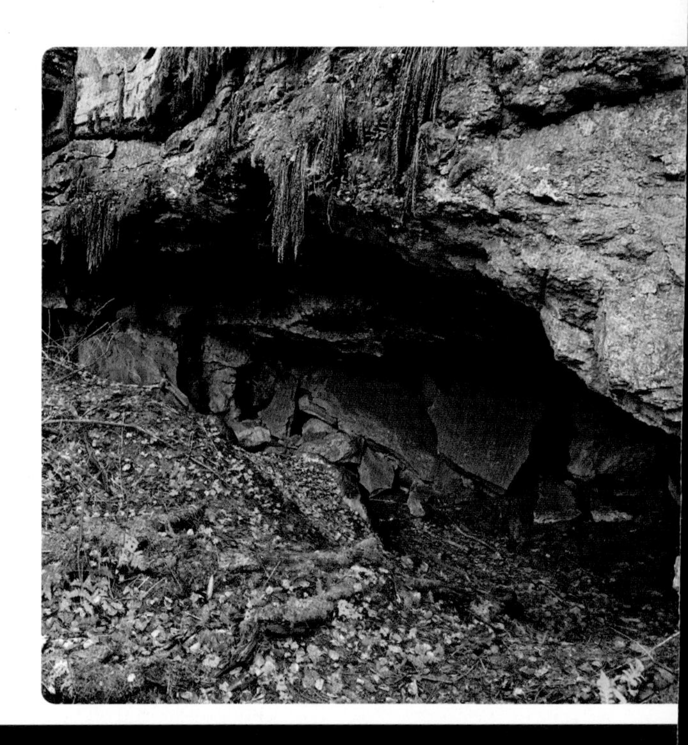

028 STEP-BY-STEP Build a Shelter from Branches and Leaves

If you can't find an enclosure like a cave or an overhang, use brush and branches to build a leafy lean-to.

STEP ONE To make a roof beam, cut a log that's 60 to 90 centimetres longer than your body. Remove its limbs.

STEP TWO Locate a tree with a low branch, and prop one end of the beam in the crotch—ideally, it should be about one and a quarter metres from the ground. If you can't find a low branch, lash the beam between trees that are 2 to 2 and a half metres apart. And if you can't find the right trees, use stumps or boulders or anything else that can serve to support the beam off the ground. Remember, you don't need to be able to stand up inside the shelter, and keeping the beam (and therefore the roof) low to the ground makes the space easier to heat with your body warmth.

STEP THREE Build a roof by leaning smaller limbs at angles against the center beam. These rafters span the space from the beam to the ground. If possible, lash the angled rafters to the beam for greater strength.

STEP FOUR For more insulation, weave lightweight limbs through the rafters. (Weaving them will keep them from sliding down or being blown off by the wind.) Once you've constructed a fairly tight roof, add insulation by piling on bark pieces, leaves, pine needles, or other small debris you find scattered around the area.

STEP FIVE Insulate the floor of the shelter with leaves or other soft matter to make it more comfortable. If you're going to sleep on the ground, you might as well make it as pleasant as possible.

029 Hole Up in a Tree Well

Snow is not necessarily an enemy in a blizzard. It's a great insulator, and if you build a proper snow shelter, it'll keep you safe and warm for a short period.

You can quickly make an effective snow shelter in a tree well (the depression in snow around a tree trunk formed by the protective canopy of branches above it). First, reinforce the natural enclosure by propping up additional branches around the lowest branches. Next, dig out the snow accumulated around the trunk. Finally, lay evergreen boughs on the floor to make a comfortable sleeping place that can be as much as 22° C warmer than the temperature outside.

030 Make a Bed in a Pinch

Too posh to sleep in a garbage bag? Not if you want to stay dry. A large plastic trash bag can serve as a waterproof body covering. For insulation, stuff the bag with leaves, pine needles, and dry grasses.

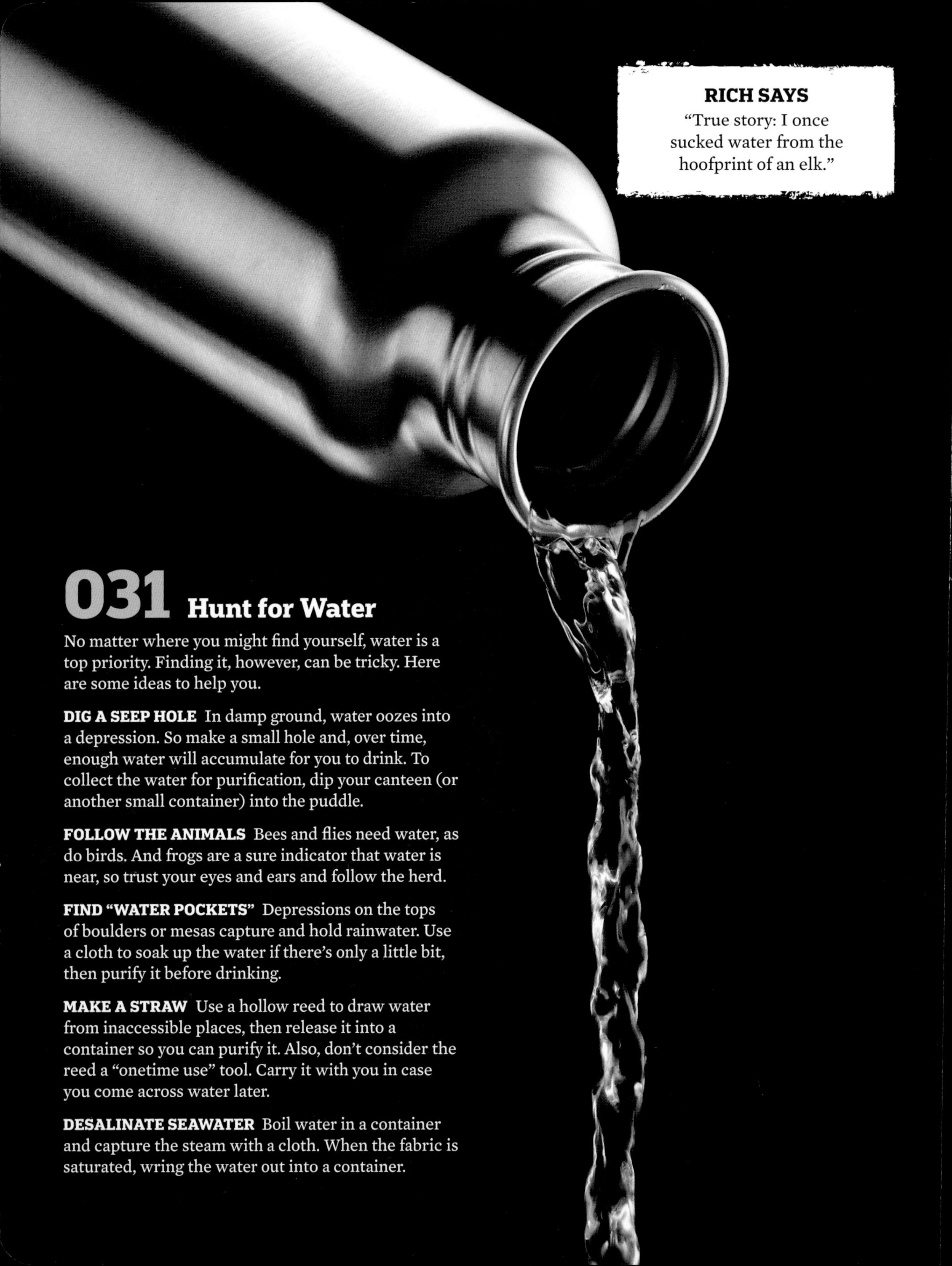

RICH SAYS
"True story: I once sucked water from the hoofprint of an elk."

031 Hunt for Water

No matter where you might find yourself, water is a top priority. Finding it, however, can be tricky. Here are some ideas to help you.

DIG A SEEP HOLE In damp ground, water oozes into a depression. So make a small hole and, over time, enough water will accumulate for you to drink. To collect the water for purification, dip your canteen (or another small container) into the puddle.

FOLLOW THE ANIMALS Bees and flies need water, as do birds. And frogs are a sure indicator that water is near, so trust your eyes and ears and follow the herd.

FIND "WATER POCKETS" Depressions on the tops of boulders or mesas capture and hold rainwater. Use a cloth to soak up the water if there's only a little bit, then purify it before drinking.

MAKE A STRAW Use a hollow reed to draw water from inaccessible places, then release it into a container so you can purify it. Also, don't consider the reed a "onetime use" tool. Carry it with you in case you come across water later.

DESALINATE SEAWATER Boil water in a container and capture the steam with a cloth. When the fabric is saturated, wring the water out into a container.

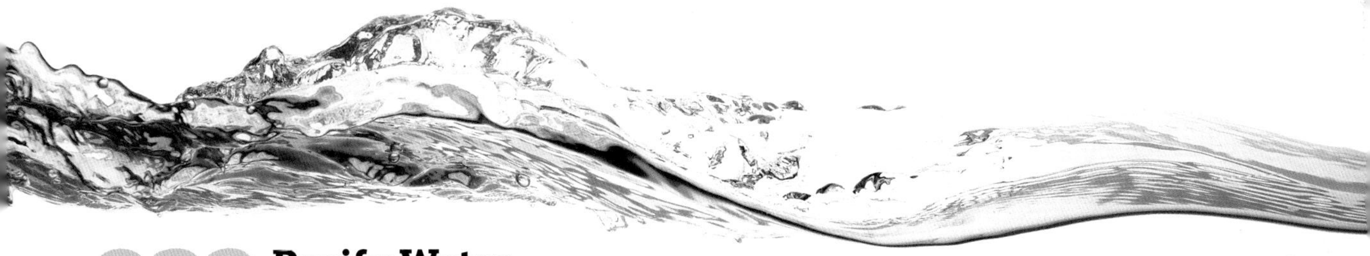

032 Purify Water in the Wild

That fresh mountain stream you see in beer commercials? It's actually chock-full of nasties that can kill you if you're not careful.

There are three steps to making water ready to drink: filtering, boiling, and treating it chemically. Start by filtering it (a coffee filter or a cloth makes a good sieve) to remove both organic and inorganic contaminants. Then kill organic critters (such as viruses and bugs) by boiling and chemically treating your water with water-purification tablets or iodine. Most survival kits include these agents, so use them—otherwise, the bad organic stuff will get you.

When faced with the prospect of drinking contaminated water, weigh the risks of illness against the risks of death from dehydration. You don't want to get sick, but choosing to drink might save your life.

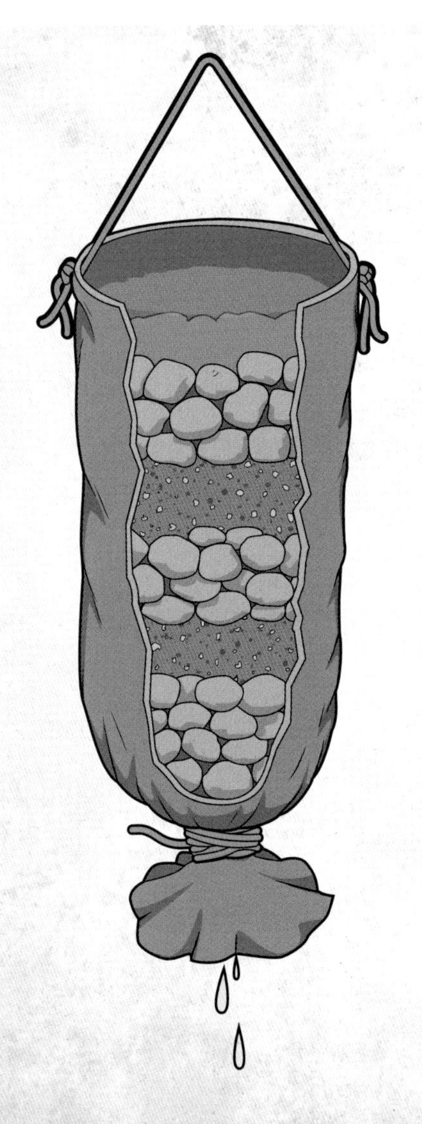

033 Filter Water with Your Pants

Yes, you can use a bag if you have one, but a cut-off pant leg makes a great water filter. Modesty must give way to survival, so don't be shy about making the most of your denim: Rescuers won't care if they find you wandering around in short shorts. To turn a pant leg into a filter, tie off the bottom and add alternating layers of gravel and sand to trap particles of debris. Slowly add water to the top of the filter, allowing it to trickle down through the layers into a catch basin. The water in this basin is ready for the next step in the purification process—boiling.

DO THIS, NOT THAT

Purifying Your Water

DO allow cloudy water to settle before filtering or chemically treating it. If water is cold, wait at least 30 minutes after chemical treatment before drinking.

DON'T drink from a stagnant pool of water where there are dead animals around—the water may have poisoned them. Safe water should also support plant life, so look for greenery. Don't consider "wild" water to be safe for consumption until you've treated it.

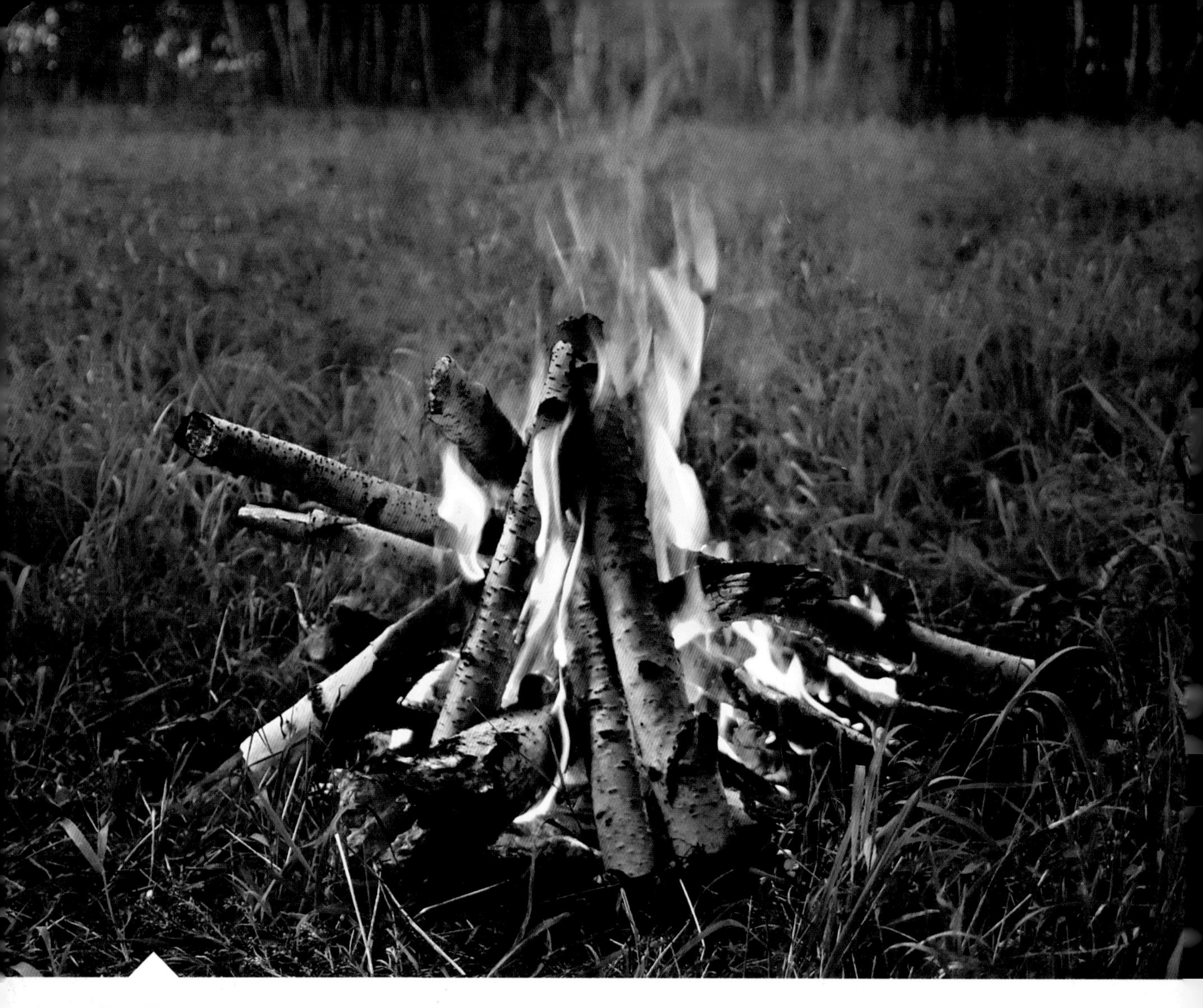

034 STEP-BY-STEP
Learn Fire-Making Basics

Where there's smoke there's fire? Not always, as someone nursing a poorly constructed fire finds out quickly. But if you want a steady blaze to cook on, keep animals away, or just warm up, follow these tips:

STEP ONE Prepare a spot with protection from wind and precipitation on dry ground (or a dry platform built up on moist ground).

STEP TWO You need three types of dry fuel: tinder, kindling, and larger pieces of wood. When you think of tinder, imagine a bird's nest, and bundle dry grasses into a nest shape. Kindling can range from the diameter of a matchstick up to the size of a wood pencil, so use splintered wood or small dry twigs snapped off a tree, or shave pencil-size twigs into "fuzz sticks." For the larger pieces of wood, look for dry branches somewhere between the size of your finger and the size of your forearm. Shattered or split wood is best.

STEP THREE In a fire pit, build a tepee of kindling and place the tinder bundle beneath it. Don't construct it too tightly, as the fire needs space to breathe. Have the larger pieces of wood close so they're handy when the fire is ready.

STEP FOUR Kneel by the tinder and kindling, using your body as a windbreak. Light the tinder bundle and feed kindling into the fire until you have a strong blaze, then start adding the smallest wood first, working gradually up to the larger pieces.

035 Make a Fire Four Ways

Even if you don't have matches or a lighter, you can still spark a blaze with the right tools and techniques. Be sure to have your tinder bundle, kindling, and fuel wood ready before you start.

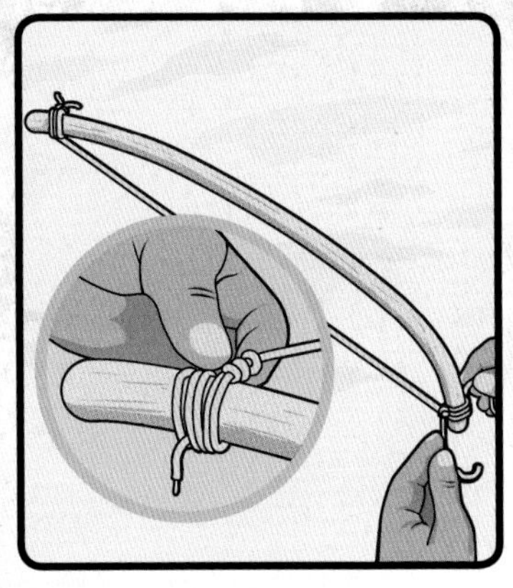

BOW DRILL METHOD Notch a board or a flat piece of bark. To make a bow, stretch a string between the ends of a flexible branch and tie it in place, then use a second stick as a vertical spindle. Place the spindle inside the bow with one end in the notched base. Turn the bow once to loop the string around the spindle, then hold the spindle's other end in place with a stone. Place a leaf under the notch and saw back and forth to create a coal. Then move it to the tinder bundle, and blow gently into flame.

FIRE PLOW No string for a bow? Friction between a board and a plow can do the trick. Carve a central groove in the board and rub a branch rapidly up and down inside this trough. It's more work than a bow drill, and it takes longer, but you can still make a coal.

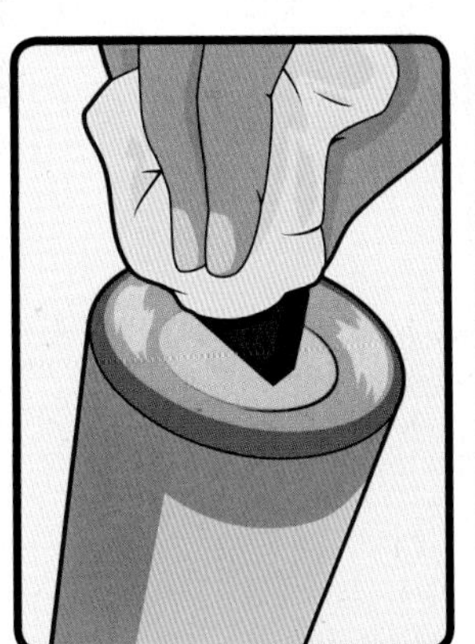

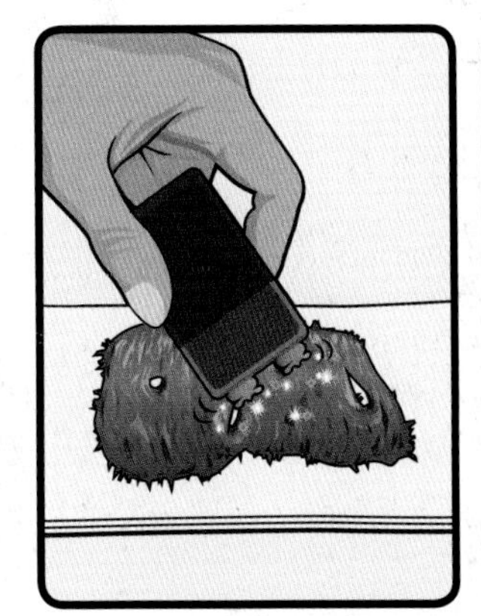

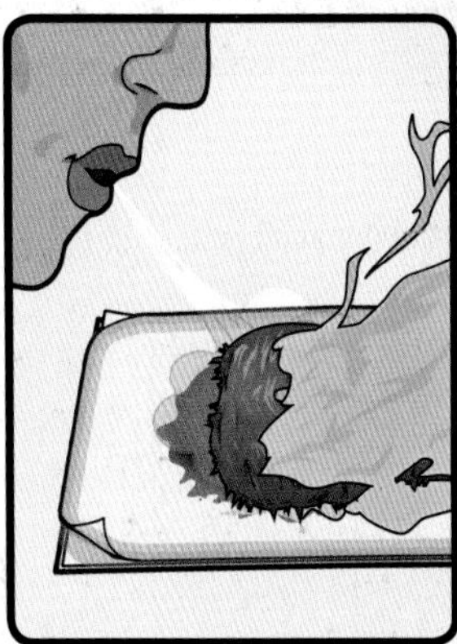

CHOCOLATE AND A SODA CAN Use cheap, waxy chocolate to polish the bottom of a soda can until it gleams like a mirror. Angle it to reflect sunlight onto the tinder bundle (no ordinary flashlight ray will do) and, with luck, the focused light will ignite a flame.

STEEL WOOL AND A BATTERY Rub the terminals of a battery against raw steel wool (not a Brillo pad). Keep at it, and electrical resistance will cause the steel wool to glow red hot. Once it does, move it to your pile of tinder and kindling, and blow the pile into flame.

036 Upgrade Your Shelter

Ducking into a temporary shelter to quickly get out of the elements is one thing, but if you need to live in that ramshackle space for a prolonged period of time, you'll want to make some home improvements.

CALL IN REINFORCEMENTS Use boulders or the upturned root system of downed trees for a basic framework. Gather heavy branches and layer them onto your exterior walls for further protection. If you have a rain poncho or tarp, spread it over the boughs to keep rainwater from pooling inside.

LAY A FOUNDATION Scrape together a deep layer of pine needles or leaves, then add tender boughs to create a soft, insulated floor about 20 centimetres thick. Position logs or stones around the perimeter to hold the floor materials in place. Do the same to a cave floor.

LOOK UP For long stays, you need food storage. You don't want to sleep with that deer carcass, so hang it away from your shelter and out of predators' reach.

LOOK DOWN May as well make yourself at home with a go-to bathroom spot. Go lower in elevation and a healthy distance downwind to dig your latrine, and, if you're sheltering near your water source, make sure to dig at least 30 metres away from it so you don't contaminate your own drinking water.

037 Let Tim Horton Keep You Warm

There are Tim Hortons outlets from coast to coast, and they still serve their piping-hot beverages in paper cups. You can recycle the cups by placing a few centimetres of dryer lint in the bottom of the cup and pouring paraffin wax over the top. Save the recycled cup and lint to use as a fire starter on your next outdoor excursion. Simply light the cup, and the lint and wax will burn like a candle to get your kindling crackling and burning in no time. Carry one in your camping kit, and keep a couple in your trunk for motoring mishaps.

038 Get Noticed by Rescuers

Let's face it: The great outdoors isn't all that great when you're stuck in the wilderness and need assistance—and quick. Ideally, you already have key rescue tools (such as fire-starting equipment and both audible and visible signal devices) at your disposal. If all else fails, use these tactics to hasten your rescue.

SCOUT WISELY Make yourself more visible by positioning yourself in a clearing or at a higher elevation. This placement allows you to be both seen and heard from a greater distance.

EMPLOY YOUR GADGETS Try your cell phone or two-way radio, and turn on your personal locator beacon (PLB). Don't leave your phone on to search for a signal, as the battery will drain quickly. Instead, turn it on at intervals as you travel, and cross your fingers.

SIGNAL WITH FIRE Set up three signal fires (widely recognized as a distress signal) and keep an ignition source handy. At any sign that a rescuer might be nearby, get all the fires going. The smoke will attract attention by day, and the flames will draw it by night.

SHINE A LIGHT Use a signal mirror during daylight hours. If you don't have a mirror handy, check your possessions for any metal object that you can work into a shine.

SPELL IT OUT Use color, contrast, and an SOS symbol on the ground to attract the eyes of searchers.

MAKE A MESS Disturb your surroundings to signal that things aren't right by beating down tall grasses, knocking over saplings, removing tree branches, and pushing rocks around.

SEND UP A FLAG Hoist a colored fabric panel to serve as a wind-driven signal flag.

039 Light Up a Signal Fire

You can use fire as an effective cry for help. Build a signal fire in a location that's open and elevated so that both the smoke and the light are visible.

THINK ABOUT CONTRAST Almost all natural fire fuel (vegetation) produces white smoke. If the weather's cloudy or foggy, no one will notice your white signal. Throw some cooking oil, brake fluid, or any other oily substance into the fire to produce black smoke, which is much more noticeable.

PREVENT RUNAWAY FIRES The middle of dry grasslands on a breezy day is a very bad place to start a big fire. And never let a fire get so big that you can't put it out with what you have on hand.

THIS HAPPENED TO ME!
When Grizzlies Attack

040 Know Your Bears

All bears are scary—but some are scarier than others. Knowing which kind you're dealing with helps you figure out just how much trouble you're in.

GRIZZLY These huge beasts can weigh 360 kilos and stand over 2 metres tall on their hind legs. They have brown fur and a distinctive hump at their shoulders, and their faces feature a dip between forehead and nose, as well as small, rounded ears. The true danger with grizzlies arises if you surprise one, or encounter a mother and cub. Do not run, as that action will likely trigger an attack. Instead, back away slowly. If this huge bear charges you, your best bet is to play dead.

BLACK BEAR Despite their name, black bears' fur ranges from blond to brown to deep black. Their faces are straight from forehead to nose, and their ears are long and pointed. Adult black bears average 135 kilos and stand about 1.5 metres tall when upright. This bear will come into camp and attack humans, but don't run: Face the bear and make yourself appear larger by waving your arms high. Fight for your life with sticks, rocks, or a knife.

041 Live Through a Grizzly Encounter

If a grizzly's mauling you, cuss yourself for getting in that fix. But do it quietly, because you're supposed to be playing dead, and corpses don't talk. The griz probably doesn't want to eat you, but you've interrupted her routine (it's most likely a female protecting cubs). And now you're going to have to pay.

TAKE YOUR MAULING The best thing you can do to avoid injury or death is to shield yourself by going face-down on the ground with your backpack (let's hope you're wearing one) protecting your back. Cover your head and neck with your hands and play dead; it's your best chance of not becoming dead for real.

KEEP QUIET Expect to be batted around, perhaps bitten a few times, and maybe clawed. Stay quiet if you can, which is a tall order when a bear has one of your body parts in her mouth.

WAIT IT OUT When the bear decides you are no longer a threat or an annoyance, she'll probably huff and wander away. Stay still until she's long gone.

042 ASSESS AND RESPOND
Handle Animal Attacks

If an animal decides to make you his dinner (or turn you into pulp just for the fun of it), you have to think—and move—fast. Knowing a bit about the beastly foes that might be lurking out there will help you survive.

Animal Profile

Method of Attack

Your Response

THE MOOSE owns everything—that's his attitude.

- The moose is one of the most dangerous wild animals because it's huge, powerful, and deceptively fast—not to mention willing to attack anyone it deems a trespasser.
- But then, it might just decide to leave you alone—not because it's afraid of you, but because it feels like it. You never can tell.

- A moose is predictably unpredictable, so exercise great caution.
- It typically executes its attacks with front hooves and antlers.
- When it's satisfied that you no longer pose a threat, it'll likely leave you alone.

- If a moose approaches you, back away.
- If it charges, run! Do not stand your ground.
- If possible, get behind a substantial barrier like a tree or boulder. If you're knocked down, scramble to get away and put something between you and that crazy moose.

THE WOLF is a tireless hunter—and the ultimate opportunist.

- Almost every continent has some version of a wolf or a close cousin that can pose a threat to humans.
- While attacks are rare, they do happen, especially in areas where these animals scavenge human leftovers and lose their fear of people.

- The greatest danger of attack is during mating season, which varies depending on hemisphere and environment, and when females are raising their pups.
- Wolves tend to hunt in packs, surrounding their victim and wearing it down by taking turns attacking it from various angles.

- When you're dealing with wolves, your response to a confrontation is key. If you try to run, they'll attack.
- If you stand your ground, face the animals, group together (if you're not alone), and approach them aggressively, the attackers will likely shy away.
- If attacked, fight back with punches and kicks to the snout.

THE MOUNTAIN LION is sneaky and powerful—and thinks you're tasty.

- Mountain lions are among the few predators to stalk humans with the intent to eat us. Isn't that special?
- Lion encounters have grown in frequency with loss of habitat. Many lions, especially juveniles, find themselves on the fringes of development, where backyard hunting provides easy prey.

- They sneak in from above and behind as you walk or bike a trail, then pounce at an opportune moment.
- The cougar will go for your neck or throat and use sweeping attacks with its claws.
- If it takes you down, it will try to drag you into the bushes where it will conceal you for later meals.

- When faced with a cougar, do not run and do not turn your back. Either action will trigger an attack and leave you vulnerable.
- Stand your ground. Make yourself appear larger by extending your arms and waving.
- Arm yourself with a club, rock, or knife, and prepare to fight.

043 Stand Your Ground Against a Lion

It doesn't take much education to figure out that lions are fully capable of eating you as a snack. The best way to avoid turning into this guy's chew toy is to stay away, especially during mating (which can occur at any time during the year), when the males become extremely aggressive, and when a lioness is with her cubs.

OBSERVE CURFEW Lions are nocturnal hunters, so most attacks happen at night. That makes blundering through the bush at midnight a no-no. Avoid camping in lion country, and keep watch throughout the night if you must be in an area where lions roam.

STAND UP FOR YOURSELF Most lion charges aren't serious attacks—but don't bet your life on it. The best survival strategy is to stand your ground. Never turn your back on a lion, and never run, because that will make this ferocious cat chase you. Instead, clap your hands, stand tall, and shout while waving your arms or a jacket. If your shouting happens to take the form of a loud prayer, I won't blame you.

044 Beware Africa's Deadliest Beasts

HIPPOPOTAMUS At 360 kilos and up, and armed with a huge mouth full of sharp teeth, the hippo is so fierce it will even attack boats.

MOSQUITO Don't let their small size fool you: Mosquitoes spread malaria, dengue fever, and other deadly diseases. Plus, they're pretty inescapable.

BLACK MAMBA Slithering atclose to 20 kilometres per hour, the black mamba is faster than a sprinting person—and definitely more venomous than one.

CROCODILE The Nile crocodile kills hundreds of people per year, primarily fishermen and folks gathering water at a river's edge.

CAPE BUFFALO Normally not aggressive, a Cape buffalo will get extremely defensive if calves or nursing mothers are threatened.

045 Live Through a Stampede

A dust cloud in the distance and a growing rumble beneath your feet alert you that you're in the path of a stampeding herd. No matter what kind of animal is stampeding, you're not going to be able to outrun it.

LOOK AROUND Are there any trees or boulders close by? If so, climb one, or at least take cover behind the largest one you see.

DIVE IN No trees? How about water? Many animals won't stampede through water, so that's a wise place for you to take cover. Granted, water brings its own hazards, such as crocodiles, so look before you leap.

ACT LIKE AN OBSTACLE No tree, no boulders, and no water nearby? Your final resort is to make like a log. Lie down, cover the back of your head with your arms, and hope for the best. Animals avoid stepping on things like logs, since a broken leg usually means certain death. That should give you something to think about while you're lying prone with all those hooves pounding around you.

046 Navigate Tall Grass

Tall grass poses two problems: If the grass is taller than your head, you can't see where you're going. In that case, you have to navigate by compass.

The other problem is that living things hide in tall grass: snakes, insects, spiders, and predators. Carry a walking staff and use it to probe the area ahead. Make noise to alert animals of your approach. Wear long sleeves, long pants, high boots (or tuck your pants into your boots), gloves, and a hat to protect against bugs and bites.

047

Avoid a Raging Bison

Bison injure more people every year than bears do. Stay at least 100 metres from a bison, and never startle them. They're unpredictable and have been known to have temper tantrums worse than a spoiled toddler. If they show aggressive behavior—pawing the ground or swinging their heads—walk away slowly and cautiously. If you're charged, run for cover. They are fast and you'll have little time, so stay alert and don't act aggressive. Bison are persistent; you may have to get behind a tree or large rock to dodge them. If you have more stamina than the bison, you can avoid being trampled or horned.

048 Face Down a Black Bear

Not all bears will deliver a cute public service message like Smokey the Bear, and knowing what to do when one wants to make you his lunch could save your life. Black bears are prominent across Canada and account for the majority of bear attacks in our country. Handling one is much different than fending off a grizzly.

Stand your ground and make yourself as big as possible by raising your arms wide above your head. Be as loud and intimidating as you can.

Don't run, as it will draw the bear to chase you. And stay on the ground; black bears are better at climbing trees than humans.

Fight to the bitter end. Playing dead is not a good idea with a black bear. Punch it in the nose or boot it in the groin and inflict pain any way possible.

049

STEP-BY-STEP

Chow Down on a Ground Squirrel

Ground squirrels are abundant throughout most of Canada, with species from the high Arctic to the prairies and mountains, and they are easy to approach and catch. First Nations people consider ground squirrel a delicacy and roast them whole. Cooking them whole keeps them moist and allows you to pick them up without using utensils.

STEP ONE Build a fire so it will burn down leaving a hot bed of coals.

STEP TWO Lay squirrel directly on the coals and turn every couple of minutes.

STEP THREE The hair will burn off and you can snap the head off and pull it down towards the belly in order to remove the innards.

STEP FOUR Pull or scrape skin off the squirrel and chow down on your tasty dinner.

050

STEP-BY-STEP

Dress a Muskrat

Muskrat inhabit the waterways across Canada, and they can be easily snared or trapped.

STEP ONE Take the sharp point of a knife and make a cut around the top of the back feet. Cut up the back of the legs to the vent and around the base of the tail.

STEP TWO Push your fingers in under the skin, where you've made the incision, and work the skin off the flesh. Once loose, you can grab the skin and turn it inside out as you pull it up toward the head and over the front legs of the muskrat.

STEP THREE Clean out the body cavity, cut the meat into portions, and cook or smoke, as you would chicken or rabbit.

051 Navigate Bogs and Muskeg

In the west these soft-bottomed lowlands are referred to as muskeg, where in the east they are often called bogs. Muskeg is a Cree term, meaning low-lying marsh. There is no easy way to travel with a vehicle or walk through muskeg. Dense stands of black spruce and willow make it difficult to navigate a straight path.

NAVIGATE CAREFULLY Muskeg and peat bogs can be over 30 metres deep and walking on the pillowy-soft clouds of moss can be a workout. The peat has the ability to hold tremendous amounts of water, and if you break through the surface it can be a quagmire to get out of. The surface is held together by vegetation and its root systems. Large-soled rubber boots act like snow shoes and give you more surface area to distribute your weight. Tread lightly and test each step before moving forward. Try to pick something in the distance to watch and maintain your direction of travel. Head for higher ground by watching for a ridge or tree tops that extend higher than everything else in the lowlands you're navigating.

AVOID STANDING WATER The water table is always close to the surface in a muskeg, so avoid open water at all costs. The peat and moss around open water is saturated, turning it into a soup that can swallow you up. Muskeg is made of dead plant material like moss, decaying trees, and sedges. The drier it is, the less likely the earth will give way underfoot.

DON'T GET STUCK Muskeg has been known to swallow vehicles and traveling with an ATV is risky. Well-rooted clumps of willow may be the only things to winch to, that is if you're lucky enough to find one close by. If walking, always carry a stick and probe the ground in front of you. Identifying sink holes that will give you a soaker, or worse, swallow you past the knee, can be avoided. If possible, you are always better to travel on muskeg edges and not through the center of these often vast, soggy wetlands.

052 STEP-BY-STEP Build a Swamp Shelter

You're in the swamp. The ground is wet. The air is wet. And the vegetation is bloated with water, which makes it a poor building material. As a result, one of the most challenging things to do is erect a dry shelter.

STEP ONE Find a dry spot. Of course, "dry" is relative, but a slight hill should be less wet than areas of lower elevation. It's also a good idea to learn how to spot and avoid run-offs. These sparsely vegetated, eroded spots are prone to flash floods, so they're not ideal for a shelter, especially when rainfall is likely.

STEP TWO Look for a space that's at least a little longer than your body and twice as wide, ideally with four trees at the corners. If you can't find a place with well-spaced trees, try driving sturdy wooden stakes into the ground. (Bamboo works nicely.) A rare benefit of building a shelter in a swamp is that it's relatively easy to plunge stakes into the soggy ground.

STEP THREE Measure and cut branches to build a frame. You'll need two rails that are longer than your body and long enough to connect to your trees or poles. Use a square lashing to secure each rail to the trees or posts. If you don't have rope, gather vines, which you can usually find in most swamp and jungle areas.

STEP FOUR Once the frame is in place, cut shorter branches to lay across the frame as a platform, and tie them to the rails. When you're done, your swamp shelter should be strong enough to hold your full weight, and keep you off the ground and at least somewhat drier.

STEP FIVE For padding and insulation, top off the platform with large leaves or cut sections of moss. And there you've got it: a fairly comfortable bed that's high above the moisture, not to mention beyond the reach of many animals and insects.

053 Keep Bugs Out of Your Pants

Even one bug bite can be too many—especially when you're in a wet environment, where the infection risk is high and the availability of calamine lotion is low.

To keep bugs from crawling inside your sleeves and pant legs, fold under the cuffs, then tie something around them. You can use spare shoelaces or elastic blousing bands, available at military surplus stores. The Velcro® cuff straps sported by commuter cyclists everywhere are also a good bet; you can find them in bike shops. And as in so many other situations, duct tape will do the trick in a pinch.

054 STEP-BY-STEP Tie a Square Lashing

When you need to build a temporary structure in a hurry, go with a square lashing: It's a quick and an effective way to secure two posts together.

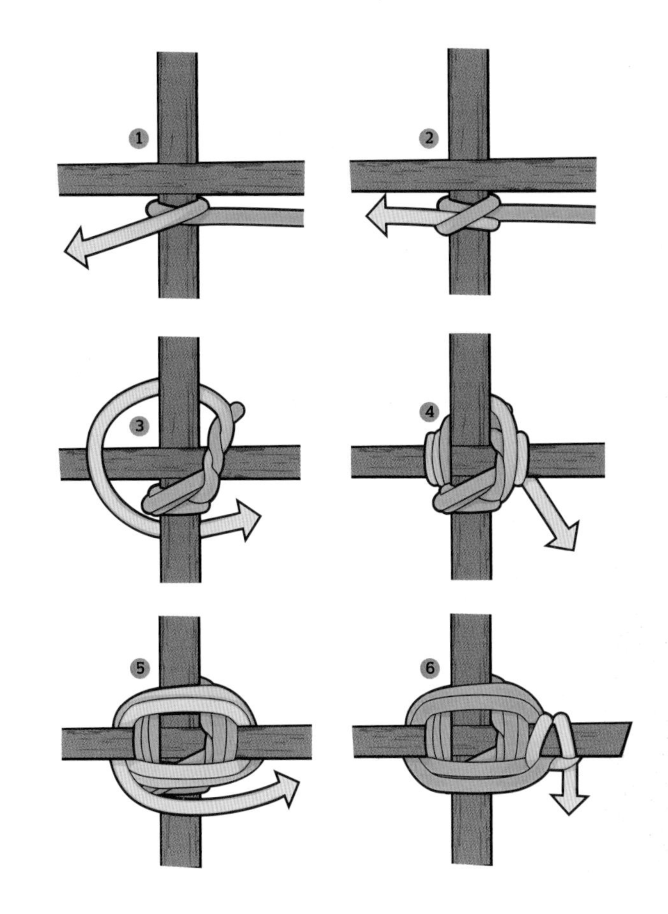

STEP ONE Cross the poles. Wrap the rope around the bottom post, with the active end—the end that you'll be looping around the poles—on top. Leave yourself a fair amount of rope on the active end.

STEP TWO Wrap the active end around the post, threading it under the first wrap. (This is called a clove hitch, and it's the basis of your knot.)

STEP THREE Twist the static end around the rope's active end. Then weave the active end around the posts, wrapping so the rope goes behind the vertical post, over the horizontal post, and under the vertical post again.

STEP FOUR Repeat this wrap two more times, pulling on the rope to tighten as you go.

STEP FIVE Wrap the rope so that it now crosses in front of the vertical post and behind the horizontal one. Repeat several times.

STEP SIX When your knot is sturdy enough, tie it off with a clove hitch, wrapping the active end once around the horizontal pole to make a loop, then looping around the pole again and threading it through the first loop.

055 Avoid Dreaded Trench Foot

This malady gets its name from a painful condition many soldiers experienced during World War I, when they stood in the trenches for days and weeks in cold, waterlogged, filthy boots. Gradually their feet would numb and their skin would turn red or blue. Without treatment, gangrene would set in, leading to amputation. Even today, trench foot impacts unprepared outdoorsmen. Don't be one of its victims.

Prevent the problem by wearing waterproof boots and wool socks. It's also a good idea to shed your boots and socks periodically, air out and massage your feet to promote circulation, and then put on fresh socks if you have them. Your feet will feel better and smell fresher. Best of all, you'll get to keep them.

056 Set a Snare for Small Animals

To catch small game, find a trail with a sapling nearby. Stick a forked branch into the path, then make a snare loop (a circle of rope that tightens when tugged). Tie the rope to a twig and bend the sapling over, and then tie the rope's other end to it. Bait a stick, and sandwich it between the twig and the fork to keep the sapling bent. When game trips the trap, dinner's on.

058 Dig a Hole Trap

Another way to catch an animal is to dig a hole 1 metre deep with an opening as big as your fist and walls that get wider toward the bottom. Lay a small log, elevated slightly by stones or other debris, over the top of the hole. With any luck, a critter will scurry under the log for cover and fall into the hole, and the hole's sloped walls will prevent it from climbing out.

057 Make a Jaw Spear

A jaw spear is great for catching fish, frogs, and other tasty morsels. Split one end of a green sapling 15 to 20 centimetres, then carve sharp, rear-angling teeth into the two inner sides of the split. Use a cord to bind the split's upper end so it won't split further. Finally, open the "jaws" and separate them with a twig strong enough to keep them apart. When you thrust the spear at your prey, the twig will be knocked away and the jaws will snap shut, holding the animal firmly in place. Remember, frogs' legs are a delicacy in France.

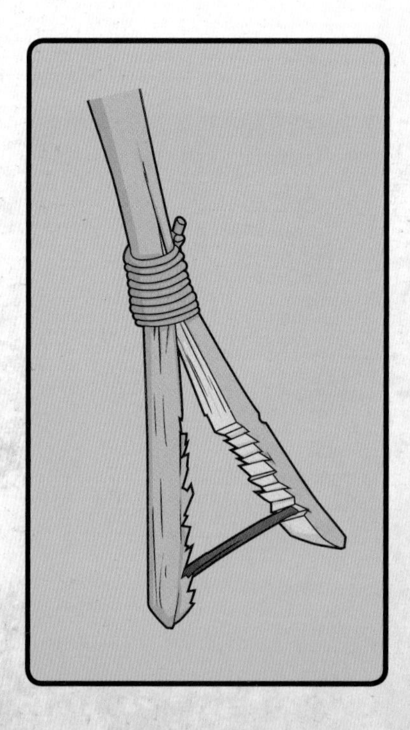

059 Fish with Your Shirt

Fishing is a great way to supplement your survival diet. If you don't have a rod and reel handy, you can use this makeshift net to catch small fish. Insert two poles through the sleeves of a basic T-shirt and out through the shirt's bottom. You can tie off the excess fabric with simple overhand knots if desired, but spreading the poles apart should be enough to keep the "net" in place. Now simply herd fish into the shallows, or scoop them up with the net.

060 Improvise a Skewer Hook

If you don't have a regular skewer hook, you can make one from a needle-shape sliver of sharpened hardwood or bone. Tie a line to the middle of the skewer, and put a daub of tree sap on the knot to keep it from slipping off. Then turn the skewer parallel with the fishing line and bury it in the bait. When the fish takes the bait, the skewer turns sideways, hooking the fish. And there you have it—fresh fish for supper!

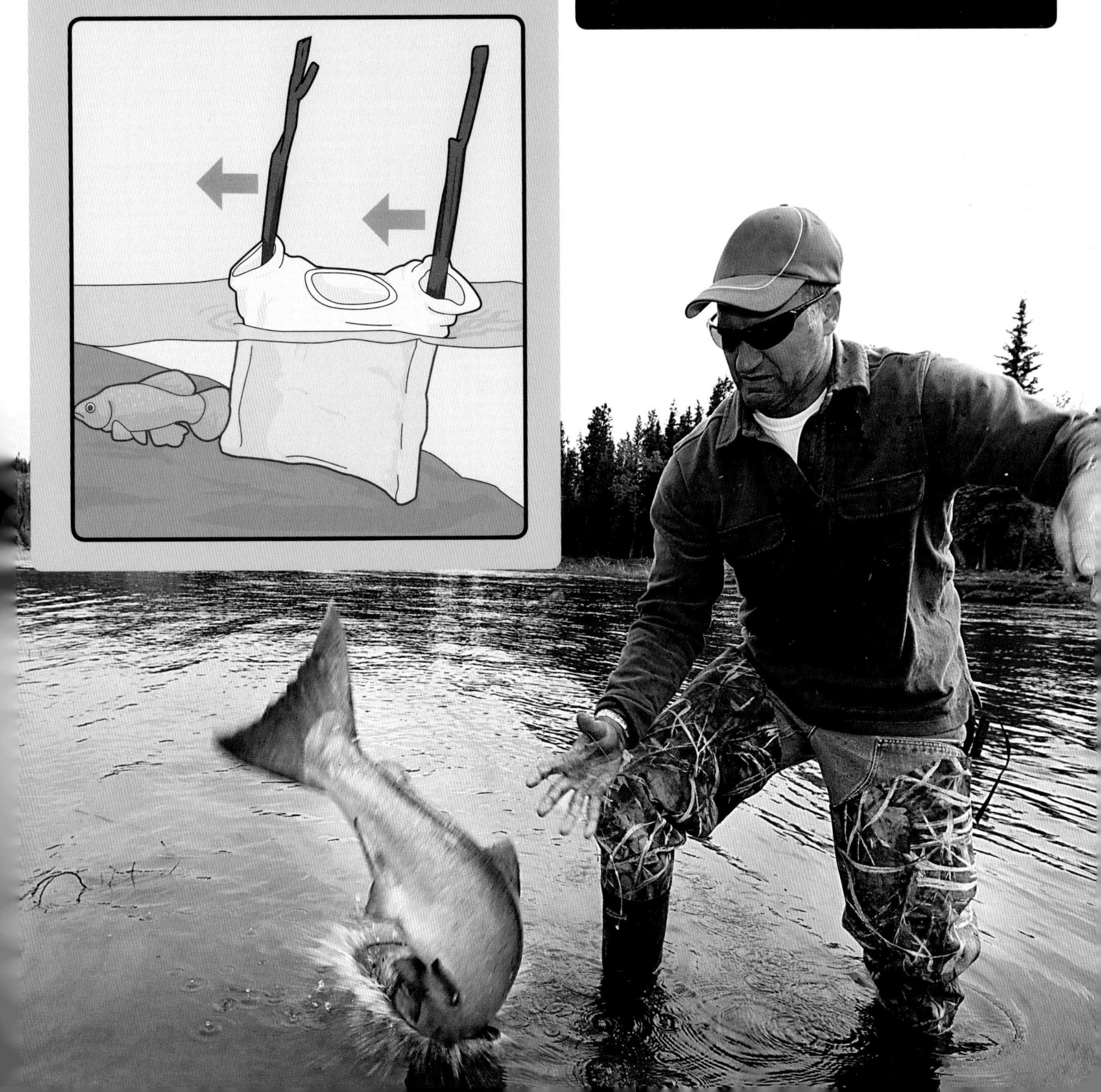

061 Shoo Away Flies

After a long winter, outdoor activities are extremely popular, but we inevitably change our fear of frostbite for the warm-weather wrath and nasty bites of black flies, horse flies, and deer flies. They are the worst, leaving festering wounds that can last for weeks.

COVER UP Protect as much skin as possible by wearing long-sleeved shirts and long pants when outside. Make sure to leave the black- and dark-colored garments at home, as you will overheat in the sun and actually attract those pesky biting flies. In addition, putting a thin coat of petroleum jelly on exposed skin, like the back of your hands, neck and ears, creates a barrier the insects can't get through.

REPEL THEM Use an insect repellent intended for biting flies with the highest DEET content possible. Canadians are restricted to a very effective maximum of 30 percent DEET in repellants, but you can still get higher-potency sprays and gels if travelling to neighboring countries. You can also use fly repellent candles or coils and set them up on the perimeter of your campsite, patio, or working area to keep bites at bay. Or, throw a few green spruce bows on the fire to "smudge" your way through a bite-free evening.

GET A FAN When sitting on your porch or patio, set up a large fan to create constant air movement where you intend to spend most of your time. It will help move the majority of bugs from your outdoor fun.

GET STINKY Northern explorers never used to bathe, thinking it helped keep the bugs away or maybe just leave a bad taste in their mouth. There could be some truth to the old tactic—at the very least, avid canoe paddlers in the north also swear by Vick's Vapo Rub used sparingly on your hands and neck. The heavy menthol aroma irritates insects and will give you a fresh scent just in case you're trying the "not bathing" tactic.

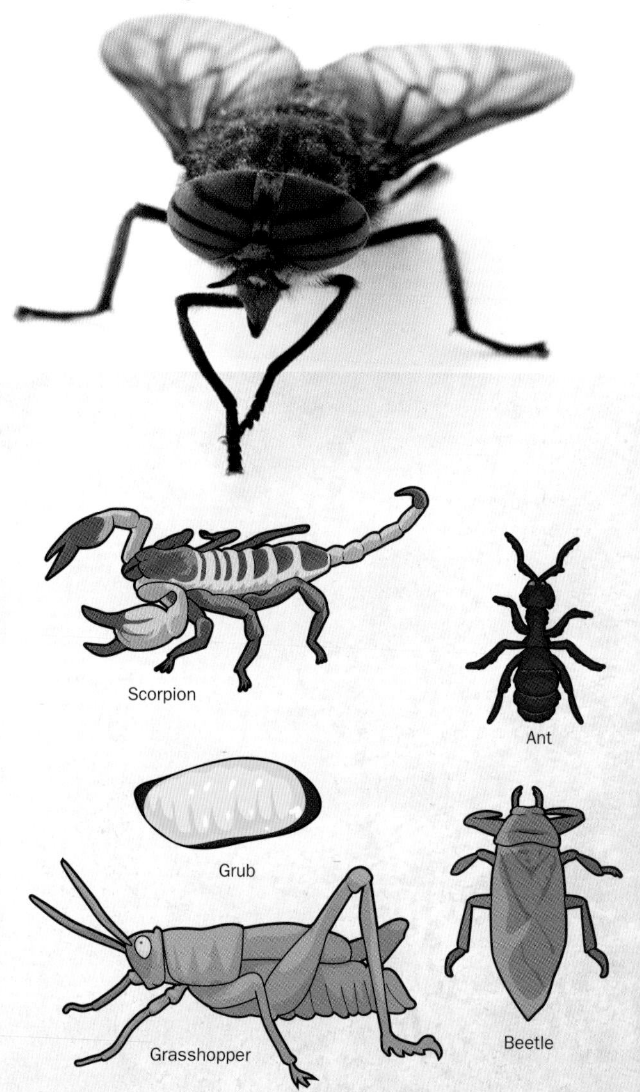

062 Gobble Up Bugs

Don't be deceived by their less-than-delicious appearance: Some bugs are edible, while others contain toxins. These are your safest bets:

ANTS These trail snacks taste like lemon drops, thanks to the formic acid in their systems. Just pop them in your mouth and chew—unless it's a fire ant, a bullet ant, or another ant that bites. Avoid those!

GRUBS Beetle larvae are fine to eat plain and live or, if you want to be fancy, as an addition to soup.

GRASSHOPPERS Skewer grasshoppers on a thin stick and roast them over the coals of your campfire.

SCORPIONS Pin the critter down with a knife, cut off its claws and stinger, and roast or toss in soup.

BEETLES Some are edible; some will make you sick. Don't eat them unless you gain local knowledge first.

063 Rid Big Game of Harmful Bacteria

In a long-term survival situation, you'll need to hunt or trap animals for food. Almost all animal life is edible, but there are safety concerns.

BUGS, TINY AND BIG Handling game animals puts you at risk of bacterial diseases such as tularemia. To avoid bites from infected insects, apply insect repellent. When butchering animals, wear long sleeves and pants—and gloves, if possible. And even if you like your steak rare when you're in civilization, cook meat you've hunted until it's well done.

HANTAVIRUS When butchering any animal, don't inhale the dust near its droppings and urine—it could carry this virus, which affects the pulmonary system.

PLAGUE Fleas from infected animals transmit plague to humans. Even after the animal is dead, the fleas will be active, but your gloves, long sleeves, and long pants—you are wearing them, right?—will protect you.

POOP When preparing an animal that you've shot in the gut, clean away matter from the digestive tract. And, as always, cook it thoroughly.

064 Spit-Roast That Bunny

A caveman and cowboy movie cliché, spit roasting is one of the simplest cooking methods. For the spit, choose wood like green oak or hickory that won't give a bad taste to the food. Ideally, the stick has a fork at one end that you can use for turning. Sharpen the other end to push through the meat. Shave the middle to flatten it along two opposite sides (this prevents the stick from rotating inside the food, so you're rotating the meat, not just the stick). Baste with drippings caught in a pan or on some bark.

065 STEP-BY-STEP Butcher a Deer Leg

Chances are you'll be limited in your butchering tools in a survival situation, so the traditional method of using a saw to cut through bones might not be feasible. But you can still fillet a deer leg with a knife.

STEP ONE After skinning the hind leg, place it on a stump or boulder with the outside of the leg facing up.

STEP TWO Slice through the connective tissue (called "silverskin") along the natural seam between the top round and the sirloin tip. Then pull the top round and the eye of round away from the bone.

STEP THREE Cut away the rest of the silverskin to yield the rump at the top of the hip bone.

STEP FOUR Turn the leg over and separate the round from the sirloin tip by pulling apart the natural seam with your fingers. Then slice the cuts away from the bone, trimming away any other meat by cutting through the connective tissue.

STEP FIVE Pull the shank off the bone. There's not a lot of meat there, but every bite counts. Who knows when you'll eat again?

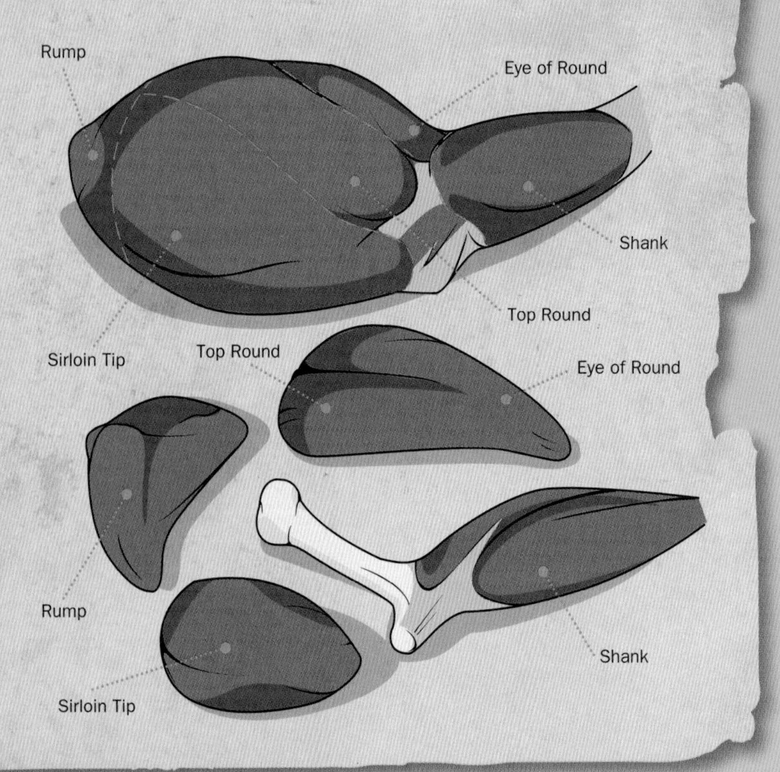

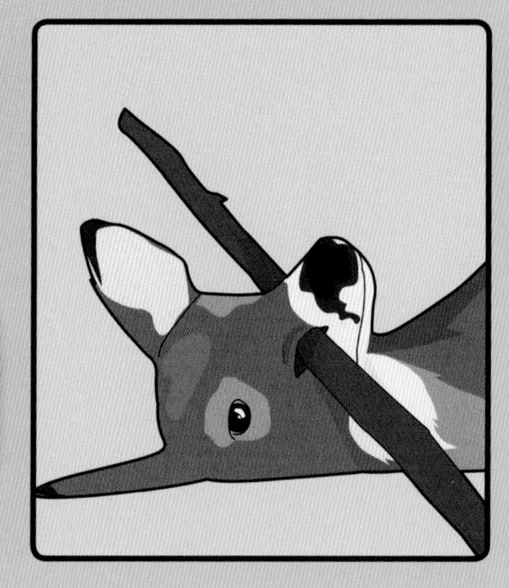

066 Drag a Deer

So you've snagged a deer—now what? Dragging that vital meat back to your shelter is hard work. Here's how to avoid hefting the carcass over your shoulders and trying to hoof it back.

Use the deer's anatomy to your advantage by cutting a 2.5-cm slit in the muzzle, just behind the black part of the nose. Push a sturdy stick through the opening, grasp the ends with both hands behind your back, and walk back to camp. The bone structure of the deer's head will bear the weight as you pull it along. Sure, it's a long haul, but you'll use less energy pulling than you would carrying—energy that you'll need to butcher that deer.

067 CHECKLIST Put Your Kill to Use

Venison makes a great wilderness meal, but what are you going to do with the rest of that carcass after dinner? Life in the wild demands economy of resources, so employ everything you can—waste not, want not.

- [ ] Use the entrails for bait in deadfall traps.
- [ ] Repurpose the stomach to make a water canteen.
- [ ] Crack the bones and scoop out the marrow to add to your soup.
- [ ] Use the antlers for arrow tips and spearheads.
- [ ] Whittle the bones into basic tools.
- [ ] Turn a scapula into a makeshift shovel.
- [ ] Create a fishing lure with a sinew fishing line and bone hook.
- [ ] Turn bone splinters into sewing needles.
- [ ] Secure clothing, tarps, or other cloth with fasteners or toggles made of bone.
- [ ] Fashion the hide into clothing, shoes, shelter, carry pouches, and leather thongs for lashings.

068 STEP-BY-STEP Trap a Goose

If you're lucky enough to be near a flock of geese, you might have a feast of fowl within your grasp. This simple, tried-and-true goose trench takes advantage of natural terrain and a goose's lack of, well, intelligence.

STEP ONE Figure out where geese are gathering in the evening by looking for plenty of droppings.

STEP TWO Dig a trench approximately 30 centimetres deep, 30 centimetres wide, and between 13 and 6 metres long. You'll want to make the trench slope gently down.

STEP THREE Scatter the displaced dirt so the trench looks natural, litter the bottom with corn or whatever nearby grain they might be feeding on, then either wait patiently out of sight or stalk back to the trap in the early morning hours.

STEP FOUR Bide your time. The geese will walk down the trench and get trapped at the end. Unable to spread its wings to fly, or turn around to walk back out of the trench, the goose is up for grabs.

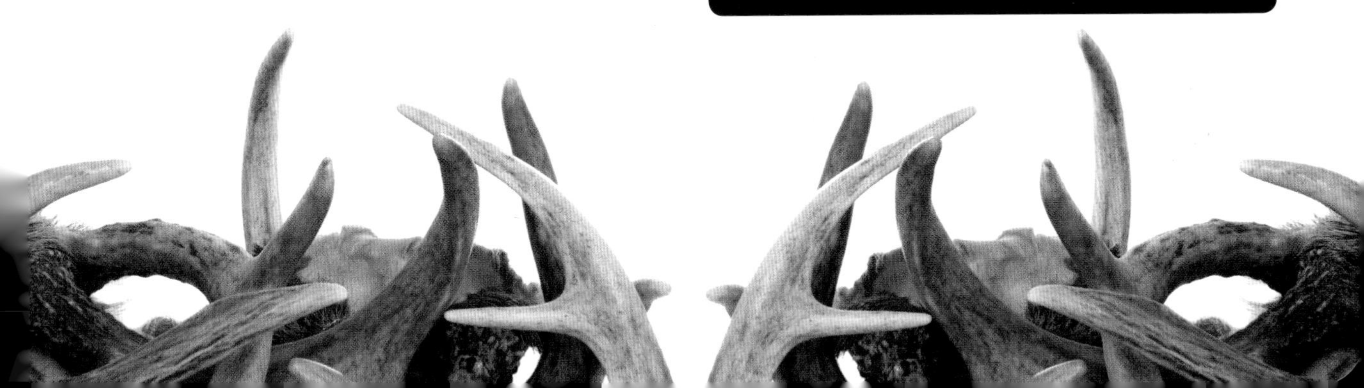

069 Steer Clear of Poisonous Plants

Call me a wimp, but I hate getting poked and stung while beating my way through the bush. To protect your skin against thorns and stinging nettles, wear long pants and long sleeves, and don leather gloves that'll let you move plants aside with ease. Use a long stick to open up a path through a thicket, and employ your well-shod feet to mash plants down out of your way. But if you can identify a plant as poisonous, don't walk through it; the itch-inducing resin collects on your clothing and boots, and might eventually get transferred to your skin.

Poison Oak

Poison Ivy

Poison Sumac

070 Remove a Tick

Great. In all your wilderness survival fun, you've managed to pick up a hitchhiker. Ticks are nasty little buggers that carry diseases. The longer one stays embedded in its host (that'd be you), the greater the chances are for exposure to the not-too-fun illnesses it may carry. Check often for ticks, especially on your head, armpits, and groin. Also look under clothes in areas like the waistband of your pants.

The best removal method is to grasp the tick near the head and pull straight back. You can use a fancy tick-removal tool if you have one; otherwise, tweezers are your best bet. Avoid squeezing the body of the tick, as that might push tick juice into the wound. Coaxing a tick to back out with a hot needle, match, or petroleum jelly is an old wives' tale. Ticks close their mouths once they've latched on to a host, and unless you pull them off, they only let go when they're done feeding.

071

Put Your Pee to Work

Question of the day: What are the top five things you can do with urine? Where's Dave Letterman when we need him?

HAVE A TEA PARTY Dip your crumpets in it and pretend it's English tea. Okay, let's get serious.

TIDY UP Use it as a disinfectant. With its high ammonia content, it's an ideal cleaning agent.

PUT UP A FENCE Urinating on "marker trees" may help establish your territory and keep potentially harmful beasties from wanting to investigate.

COOL DOWN When water is scarce and heat is intense, place a urine-soaked cloth on your head to lower body temperature.

TAKE A SWIG You can drink it, as long as you filter it and avoid drinking the first urine of the day, which contains more toxins. If you want to, you can even have mine, 'cause I'm not doing that.

072 STEP-BY-STEP Treat a Snake Bite

Snake bites happen all the time. And even a bite from a so-called harmless snake can cause infection or an allergic reaction. If you're bitten, the best course of action is to get emergency medical assistance as soon as you can. In the meantime, do the following:

STEP ONE Wash the bite with soap and water.

STEP TWO Immobilize the bitten area and, if possible, keep it lower than the heart.

STEP THREE Cover the area with a clean, cool compress or a moist dressing to minimize swelling and discomfort.

STEP FOUR Monitor vital signs, such as temperature and pulse rate.

STEP FIVE If you can't reach emergency medical care within 30 minutes, place a suction device over the bite to help draw venom up out of the wound. Only use your mouth to suck out the venom as a last resort—and be sure to spit it out. Then wrap a bandage 4 to 10 centimetres above the bite to help slow the venom's movement. Don't totally cut off circulation—the bandage should be loose enough that you can slip a finger under it.

073 Swing a Mean Machete

While a machete is fun for pretending to fight off a band of ninjas, it can also be quite useful. You can wield one to chop and split wood, or to clear vines and grasses from the trail ahead.

As with any cutting tool, the most important thing is to prevent injury to yourself. Always consider where the blade would end up if it missed its target, and make sure no part of your body is in that location. Grip the machete handle firmly, swing deliberately, and be ready to react if the blade glances off or misses. Keep the blade sharp and don't let the edge strike the ground, or it will become dull. If you're clearing vegetation, use a side-to-side sweeping action, and feel free to make lots of kung fu noises as you go.

074 ASSESS AND RESPOND
Understand Poison Types

I don't want to scare you, but you can run into dangerous stuff when you're out in the wild. So it's a good idea to know what you might be up against—and how quickly you need to get medical attention if you're bitten, clawed, or poisoned.

 Source

 Medical Effects

 Treatment

CYTOTOXIN will rarely kill you, but it'll likely leave horrible scars.

Brown recluse spiders and puff adders

 This toxin targets cells, particularly skin and muscle tissue. The bite wound spreads, and nausea and shock accompany intense pain.

 Apply ice to decrease the swelling, wash the area with cool water and mild soap, and avoid strenuous activity to reduce the toxin's spread. Get the victim to a medical facility to receive antivenin.

NEPHROTOXIN causes your kidneys to fail; you'll be dead after several days without treatment.

 Cortinarius mushrooms (also known as webcaps) and some molds

 Nephrotoxin attacks the kidneys. A fever develops, then worsens and brings about nausea, which leads to fainting, then coma, then kidney failure.

 Requires professional medical attention to remove the toxin from the body, monitor and support kidney function, and administer dialysis in severe cases.

BACTEREMIA slowly kills its victims over the course of a day or more.

 Any animal attack where the wound becomes infected

 An infected bite can lead to blood poisoning (sepsis), attacking the red and white blood cells. This can cause fever and widespread organ failure.

 Get the victim to a hospital. After he or she undergoes a blood culture to verify the infection, the infected person must receive treatment with a course of intravenous antibiotics.

HEMOTOXIN wreaks havoc on your blood, and could kill you in five hours flat.

Rattlesnakes and other vipers

 The venom damages red blood cells, resulting in dizziness and internal hemorrhaging as the toxin travels through the circulatory system.

 Keep the victim calm. Remove jewelry (because there will be swelling) and immobilize the injury below heart level, but do not wrap it. Transport the victim to a hospital as quickly as possible.

NEUROTOXIN shuts down your nervous system—some can kill in mere hours.

Gila monsters, black widow spiders, cobras, and some scorpions

 This one harms nerve cells. Excruciating cramps can lead to violent vomiting, followed by seizures and possible paralysis.

 Keep the victim as calm as possible to reduce circulation of the toxin, and get him or her to a doctor immediately to receive antivenin. Time is of the essence.

075 Heal with Bugs

Typically, you want to avoid bugs as much as possible. That is, of course, unless they can be of use to you.

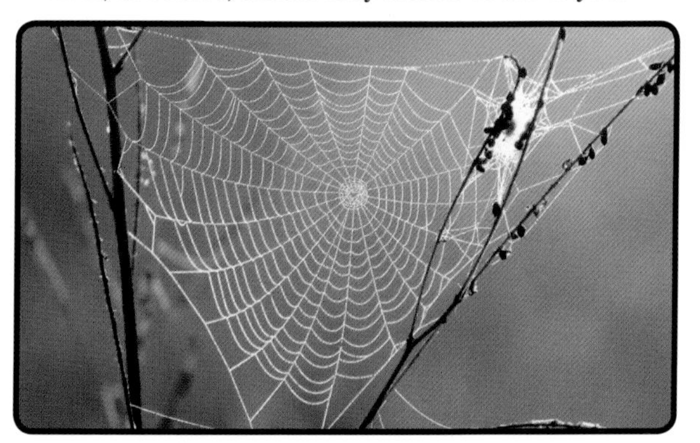

WEB BANDAGES A spiderweb can make a sterile bandage for a small cut or abrasion. Find a web and smear it over the injury to prevent infection.

TISSUE THERAPY Maggots are great for removing decayed flesh. Place the insects in a wound and let them feast until only healthy pink tissue remains.

ANT SUTURES Use ants to close a wound. Let them bite both sides of a laceration, then break off their bodies, leaving their heads and mandibles attached.

076 Remove a Leech

Leeches are sneaky, waterborne, bloodsucking worms that attach themselves to your skin with suckers (which, conveniently, they have at both ends). The best defense is to cover your body and tuck your pants into your boots. To dislodge a leech, slide your fingernail under a sucker. Work fast, since the leech will try to reattach itself while you're working on the sucker at the opposite end. Clean the wound to prevent infection.

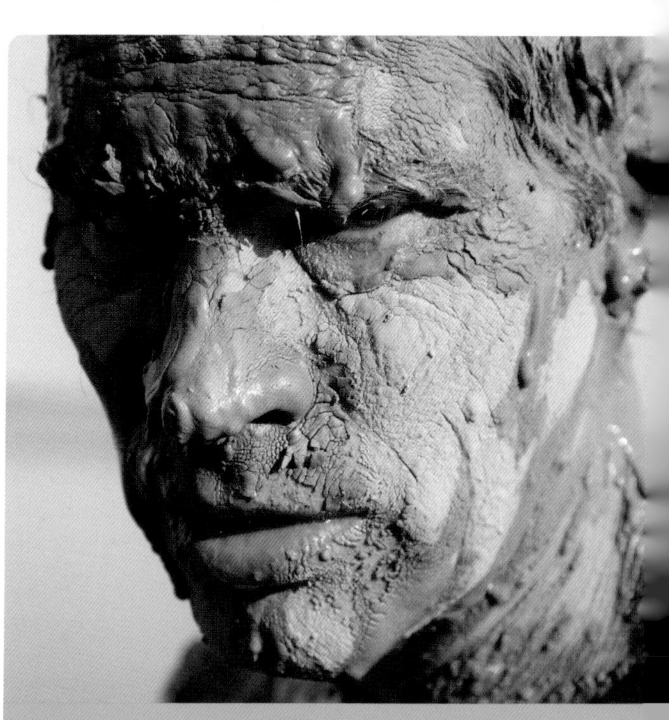

077 Keep Mosquitoes at Bay

Mosquitoes are attracted to dark clothing, perspiration, carbon dioxide from your breath, lactic acid produced by exercise, and sweet smells like perfume and deodorant. So don't wear dark clothes, and when you exercise, don't get sweaty or breathe heavily. And don't wear aftershave.

Those things are easier said than done (except for shunning aftershave), but there are lots of ways to avoid mosquito bites. Natural repellents include oils made from cinnamon, cedar, eucalyptus, and several types of flowers. In the wild, where those oils might be unavailable, coat your skin with mud and sit near a smoky fire. Making camp on a windy ridgeline also helps keep mosquitoes away.

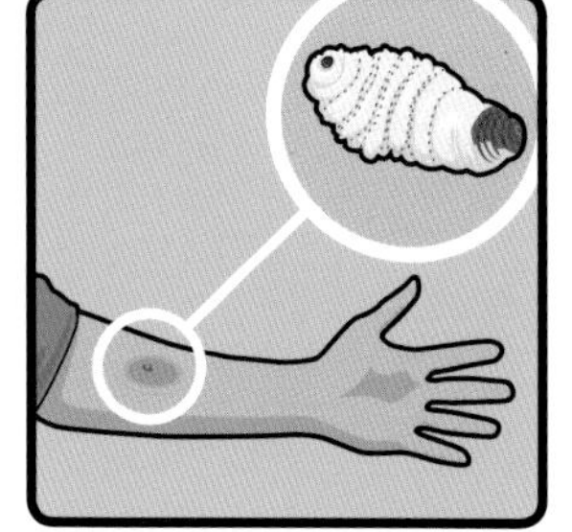

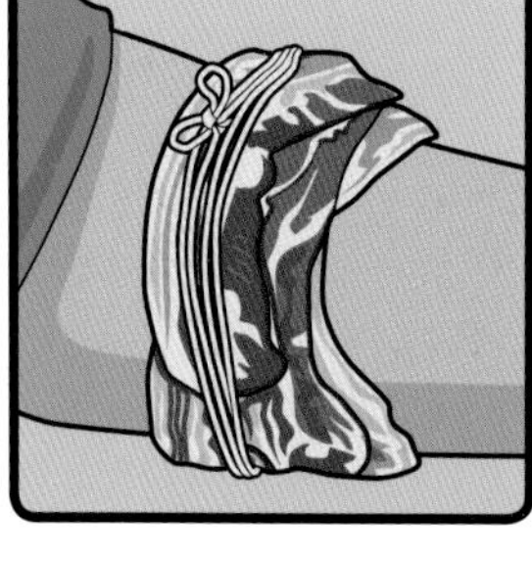

078 Banish a Botfly

The botfly is native to Central and South America, and it likes to procreate by depositing its eggs on the flesh of human hosts (yes, you). And those eggs grow into larvae that burrow inside (yes, inside you). Best of all, the larvae have spines that create pain.

To coax out an invader, tie raw bacon over the area for three days; when you take it off, you'll see that the offender has burrowed out of your arm into the meat.

If you'd rather see it dead, suffocate it by putting tree sap, nail polish, or petroleum jelly over the wound, then squeeze out its corpse the next day.

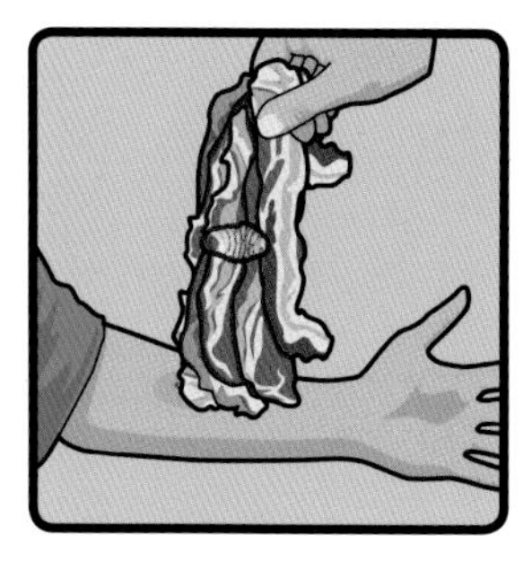

079 Know Your Amphibians

Boreal, chorus, and bull frogs, and a host of other croakers are abundant in Canada and can be a good source of protein if nothing else is available. They are easy to catch, clean, and prepare and could mean the difference between starving and enjoying some fresh-frog table fare.

Knowing amphibian basics is critical in our neck of the woods, and connoisseurs need to know the difference between frogs and toads. Be aware of Canadian and boreal toads, as their skin produces toxins that could lead to more than a belly ache. Don't eat ANY toads.

Generally, the easiest way to identify frogs from toads is their skin, as a frog is moist and smooth and a toad is dry and bumpy. Look for the poisonous glands behind a toad's eye, where they bulge out from the head. Most frogs have horizontal pupils, while most toads have vertical ones.

If you're not sure, don't eat it.

080

STEP-BY-STEP

Treat a Scorpion Sting

Were you even listening when I told you how to avoid a sting? Anyway, here's how to limit the damage.

STEP ONE Wash the affected area with soap and water.

STEP TWO Apply a cool compress to help reduce swelling and improve circulation.

STEP THREE If stung on an arm or a leg, elevate the limb to heart level if you can.

STEP FOUR Keep your cool. Few victims die, though you may experience unpleasant symptoms like rapid breathing, increased heart rate, and muscle weakness.

RICH SAYS

"Don't get stranded here—Disneyland this ain't! Everything out here is either needle sharp, hotter than hell, hungry for your blood, or poisonous."

081 Fight Dehydration in the Desert

The desert is a land of dangerous extremes—it can kill you with its heat or its cold—but the biggest threat is the dryness. Dehydration can take you down in a matter of hours.

WATCH THE SIGNS The symptoms come slowly, and unless you're paying attention, you won't notice them. Your blood thickens and your body's blood volume is reduced. Your pulse speeds up and your heart works harder. You become exhausted. Your mind ceases to function well, and you begin to make bad decisions. Even without mistakes, death comes soon enough, unless you can find water and drink your fill.

KEEP COOL Try to pace your activities so you don't perspire too much, and seek the shade when the sun is hot. Travel only during the cool early morning and late evening hours, then rest overnight so you're not stumbling around in the darkness.

DRINK UP Store your water in your stomach, not your canteen. Contrary to popular belief, rationing water will not extend your life. Don't eat unless you have some water to drink, because the digestion of food requires water in your system. Eating without water will dehydrate you faster. If you get desperate for water, filter and drink your urine as a last resort.

STAVE OFF THE COLD Dehydration can make hypothermia worse, and the desert can be bitterly cold at night. Find shelter before dark, get a fire started, and stay warm.

082 Navigate the Arctic

Traveling the taiga or tundra regions of the north is daunting. It is a vast region of Canada with very little infrastructure, meaning you could be out there for weeks or even months without much for resources. You have to deal with dry, extreme temperatures and everything around you will begin to look the same.

SEASONAL CHALLENGES In the winter the Arctic is a barren landscape covered in hard-packed snow. It can be difficult to tell whether you're traveling on ground or ice, and avoiding frost bite or hypothermia is always a challenge. In the summer months white snow is replaced with gravel, lichen-covered rocks, and low growing vegetation. The incredible amount of water makes it hard to navigate the spiderweb of rivers and lakes and at times you'll feel like the black flies could pick you up and carry you away.

WATCH THE SUN AND STARS In the summer there can be close to 24 hours of daylight. Use the sun as your navigational point, knowing it will travel across the sky from east to west over a longer period of time. The sun travels in a big circle so keeping track of what time of day it is can be key to using the sun for navigation. In the winter it can be virtually dark both day and night. Using the stars can be the only way to navigate when the skies are clear enough to allow it.

BUILD AN INUKSHUK In the arctic every hill looks the same and it is easy to walk in circles. The Inuit build inuksuit, the plural of inukshuk, as navigational aids to tell others someone was there or to simply identify the right path. Each stone monument, built in the likeness of man, should be distinct and identifiable so you can use it as a reference point. You'll have to dig deep and remember the days when you played with building blocks. Mark your path with inuksuit by building the figures along the trail and mark where you've stashed supplies or found abundant food.

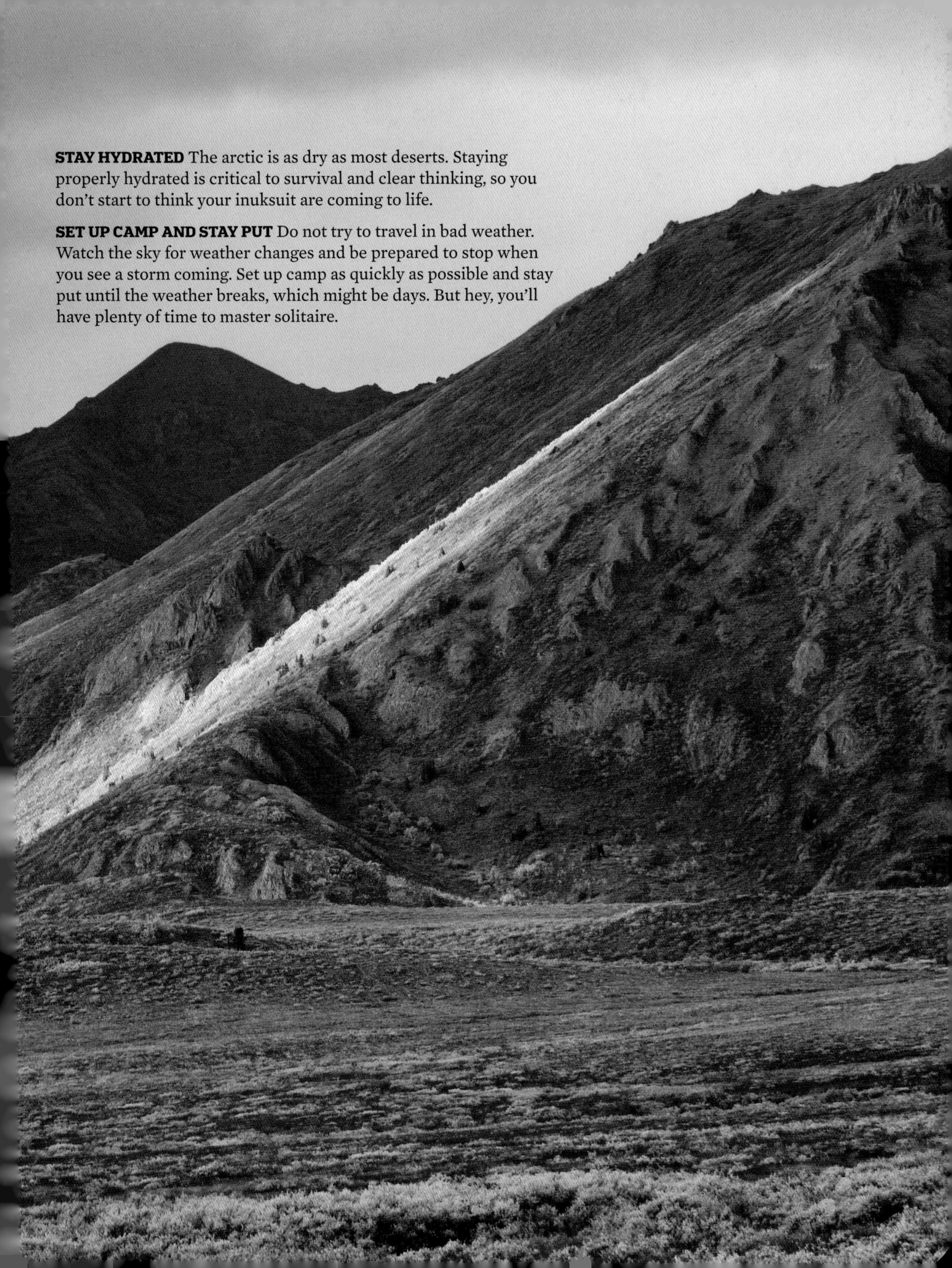

STAY HYDRATED The arctic is as dry as most deserts. Staying properly hydrated is critical to survival and clear thinking, so you don't start to think your inuksuit are coming to life.

SET UP CAMP AND STAY PUT Do not try to travel in bad weather. Watch the sky for weather changes and be prepared to stop when you see a storm coming. Set up camp as quickly as possible and stay put until the weather breaks, which might be days. But hey, you'll have plenty of time to master solitaire.

083 Make a Solar Still

With a bit of ingenuity, you can gather water in a seemingly bone-dry landscape; just rig up this solar still and, during daylight hours, water vapor will condense beneath the tarp and drip from its lowest point into a container.

Start by digging a hole in the sand (make sure the hole is deep enough to reach the damper subsoil) and putting in a container to collect water. Thread tubing from the container to the surface—you'll drink out of this—and cover the whole shebang with a tarp. Then anchor the tarp with rocks, seal any airholes with sand, put a rock in the center of the tarp, and wait for water to condense.

084 Scout for Water in the Desert

The desert is a place of such contrast that you can see any green vegetation at quite a distance. It stands out from the rest of the dry environment, like a drink of water just waiting to be gulped.

Tracking down the rare lush patches that dot an otherwise arid landscape can help lead you to water. It might be below the surface, but it's there, and it's worth digging for. Scan the distant horizon; if you see a pattern of green, go to it. It might be grasses, or even large trees, fed by an underground spring or puddles remaining from the last rainstorm. Also keep an eye out for dampness near the deepest natural depressions of dry streambeds. If you find moisture, dig, dig, dig. Then place the damp soil in a T-shirt, hold it overhead, and wring it to release water.

THIS HAPPENED TO ME!

Trapped in a Canyon

I TOOK OFF ON A DAY TRIP TO A NEARBY DESERT, HOPING TO TAKE PHOTOS OF PLANTS AND ROCK FORMATIONS. I LET MY ROOMMATE KNOW WHERE I WAS HEADED AND WHEN I'D BE BACK. I WAS FAMILIAR WITH THE AREA, SO I WASN'T WORRIED.

085 Seek Water in a Canyon

Springs tend to surface at lower levels in canyons, so to find water, start near the canyon mouth and work your way upstream. Moving this way, up-canyon, is safer, as it lessens the chance of your descending a drop-off that you can't climb back up.

In addition to springs, look for "seeps"—moist spots in the canyon floor where water rises up from an underground source. Seeps often result in puddles substantial enough to drink from (although you should, of course, purify the water before doing so).

Beware of both pools and hot springs. Canyon-floor pools can be deceptively cold and deep, and may be difficult to escape should you fall or jump in. The sulfurous fumes of hot springs can overcome you, and the water can be hot enough to literally boil you alive. Steer clear, no matter how tempting a nice warm wilderness bath might sound.

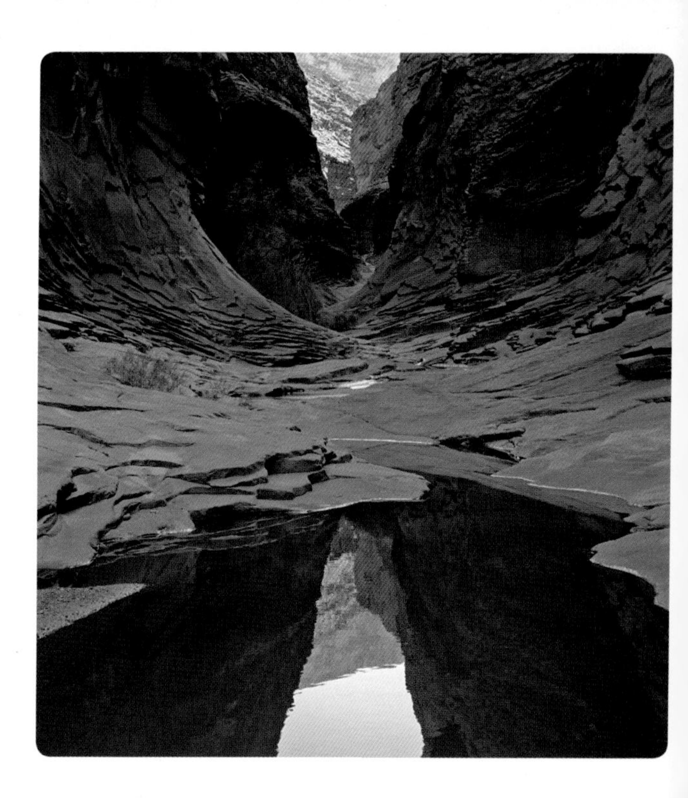

086 Maximize Heat from a Campfire

The problem with campfires is that most of the heat escapes, so the fire warms only the side of your body that faces the flames. The ideal is to build a fire between two reflective surfaces and then station yourself in between them so you can absorb warmth. Set up a campfire 2 to 2 and a half metres from a natural reflector, such as a rock wall, then erect a stone or green log on the other side of the fire. Position yourself in the space between the fire and the wall, and prepare to get toasty.

087 STEP-BY-STEP Scale a Canyon

Stuck in a canyon? Take a tip from Santa Claus and shimmy up a chimney, a narrow slot that's sometimes the only escape route in a rock canyon. The trick to climbing it is to use opposing forces.

STEP ONE Put your back to one wall of the chimney and one foot about knee-high against the wall in front of you.

STEP TWO Place your other foot on the wall behind you, bending your knee. Put your hands behind your back.

STEP THREE Push up with your legs and arms, straightening your bent leg and "stepping" up the chimney wall. Then repeat, stepping up with your other leg. Keep going until you're at the top.

088

CHECKLIST

Equip Yourself for the Mountains

Choosing the right gear requires a balance between having what you need and avoiding overload—which is never a good idea, but particularly unwise in the mountains, where you may fatigue easily. In addition to the essentials in your wilderness survival kit, consider the following for extreme survival conditions:

- ☐ Mountaineering harness, ropes, and carabiners. Even if you don't plan on doing any technical climbing, this gear could end up saving your life.
- ☐ Ice axe. You might not expect to encounter ice where you're going, but weather may force you to change course.
- ☐ Crampons. Like the ice axe, this piece of equipment might be the difference between being stuck and being able to hike out to safety.
- ☐ Collapsible snow shovel. If you end up in a blizzard, and a snow shelter is all that separates you from surviving or freezing to death, you'll be glad to have this handy item close by.
- ☐ Personal locator beacon (PLB). In this day and age, there's no reason to go anywhere without one. They're affordable, and as long as you have a clear line of sight, rescuers can locate you in even the remotest backcountry.
- ☐ Insulated pad for sleeping on snow. You can freeze without one.
- ☐ Helmet. You only have one head. When a single misstep can mean a concussion or worse, wearing a helmet seems like a no-brainer.

089 Be a Modern Caveman

There's a reason why bears and other beasts hole up in caves: They're ready-made shelters that provide immediate protection from rain, snow, wind, or brutal sun. No need to work at erecting a hut—just move in and set up housekeeping.

WATCH OUT FOR WATER Make sure the cavern is high enough to be out of danger from flash floods, incoming tides, and storm surges.

PUT UP A FENCE Erect a low stone wall across the opening to help keep dirt from blowing around.

START A FIRE The stone walls make good reflectors for the campfire, and there's no worry of the fire spreading to nearby vegetation and getting out of control. To keep campfire smoke from becoming a problem, build the fire near the cave entrance.

BEAT THE DRAFT Because they are made of rock, caves generally retain the cold. They're good places to escape the heat of a hot desert, but not so desirable in the dead of winter. Unless you can get a good fire going or partition a section of the cavern into a small room, cold air will always surround you.

090 Stay Safe in a Cave

Like any neighborhood, a cave has its advantages and disadvantages. Before you can move in, you need to make sure it isn't already occupied. Depending on where you are, caves might be favored dwellings for venomous snakes, bats, wolves, bears, cougars—you get the picture. Even if the only cave dwellers are rats, mice, or squirrels, you might become ill from contact with hantavirus in their urine or feces, so look for a clean cave floor. One other caution: Caves exist because the ceiling "caved" in from some type of erosion. If you see evidence of instability overhead or fresh rockfalls on the floor, or if there's water flowing through the cave, it's probably not structurally sound. I'd move on.

091 Find Food Above the Tree Line

The farther north you go, the lower the tree line. But life—and hence food—exists even where trees do not. Depending on where you are in the world, the fauna and flora will vary, but small animals and birds are probably your best bet. They live among the rocks and low-growing foliage, where you can set snare traps along their preferred routes of travel. In subalpine regions, ruffed grouse (called "dumb chickens" for a reason) are easy to approach and kill. Also use the offal of a previously killed animal as bait to attract birds of prey and four-footed predators, and while they are paying attention to the bait, take them out with a stick or rock.

092 Conquer Altitude Sickness in the Mountains

The cause is simple: going too high too fast. And the higher the altitude, the longer it takes to acclimate. So when you're climbing in the mountains, slow down. Ascending beyond 2,400 metres should be done at a rate of no more than 300 metres per day. Avoid strenuous exertion for at least 24 hours after reaching new heights, and increase water intake as you go.

And if you don't follow these instructions? Watch for signs of two forms of serious altitude sickness: high-altitude pulmonary edema (HAPE)—characterized by breathlessness, fatigue, dry cough, and blue lips and nails—and high-altitude cerebral edema (HACE), which typically features a severe headache, loss of coordination, and confusion. Both are potentially deadly. Victims must immediately descend at least 600 metres to save their lives, and then they must be evacuated to a medical facility as soon as possible.

093 Make a Musky Hand Warmer

When exploring in the high arctic, your hands are going to get cold. Really cold. Of course you've geared up properly, but here's a way to add a little more warmth.

During the summer months, musk oxen in this area rub themselves on rocks to help them shed their thick undercoats, a wooly layer known as quiviut by the local Inuit peoples. As you hike, keep an eye out for tufts of wool on rocks and shrubs.

Quiviut is highly adapted to hold heat in extreme conditions. Collect small bundles and place them in your pockets to quickly warm up your fingers and hands. Slide your hand into the quiviut and within seconds you will feel heat flowing to your fingertips.

DO THIS, NOT THAT
High Altitude

DO avoid alcohol and caffeine, and drink lots of water. If you're perspiring, use sports drinks to replace electrolytes. Staying properly hydrated will help you recognize early altitude-sickness symptoms like a headache, rather than confusing them with dehydration.

DON'T sleep more than 300 metres above the elevation at which you slept the previous night once you've climbed above 3,000 metres—even if you've trekked higher during the day. And, obviously, never go higher once you notice possible signs of sickness.

094 CASE STUDY: SNOWED IN
Avoid Getting Stranded in the Mountains

It was Saturday evening, November 25, 2006. James Kim and his wife, Kati, and their two young daughters were on a family vacation, traveling through Oregon's Coast Range on their way to the Pacific coast more than 210 kilometres away. The rain coming down on Interstate 5 meant there would be snow at elevation. Still, the family decided not to stop. The drive is simple enough, but they missed the turnoff to Interstate 42, which leads to the coast. Then they made the fateful decision not to backtrack, looking instead for an alternate route.

The Kims chose Bear Camp Road, a single-lane mountain road known to be treacherous. When they arrived at a fork, they mistakenly turned onto a logging road. Another 34 kilometres and 1[illegible]ertical metres later, running low on fuel, James Kim stopped the car for the night. When the[illegible]woke, they were stuck in the snow, out of cell-phone range, and lost in the wilderness.

The Kim family was traveling light, ill prepared for winter conditions in the Oregon mountains. They had little food and few supplies, and they waited anxiously for authorities to find them, doing everything possible to both position themselves for rescue and keep each other as warm and well fed as possible. But after a week of desperate nights in the freezing Oregon backcountry, the Kims lost hope. James decided to leave his family and hike out for help.

James was not properly clothed. He had no food, and no idea where he was. And while he started off following the road, after a little while and for reasons known only to him, he turned off the road and followed a ravine. At some point, he began shedding his clothing as he walked, which is a common sign of hypothermia.

Meanwhile, rescue searchers had tracked the Kims' cell phone and credit card records, and had narrowed in on Bear Camp Road as the likely location of the stranded family. On the ninth day, a helicopter pilot searching on his own found the car, and Kati and her two children were saved. Sadly, James Kim's body, partially undressed, was found a few days later in the waist-deep water of a frozen stream.

POST ASSESSMENT
Snowed In

The Kims' story ended tragically, no doubt. But there's a lot to learn from both their mistakes and their wiser decisions.

They shared a detailed route sheet with family and friends, which included intended overnight stays.

Initially, they remained calm and avoided immediate rash action.

They sheltered in a clearing, making them more visible from the air.

They burned signal fires (using their tires as fuel) to create columns of signal smoke.

Kati left a note on a road gate explaining where they were and what had happened.

James wrote SOS in large letters in the snow for searchers to see.

Kati breast-fed both children to keep them alive.

They continually honked the horn to scare off bears, which would also have signaled any nearby search team.

They used the car heater only intermittently, conserving fuel as long as possible, and huddled together to share heat.

They deviated from their intended route, making several wrong turns, and didn't notify friends or family that they'd gone off course.

They tried to travel overnight in unfamiliar and difficult terrain, and were not prepared for driving in rough winter conditions.

They ignored weather data, which predicted heavy snowfall and impassable roads.

They were not equipped with proper emergency supplies (such as food, water, and basic first-aid gear) or clothing appropriate for being outside in winter conditions.

When James Kim hiked out, he did so in a state of desperation: He was hungry, hopeless, and suffering from hypothermia, which caused him to head into the woods rather than hiking down the road where human contact would have been more likely.

095 Trek Across a Glacier

Glaciers are rivers of ice that move constantly, but at a rate so slow it's undetectable to human eyes—at least usually. From time to time, dynamic events happen. Ice towers can collapse, and huge chunks sometimes fall off and into surrounding water, creating icebergs. If you need to cross one of these treacherous zones, heed these warnings:

MIND THE GAPS The biggest dangers to a hiker are crevasses, which erosion forms over time, leaving great scars in the ice that reach into the belly of the glacier. Avoid visible crevasses and ice ridges, where a misstep can lead to disaster. That's the easy part; the hard part is avoiding the dangers you can't see. Snowfall can bridge crevasses, hiding them from view. If you step onto a snow bridge, you might break through and fall to your death—or become injured and trapped by the sheer walls of ice.

BE PREPARED When crossing a snow-covered glacier that might have hidden crevasses, wear crampons, carry an ice axe, rope yourself to experienced hiking partners, and know self-rescue techniques using ascenders, which allow "reverse rappeling" in case of emergency. If you are alone and must cross, use a long pole to probe the snow ahead. Carry a personal locator beacon (PLB) to call for rescue if you run into trouble.

RICH SAYS

"Lose your footing here and you become an anthropology display a thousand years from now."

096 STEP-BY-STEP Tie a Double Figure-Eight Knot

The double figure-eight knot lets you attach yourself to anchors or tie other climbers to a single rope.

STEP ONE Create a figure eight.

STEP TWO Bring the active end through the figure eight's bottom loop and form another, looser loop. Then bring the active end back up through the bottom loop.

STEP THREE Lead the active end over the top loop. Thread it under the anchored section of rope and over the figure eight.

STEP FOUR Wrap the active end behind the bottom loop, then up through the top figure eight, joining the other line.

STEP FIVE To tighten the figure eights into a secure knot, pull on the bottom loop.

097 Rappel on the Fly

If you have rope but no other climbing gear, use the "expedient rappel" method. Loop the center of your rope around an anchor (a tree or rock), allowing both ends to dangle over the cliff. Make sure both ends reach the ground below. Test your anchor, then straddle the double rope, facing uphill. Bring the rope around your right thigh to the front and diagonally across your chest. Lead the rope over your left shoulder and diagonally across your back to your right hip. Grasp the double rope ahead of you with your left hand, and the double rope behind your hip with your right hand. Walk backward over the cliff, leaning back against the rope and feeding the rope over your body to overcome friction. Keep stepping back and feeding the rope until you reach the bottom. When you're there, pull on one end of the rope to retrieve it. Kissing the ground is optional.

098 Descend a Scree Slope

Know what scree is? It's an accumulation of small rocks that have eroded from the freezing and thawing of a bigger formation above. A slope covered with scree has a loose surface, like a bunch of angular marbles. When you cross a scree slope, the surface moves under your feet, and you have no choice but to move downslope with it. Try to glide on the scree using a controlled slide, as if cross-country skiing. A small avalanche of loose rock will follow you. Aim for a point diagonally across and down the slope. Keep your feet under you at all costs, and yodel to help the mood.

099 Start a Fire in the Snow

The most challenging time to build a fire is when the ground is wet or covered with snow. Of course, when are you most in need of a fire's warmth? You guessed it. So here's what you do.

PREPARE THE GROUND Use rocks or branches to isolate the fire's base from snow-covered or damp ground. Build your fire on a platform of stones or green logs laid tightly together so the updraft of warm air doesn't draw the dampness from below. The higher and tighter the platform, the better.

HAVE FUEL READY Gather plenty of dry tinder, kindling, and fuel wood before attempting to light the fire. You don't want to be scrambling around for materials to keep the fire burning. Lay damp wood near the fire to dry it.

LOOK UP If possible, protect the fire from precipitation by sheltering it from above, but don't build it below snow-laden or dripping tree limbs. If you want to know why, read Jack London.

100 Turn Snow into Water

Need water? Melt some snow or ice. Prop up a stone slab or a metal sheet over your campfire, and make a channel of smaller stones at its center to hold the snow in place and direct runoff. The slab should be tilted slightly so that as the chunk melts, the resulting water drains into a container. This method allows you to keep the melting process going as long as needed—just use additional containers to capture more water. Make sure you purify your water before drinking it. Snow may be white, but that doesn't mean it's clean.

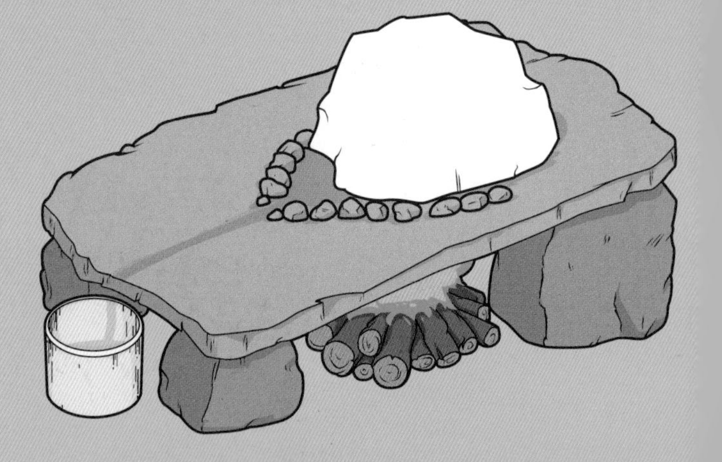

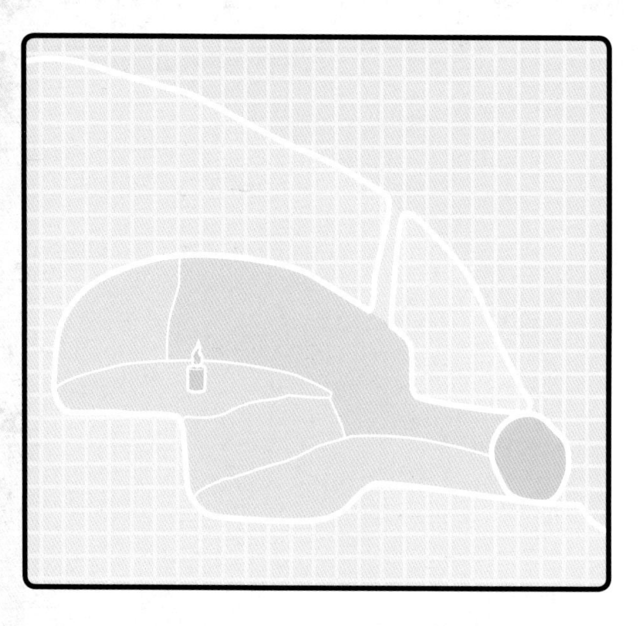

101 STEP-BY-STEP
Build a Snow Cave

So you're on a slope and there aren't many shelter options. Burrow your own snow cave and keep warm.

STEP ONE You need deep snow, preferably on a hillside so you can dig straight in. Begin with a low entrance just large enough for you to crawl inside.

STEP TWO After penetrating about 60 centimetres into the snow, start carving upward to create a dome 1.25 to 1.5 metres tall and 1.75 metres wide.

STEP THREE Against the back wall, shape a sleeping bench 60 centimetres up from the floor. Poke a small hole in the roof beside the door as an air vent.

STEP FOUR Cover the entrance with a snow block, then heat the interior with a single candle.

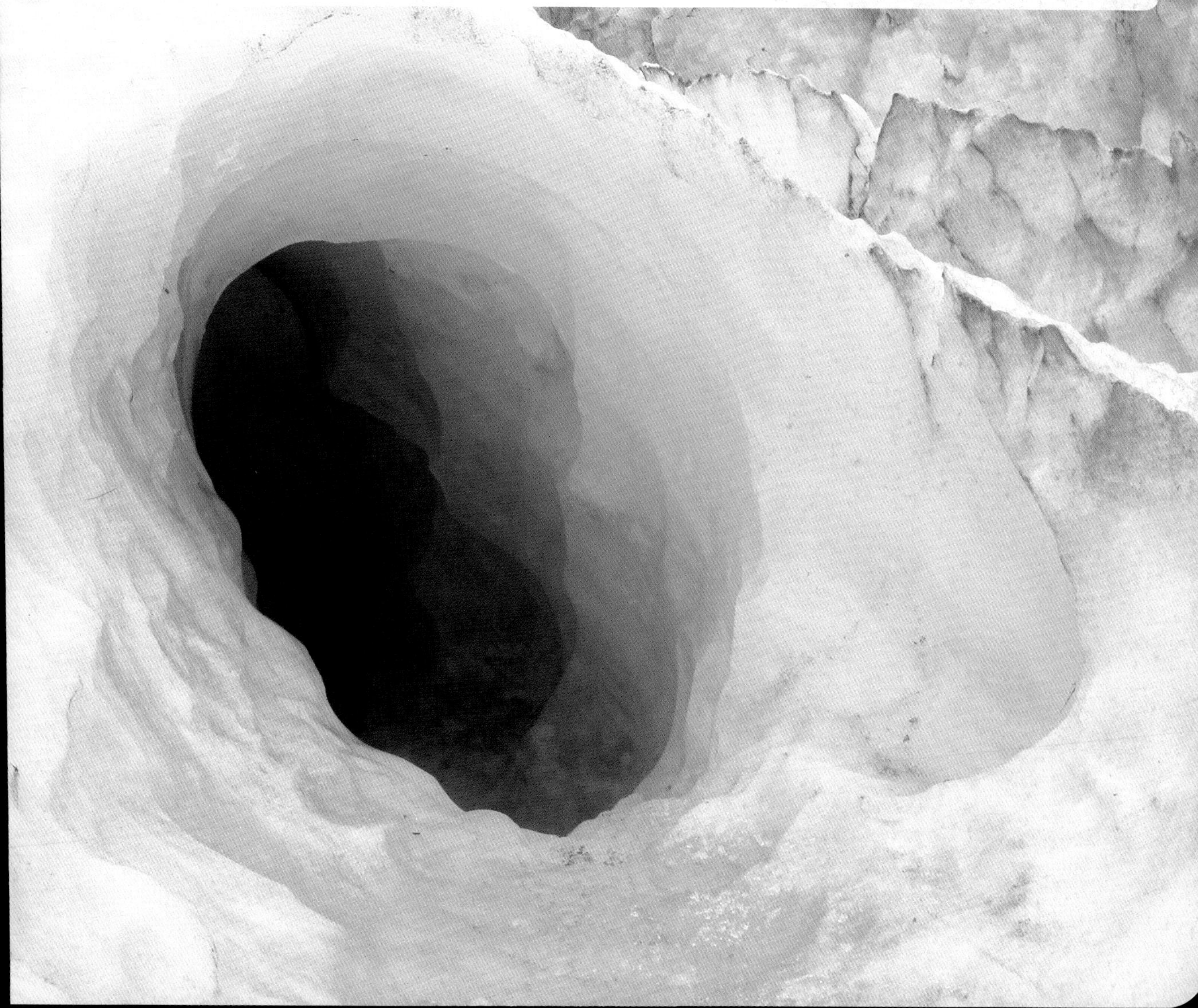

102 Traverse an Ice Floe

Say your kayak gets trapped in Arctic waters, or your plane goes down over the poles, and you end up having to leapfrog across a chain of floating ice. Sounds grim, I know.

KNOW YOUR FLOES Floes are collected chunks of ice renowned for their unpredictability. A small floating piece might flip over beneath your weight. Or you might slip between chunks and be ground to death as they clash in the current. Individual ice sheets also are popular haul-outs for marine mammals and hunting platforms for predators.

GO EASY If you have no choice but to cross a floe on foot, feel your way, probing with a pole to test each ice chunk before you commit your weight to it. As you move from berg to berg, go carefully so you don't upset their stability.

REALIZE YOUR LIMITS Are you on a frozen river? River ice is the most dangerous, because the current tosses and churns it. Get off that ride as quickly as possible.

103 Rig an Ice-Fishing Trap

And you thought *you* were hungry? Fish in a frozen lake are just as desperate for a meal, so turn their starvation to your advantage: Build several self-tending ice-fishing rigs and fish many holes at once. Start with a base stick that's twice as long as the diameter of your chosen ice hole, then lash a cross stick to the center of the base stick, with two-thirds of the cross stick on one side. Tie a baited fishing line to the short end of the cross stick, and a flag to the long end. When a fish takes the bait, the line will pull the cross stick upright and the flag will tell you a fish is on your line.

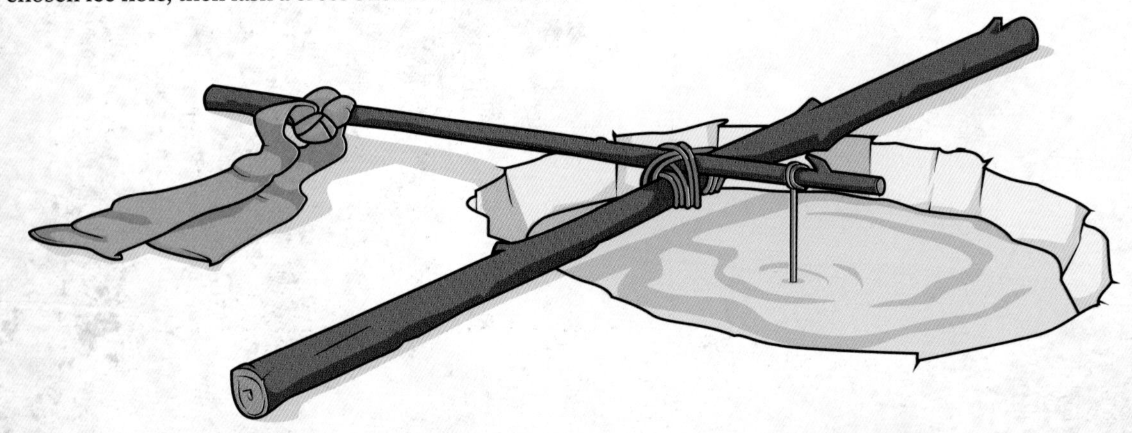

104 Improvise Snow Goggles

Snow blindness is a real danger that you can easily prevent with a good pair of sunglasses. However, you might not always have a pair handy, especially if weather conditions take you by surprise and you find yourself in a survival situation. So make like the Inuit and fashion your own goggles. First, cut a strip of duct tape 30 centimetres long and fold it over on itself lengthwise. Then, using a knife or razor blade, cut a single long slit in the folded duct tape. Next, fasten the makeshift goggles around your head with more tape. For added protection, blacken your cheeks with soot or other dark material to help absorb sunlight.

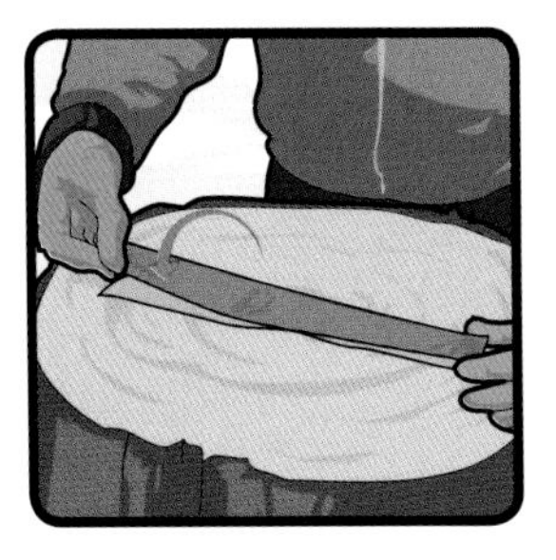

105

STEP-BY-STEP

Make Emergency Snowshoes

Walking through deep snow is tough work that will drain you of crucial energy. These snowshoes will help you glide across—not plow through—the snow's surface.

STEP ONE Start by cutting two pine boughs with ample foliage to about 1 metre long.

STEP TWO Tie a string near the base of the branch, where you cut it. Then flip the branch over and tie an overhand knot on the opposite side.

STEP THREE Place the branch so that its top (the side that faces upward when the branch is on the tree) is face down in the snow, with the foliage bending upward. Step on it, tie the string to your shoe, and thread the line through the shoelace eyelets.

STEP FOUR Once you're strapped in, walk normally across the snow. Your boot will naturally come up from the branch about 30 degrees when you walk, which will keep you from sinking into the snow.

KNOW THE NUMBERS
Thin Ice

10 CENTIMETRES Minimum ice thickness that can support a person.

689 Number of hypothermia-related fatalities each year in the United States.

10 TO 60 SECONDS Time you have to escape an automobile before it sinks after crashing through the ice.

1 TO 3 HOURS Time that someone who is using a flotation device can stay alive in 4° C water.

57 METRES Record distance for an under-ice swim, set by Wim Hof in 2000 at the Finnish village of Kolari.

15 TO 45 MINUTES Amount of time a person will likely remain alive in the water after falling through ice, provided he or she gets immediate medical attention after rescue.

106 Cross an Icy Pond

Before you venture across that frozen pond, it's a good idea to understand what's going on with the ice. If you grew up playing hockey outside, you probably already know this stuff. But if you grew up where ice was mainly something you put in a drink, these tips just might come in handy.

NEVER ASSUME THE ICE IS SAFE Many factors can compromise ice strength. For instance, rain weakens ice, and moving water, which you might find around the edges of a pond or in the middle of a brook, can reduce ice strength by as much as 15 percent. Always figure those factors into your equation.

CAREFULLY OBSERVE ICE CONDITIONS Slack ice, where chunks of ice have frozen together and are floating over water, is new and weak; clear blue ice is typically the strongest. Be wary of slushy ice late in the season. Also watch for ice-weakening features such as vegetation growing through the ice—and, of course, cracks.

GET LOCAL INFORMATION If no one else is crossing that frozen pond, chances are you shouldn't, either. Before heading into the backcountry, check in with local ice alerts and outdoor stores for advice.

TEST THE THICKNESS The only effective way to measure the ice's thickness is by cutting a hole in it. With luck, that thickness will be uniform throughout. If it's less than 10 centimetres thick, just go around the pond. If it's between 10 and 15 centimetres thick, it's safe to walk on. And between 15 and 25 centimetres thick, you could drive on it—if you had to.

HAVE A SAFETY PLAN IN PLACE Don't cross ice by yourself—even if you think it's thick enough. In this scenario, being just a smidge wrong could be deadly.

STRIP BEFORE CROSSING It may sound insane, but it's best to remove your clothes before crossing the ice. That way, if you do end up taking a frigid plunge, you'll have warm clothes to put on after you crawl out.

107 STEP-BY-STEP Get Out of Broken Ice

Forget hypothermia: The first thing to worry about when you've fallen into ice is getting yourself out. Assuming you have your pitons (because you planned ahead like a good survivalist), here's what to do:

STEP ONE Turn around in the water so you're facing the way you came. That's probably the strongest ice.

STEP TWO Jam the points of the pitons into the ice.

STEP THREE While kicking your feet vigorously, haul yourself out of the ice.

STEP FOUR As soon as you're on the ice, roll (don't crawl) away from the edge of the hole. Get off the ice, and get warm immediately.

108 Save Someone from a Chilly Demise

If you see someone fall through ice, resist the urge to be a hero and run out on the ice to help. If the ice wasn't strong enough to support that person, it won't be strong enough to support you, either.

KEEP TALKING Let the victim know you're there to help, and encourage him or her to keep swimming.

REACH OUT Extend anything—a rope, a tree branch, a boat oar, or even a set of jumper cables—as a lifeline that the victim can grab, then pull him or her out.

FLOAT A BOAT Push a small boat out onto the ice and help the victim over the side. If the ice breaks again, you'll end up floating in the boat instead of swimming.

109 Swim Across a Raging River

Even for experienced outdoorsfolk, swimming across deep, moving water is unsettling.

STRIP DOWN Swimming nude is much easier than fighting the weight of waterlogged clothing. Use a trash bag or poncho to keep your things dry—and the bundle can do double duty as a flotation device.

AIM DOWNSTREAM In rapids, you won't be swimming freestyle across the river. The current is going to pull you downstream fast, so position yourself on your back, with your feet facing downstream. This position will help protect you against impacts with rocks and submerged snags.

PADDLE Use your hands, both to paddle and to guide yourself toward the far bank. It takes a while to cross rapidly moving water, so plan to swim deliberately, and expect to end up a long way downstream.

110 STEP-BY-STEP Wade Across a River

There's a river in your way, but luck's in your favor: It's shallow enough for you to wade across. Here's how to stay on your feet as you go.

STEP ONE Drag is, well, a drag. To cut down on it, remove your clothing, except for your boots or shoes, as they'll protect your feet from jagged river rocks.

STEP TWO Carry your clothes above your head, so you'll have dry clothes when you reach the other side.

STEP THREE Wade against the flow at a 45-degree angle; you'll be less likely to be swept off your feet.

STEP FOUR If the current threatens to sweep your feet from under you, use a pole to stabilize yourself. Keep it on the upstream side of your body, because in that position, it's easier to hold onto the pole and stay in place.

STEP FIVE Use the pole to probe the water ahead of you for solid footing, holes, snags, and hidden boulders and tree limbs.

STEP SIX Make sure you're on a steady surface before taking each step. If you lose your balance and get swept away, it'll be tough to regain your footing

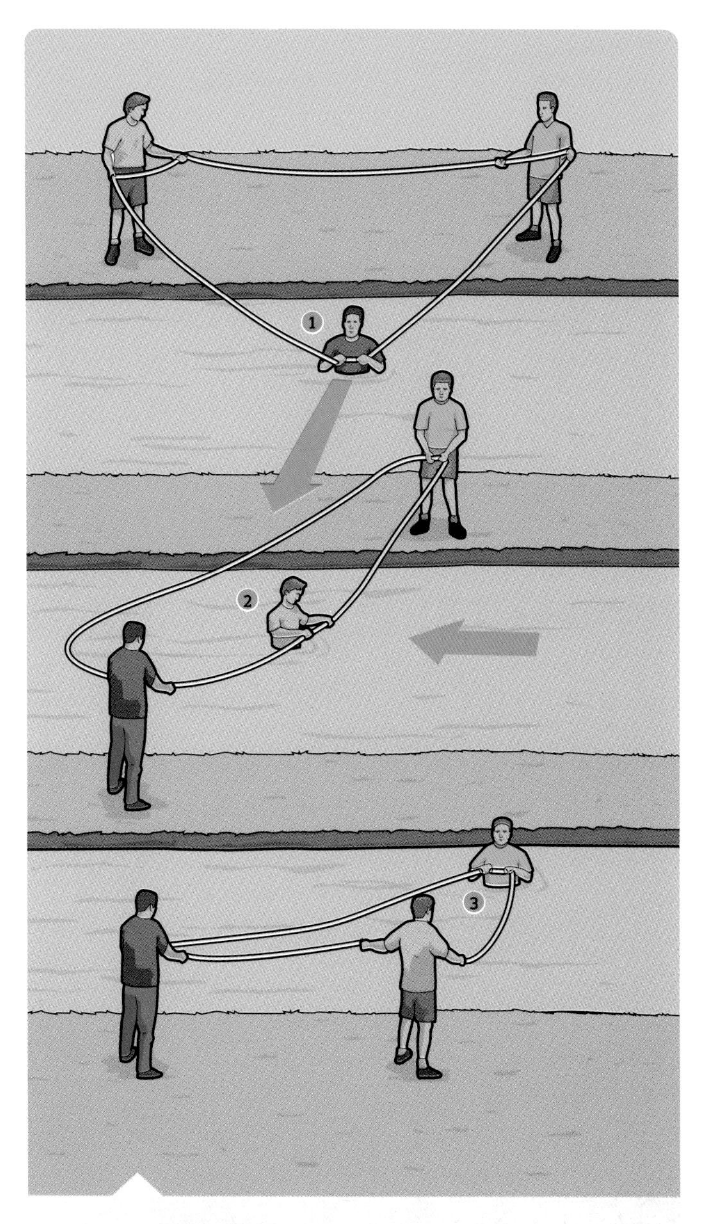

111 Ford a River with Friends

Remember geometry from grade school? Good, because basic knowledge of triangles can keep you from getting sucked into a fast-moving river. If the person braving the current is backed up by two friends on shore—with a sturdy rope loop connecting all three—the two on land will be able to help the one in the water, even if he or she loses footing. Once the first person has reached the far bank, the second can cross, using the rope stretched between the banks as a safety line. When the last person is ready to cross, he or she enters the water, and the others pull him or her across.

112

STEP-BY-STEP
Tie a Fisherman's Knot

Got two short ropes, but need a long one? A fisherman's knot can join the short ones together.

STEP ONE Loop one rope's end around the other rope, then bring it over both ropes.

STEP TWO Bring the same end up and behind both ropes, creating two loops, then thread it through both loops and pull to tighten.

STEP THREE Loop the other rope's end behind the two ropes.

STEP FOUR Bring that rope up and over both ropes, and then behind them again, creating two loops.

STEP FIVE Thread this rope's end through the two loops. Pull both anchored ends to tighten.

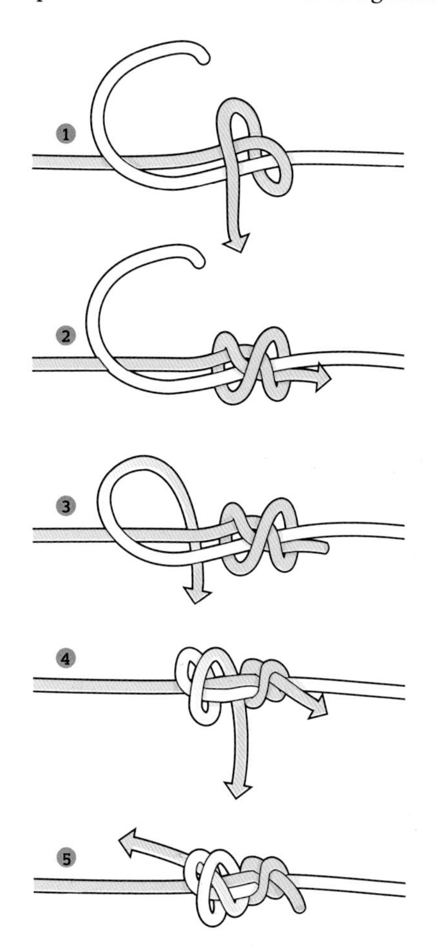

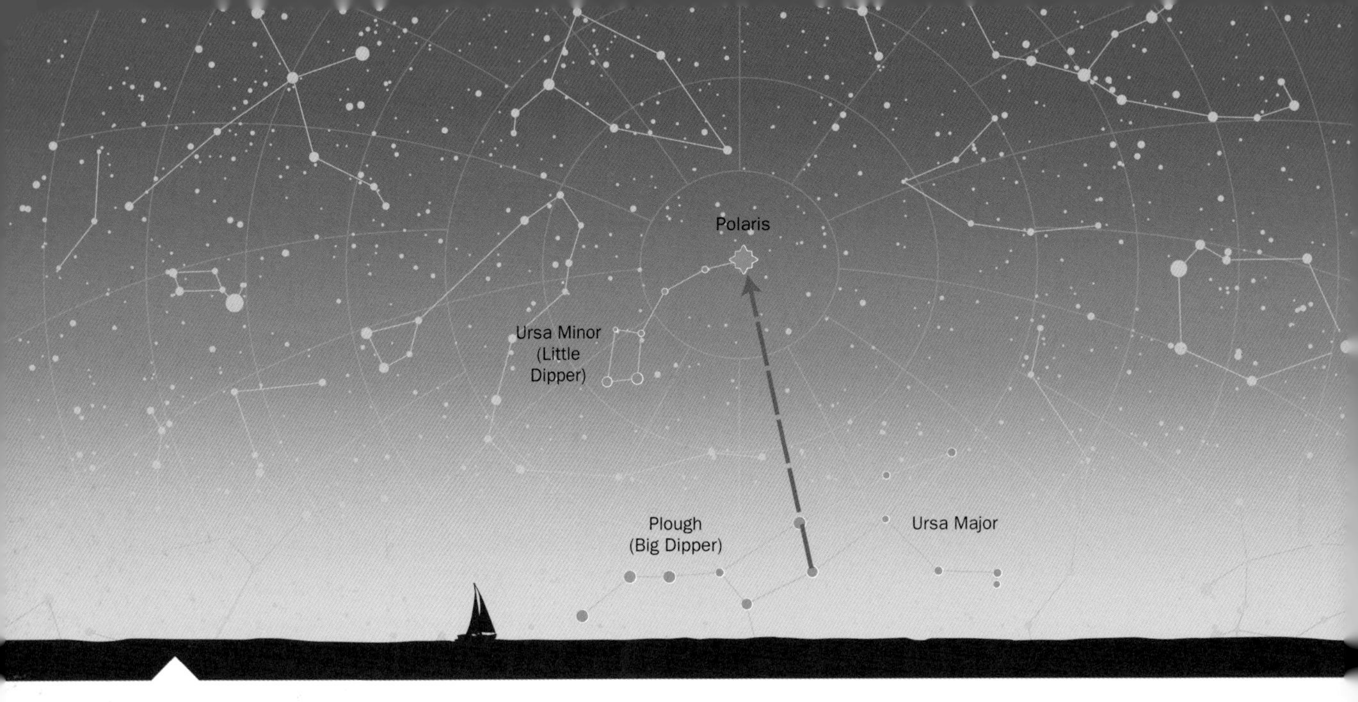

113 Orient Yourself by the Stars

FIND THE NORTH STAR To find Polaris, the prominent star that's close to the north celestial pole, look for the famous pattern of stars called the Big Dipper or the Plough in the constellation Ursa Major. Mentally draw a line connecting the stars at the end of the Big Dipper's "bowl," then extend that line out five times its length to arrive at Polaris. It's hard to miss, since it's the brightest star in Ursa Minor, or the Little Dipper.

SEEK THE SOUTH POLE Traveling below the equator? Find the Southern Cross's long axis and extend a line down four and a half times the axis length. Then locate the bright stars Rigil Kent and Hadar to the left of the Southern Cross. Figure the midpoint between these two stars, then imagine a perpendicular line from that point to the end of the line drawn from the Southern Cross. That intersection marks the South Pole.

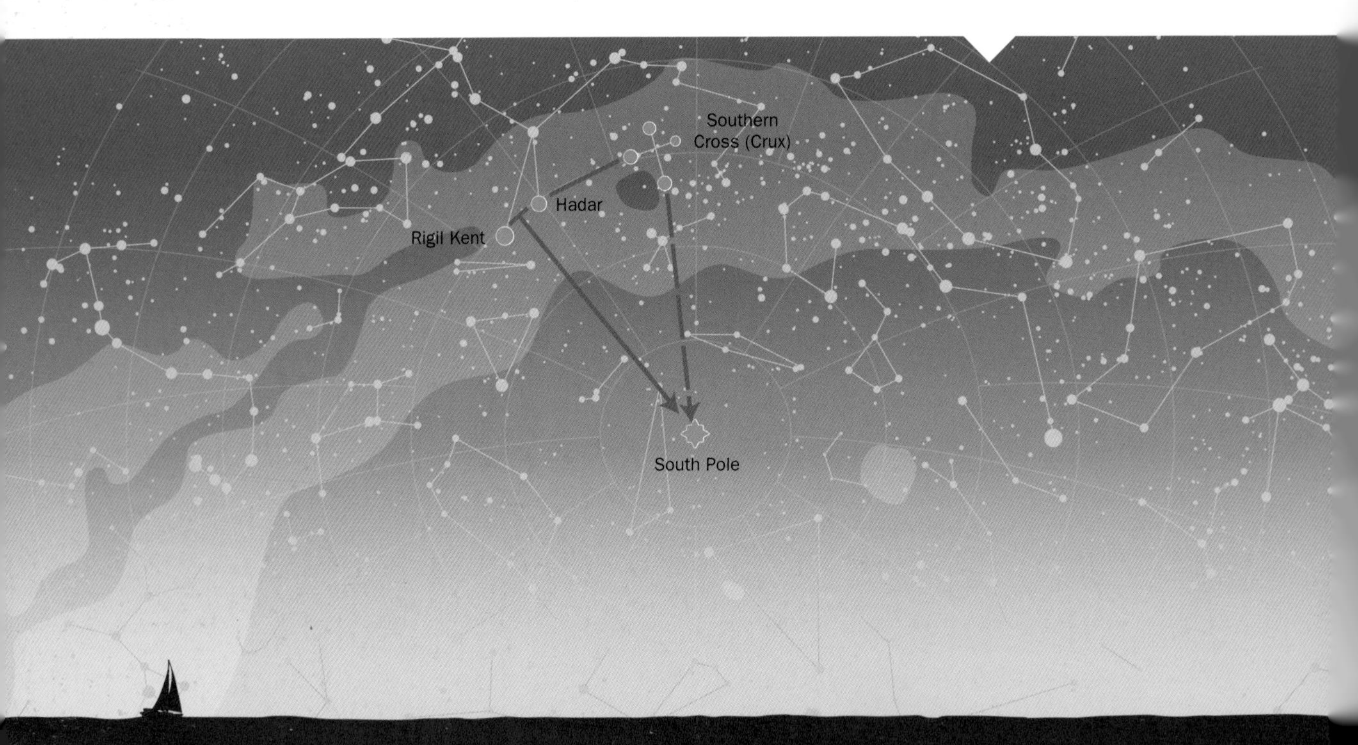

KNOW THE NUMBERS

Out to Sea

2.6 Average number of cruise-ship passengers that are lost per year.

500 Number of ships weighing 450,000 kilos or more that are lost at sea per year.

161 METRES Farthest distance that a shout at sea is likely to be heard.

30 TO 90 METRES Distance an average person can swim in 4° C water before he or she succumbs to the elements.

85 HOURS World record for longest time treading water. Don't try to beat it.

108 KILOMETRES Longest distance ever swum in open ocean water—a feat accomplished by Australia's Penny Palfrey, a world-class athlete. Again, don't even try to beat it. Really.

169 KILOMETRES Farthest recorded distance from which a signal mirror's flash has been spotted.

114 Signal a Boat

At sea, you're rarely more than a few kilometres from land. The trouble is, that land is under hundreds or thousands of metres of water, so walking to it is out of the question. Here's how to get rescued.

SAY IT WITH A SATELLITE The most effective signaling device is an emergency position-indicating radio beacon (EPIRB), which notifies rescuers via a global satellite system. The next best device is a very-high-frequency (VHF) or single-sideband (SSB) radio.

BE CALM AND CLEAR When making a Mayday call, state your GPS coordinates, the nature of your emergency, a description of your vessel, and the number of people on board.

LIGHT THE WAY Use visual signals like aerial flares, smoke, and dye markers. Don't fire a flare unless you know someone is close enough to see it, and hold it over the water so you don't risk setting your boat on fire. Use a mirror in daylight, flashing it at the horizon.

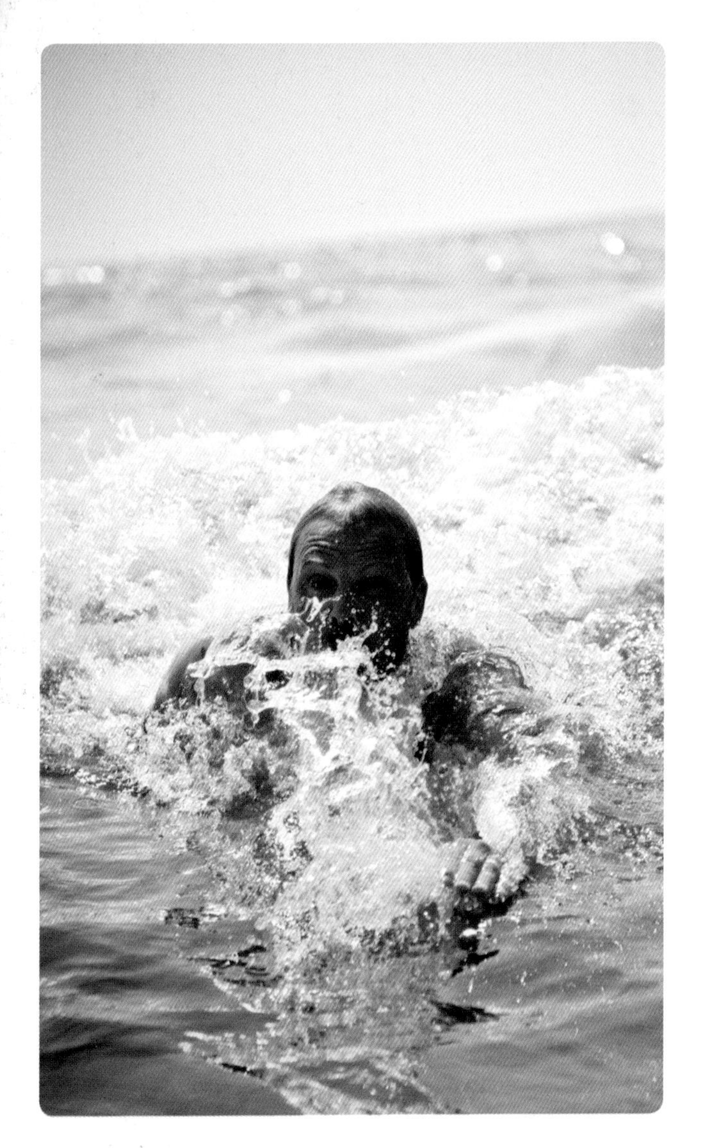

115 CHECKLIST Improvise a Float

Drowning is the number one cause of death in boating accidents, so once you've wound up in the water, your goal is simple: Stay afloat. The longer you do, the greater your chance of rescue. The best flotation device is a life jacket, but if you don't have one, grab onto anything that's floating (including the boat itself). If possible, tie items together to make a raft that will be easier to hold or lie on. Look for any of these buoyant objects:

- [ ] Cockpit cushion
- [ ] Life ring or horseshoe ring
- [ ] Wet suit
- [ ] Scuba tank and buoyancy vest
- [ ] Ice chest
- [ ] Piece of wood
- [ ] Bit of polystyrene foam
- [ ] Boat fender (aka "bumper")
- [ ] Crab pot or shrimp trap buoy
- [ ] Fishing-net float
- [ ] Plastic garbage sack that you fill with air
- [ ] A bucket that you can turn over to trap air inside
- [ ] A fuel tank
- [ ] Empty jerry can
- [ ] Plastic bottle that you empty and fill with air

116 Beat Hypothermia in the Water

Water cools us down—sometimes in ways that are hazardous to our health. Even in tropical "warm" water, you'll eventually suffer hypothermia if you stay in too long. Follow these steps to hold on to your heat.

GET DRY If you're in the water, get out immediately if you can. If your boat has capsized, attempt to right it, and then crawl back inside and bail out the water. If you're on land, stay dry and out of the wind.

GET WARM Remove your wet clothing and put on dry clothes if they're available. Otherwise, dry out the wet clothes before re-dressing. If you're with others, huddle together to share warmth.

WORK AS A TEAM When you're stranded with a group in the water, you can cling together for shared warmth. Face inward, hold on tightly, and tread water to conserve heat. If you're out of the water, huddle the same way to stay warmer in the wind.

ASSUME THE POSITION If you're wearing a life vest, assume the heat escape lessening posture (HELP) by drawing your legs up, folding your arms across your chest, and keeping your face out of the water.

KEEP YOUR WITS Remain calm and still. Don't try to swim, since that circulates cold water around your body and reduces core temperature.

117 Find Drinking Water at Sea

Water, water, everywhere—and not a drop to drink? Not if you're prepared, resourceful, and willing to put effort into collecting drinkable water. And you should be: It will save your life.

TRAP MOISTURE Outfit your vessel with a plastic tarp to catch rainwater and drain it into containers, allowing the first drops of rain to wash the salt off the tarp. If you don't have a tarp, use fabric to absorb moisture, then wring it out into containers. Never drink saltwater—it will make you ill and speed dehydration and death.

PULL A MACGYVER When you've been adrift at sea for a period of time, all your clothes end up encrusted with salt crystals. At the first sign of rain, give all your clothes and other fabric a seawater bath. Yes, it's salty, but not as salty as the salt residue, which will make any water it contacts undrinkable. If you have sails, make a bowl out of them to capture the water. Tarps, shirts, plastic sheets, and even the raft itself can all collect water. Any can, bottle, or other container can store it. The first water you collect will have a high salt content, so store it separately, and use it to clean wounds or to wash food before eating.

118 Catch Fish in Open Waters

Stranded at sea? If you're in a life raft, small fish often gather beneath the raft, either out of curiosity or because they feel sheltered there. Who knows? But catching those fish might satisfy your need for nourishment. Troll a handline with a hook and anything flashy to serve as a lure. Jig the lure up and down a few metres below the surface, being careful not to snag the life raft with the hook. After catching a fish, use the guts as bait to catch more.

119 Stay Alive at Sea

The Canadian coastline is vast, flanked by three oceans to the west, north, and east. It can be easy to get stranded at sea and left adrift at the whim of the ocean currents. Don't panic, get organized, and develop a plan to get to shore or reach help safely.

SIGNAL FOR HELP Use your radio to verbally transmit the international signal for distress, Mayday Mayday, or if you're not about to die but you might soon, you can also use the urgent signal of pan-pan. Try to reach close boats using very high frequency (VHF) radio messages on channel 16. The high frequency (HF) can be used for longer range communications on 2182 kHz. A mirror can also be used as a signaling device using the Morse code of SOS, which over time became associated with phrases such as "save our ship" or "save our souls". It is three dots followed by three dashes and ending with three dots. Signal as one code, without breaks between the dots and dashes. If you don't have a mirror, raise and lower both arms repeatedly from your sides, outstretched from shoulder height to above you head.

POWER YOUR CRAFT The tide will move your boat in the direction of its ebbs and flows so if you know which direction land is, use the movement to steer your craft. You can use your dead motor, or fashion a rudder, to steer across the flow of the tide to get you closer to shore, rather than head further into unknown territory. Make a sail out of tarps, towels, or other fabrics to power your craft, allowing you more control when steering. If you know where land is anchor up when the tide would pull you away and drift when it will take you towards shore.

RATION FOOD AND WATER Prepare for the worst and only use food and water when necessary. You don't know how long you will be at sea, so making the most of what you have is critical. You can survive for days without water, so drink once a day. When you do, sip the water to try to satisfy your thirst and make it last as long as possible. Avoid diuretics, like caffeine, which can rob you of valuable hydration. Eat only what you need to stay alert and prevent delirium from setting in.

DO SOME BIRD WATCHING Watch for sea birds, as they tend to head back to land after feeding. They fish out at sea and return to nesting areas to feed their young. Explorers and hunters on the Arctic Ocean counted on the birds to get them to the closest land when in open seas.

TAKE INVENTORY Know where your survival gear is in case you need it. Life jackets, flares, survival suits, and inflatable rafts should be easy to access in case of need.

SLEEP IN SHIFTS You don't want to miss any opportunity to get help so make sure someone is watching the surroundings out to the horizons, at all times. This will mean sleeping in shifts to make sure someone is alert and awake to spot and signal potential help. Use a vantage point for watching to give you every advantage possible.

120 Right a Capsized Boat

Small sailboats capsize easily, but luckily, they're easy to right. Crawl up onto the overturned hull, grab the centerboard (keel), and lean back, using your weight against the centerboard as a lever to flip the boat over. When it's upright, crawl aboard and bail out the water.

If your capsized boat is a motorboat without a centerboard, righting it will take a bit more doing. Tie one end of a rope to something secure in the middle of the boat, like an oarlock. Toss the free end of the rope up onto the hull. Crawl onto the hull to grab the free end of the rope, facing the side where the rope is tied. Back up toward the water and lean back, using your weight against the rope to pull the boat over. Once it's upright, scramble on and start bailing.

121 STEP-BY-STEP Put Out a Boat Fire

A fire on a boat is a life-threatening catastrophe, so it's wise to have a plan in place before you leave shore.

STEP ONE Store fresh fire extinguishers in locations near the galley and the engine compartment, the two most likely locations for fire.

STEP TWO If fire breaks out, move everyone out of the cabin and get them into life vests. Call VHF channel 16 to report the emergency. Prepare to abandon ship.

STEP THREE Fight the fire with extinguishers, keeping a clear escape route behind you at all times. Always extinguish fires from the bottom up.

122 STEP-BY-STEP **Start a Flooded Motor**

Do the following to start a flooded outboard motor:

STEP ONE Remove any spark plugs and wipe them dry.

STEP TWO Crank the motor several times to blow excess fuel out of the combustion chamber.

STEP THREE Reinstall the spark plugs and then reconnect the wires.

STEP FOUR Raise the warm-up or fast-idle lever and crank the starter no more than 8 to 10 seconds before pausing.

STEP FIVE If the motor doesn't start, crank the starter again.

STEP SIX After the engine starts, leave the fast-idle lever up until the motor runs smoothly. Then, with luck, you're good to go.

123 Plug a Leak

Water is supposed to stay on the outside of a boat, but inevitably some gets inside due to rain or waves coming over the bow. That's not a big problem. However, when water invades because of a leak, the problem becomes quite real.

FIND THE TROUBLE SPOT Your top priority is to locate the leak. If you can't find it, head for dry land fast. Check to see that the boat's drain plug is closed—if it's open, that's your culprit.

HEAL YOUR HULL If the leak is caused by a failed thru-hull fitting, stop it with a conical soft-wood plug that should be tethered to the hull.

PROTECT WITH PLASTIC If the hull is fractured due to impact, place a large plastic sheet across the leak on the outside of the hull. Secure the plastic with ropes. Water pressure will help hold it in place as you carefully head for land.

USE OLD FAITHFUL If all else fails, you can repair small cracks with duct tape.

124 Avoid Shark Bites

Sharks don't usually hunt people as a food source, which is why most shark bites stop there: Once the shark realizes you're not a nice blubbery seal, it leaves you alone. Unfortunately, that little "mistake" isn't all that little for the human on the receiving end of those chompers. Here's how to avoid those nasty bites:

CEDE THE SEA While there certainly are open-ocean predators, most shark threats are in the shallows and near food sources. Coral reefs are popular hangouts—and also happen to be the most desirable dive sites. If you're diving in these areas, be aware of the shark risk before you enter the water, and dive with at least one partner, as sharks are less likely to mess with a group.

GET AWAY If you do suddenly find yourself in close quarters with one of these beasts, your best bet is to get out of the water, swimming away with smooth, even strokes that won't attract its attention.

FACE YOUR FOE When a shark wants to eat you, you'll know in advance: It will hunch its back, lower its fins, and rush at you in a zigzag. Thrust your spear gun, camera housing, knife, or whatever else you're packing to discourage it. If you can, punch its supersensitive nose or stab at its eyes or gills.

SUBMERGE Divers report successful evasion by descending to the seafloor and waiting for the sharks to leave. But that only works if you've got an air tank.

125 Make Peace with a Man-of-War

The Portuguese man-of-war isn't a true jellyfish, but it stings just as badly—or worse. Responsible for up to 10,000 stings in Australia alone each year, the man-of-war haunts warm waters and is equipped with long, threadlike tentacles that deliver a nasty venom. And the poor recipient of that venom can look forward to days of agony, muscle spasms, and welts, if not death.

So how can you skip this tropical water experience? Unfortunately, the only way to avoid getting stung is to sport a full-coverage wet suit in waters where these creatures lurk. But if you are stung by a man-of-war (and you'll know if you see its inflated blue, purple, or pink top section), remember that its venom differs from that of a true jellyfish, and requires different treatment. If you're stung, use tweezers to remove the tentacle remnants, then flush with saltwater. Don't scrub the area, as that can release toxins into your skin. Follow with hot saltwater or a compress that's at least 45° C. Skip vinegar and freshwater rinses—they'll only make a bad thing worse.

126 Deal with Sea Caves

People are drawn to dangerous things. So when you're scuba diving and you find a shipwreck or an underwater cave, it's hard to resist exploring.

BE PREPARED Being certified to dive in open waters doesn't give you carte blanche to explore underwater caves. That requires a separate training certificate, and for your safety you should get the necessary schooling and gear before you venture into such treacherous territory.

BUY A MAP Divers have already explored many shipwrecks and caves, so use the knowledge they've gained. First of all, you'll find cooler sites. Second, you'll avoid hazardous situations. Before diving, check with local authorities about potential danger zones.

BE AWARE If you get lost in a cave or a sunken vessel, you'll have limited time to get out before you run out of air. Before going in, tie a piece of strong line to help you retrace your path. Have a standby diver monitor that line to ensure that it doesn't come undone.

127 Escape Kelp Entanglement

Kelp forests are a favorite habitat for fish and for divers wanting to get close to fish. Alas, when it comes to kelp, getting close can mean getting caught.

DETANGLE YOURSELF It's virtually impossible to break kelp by hand, so you have to untangle those slippery organic ropes. (Pro tip: Strap a knife to your ankle before you descend; it'll help you cut your way to freedom.) Slow your breathing and methodically undo the tangle. Kelp snags easily on your fins, mask, snorkel, dive tanks, and regulators, so release each component in turn.

MAKE IT A TEAM EFFORT If you're diving with a buddy (and you always should be), untangle each other.

TAKE THE EXPRESS LANE Try descending to where the kelp rises up from the sea floor. At this depth, the foliage isn't as thick and currents don't move the stalks as much, so you can then swim to a clearing and ascend.

128 Keep Track of Time at the Equator

Stranded near the equator? Rejoice: Sunrise and sunset come at around 7:00 a.m. and 7:00 p.m. year-round, which makes keeping track of time easy.

First, find a level spot and drive a stick into the ground. Face south and, when the sun comes up, use a rock to mark the stick's shadow as 7:00 a.m. When the sun sets, the shadow will be on the opposite side, indicating 7:00 p.m.; mark its end with another rock. Then, place a rock halfway between these rocks—that's 1:00 p.m. Mark the halfway points between these three rocks to note 10:00 a.m. and 4:00 p.m. Halfway between each of these five rocks you can mark as 8:30 a.m., 11:30 a.m., 2:30 p.m., and 5:30 p.m. Now, check your dial: The marker on which the shadow falls indicates the hour. And you'll always know what time it is—at least during the day.

129 Find Lunch in a Tide Pool

There's usually a lot to eat in a tide pool, though what you find depends on the latitude. So, what to look for? You'll find many edible creatures, from octopuses to small fish. Tide pools also harbor a variety of small crabs and crustaceans, like mussels. Most monopods are edible, but some are dangerous (such as the venomous cone snails of the South Pacific), so gain local knowledge before harvesting. While you can plunder much of the tide pool by hand, some common tools also come in handy. Make a dip net for shrimp and small fish by stretching a shirt over a pair of sticks. A makeshift spear is useful for larger fish and spiny urchins, which can be harvested for their roe. With all that bounty, it's helpful to have a bag or basket of some sort to carry your catch.

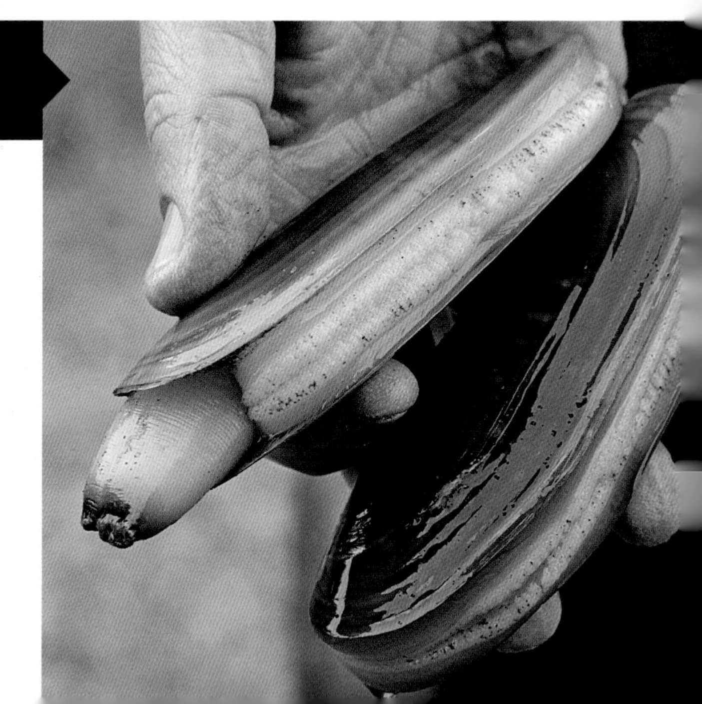

130 Swim Against a Riptide

Feel like you're swimming hard but going nowhere? You're in a rip current, which forms when waves come ashore, then wash back out across an underwater sandbar. The worst ones occur when the sandbar is breached, creating a funnel where outgoing water moves swiftly with a powerful current.

Don't fight a rip current; it will exhaust you, and you can easily drown. The best survival tactic is to allow the current to carry you out to sea until it weakens. Then swim parallel to the shoreline to a spot where the current is not running, and swim back ashore.

131 Make the Most of a Coconut

If you're lucky enough to wash ashore where coconuts grow, survival will be much easier. In addition to food and drink, the coconut palm provides materials for shelter, rope, fire making, and clothing.

DRINK THE JUICE If you've got young, green coconuts, you're in luck: These contain sweet water that's high in sugar, fiber, protein, antioxidants, vitamins, and minerals to balance your electrolytes. To save the water, drain the coconut by punching a hole in one of the soft "eyes" at the end.

EAT UP All coconuts are rich in calories, regardless of their age. This meat provides the same benefits as the water, plus carbohydrates and fats. But green coconuts come with a special treat: At their center is a delicious marshmallow-soft jelly. To get at all that goodness, rap the coconut smartly on its equator, rotate it, and rap until the shell cracks open.

WEAR IT You can use the husk to make rope, sandals, and clothing. And the shell can function as a bowl, a scraper, and even as a bra. Heck, I've seen weirder things.

132 Assess a Deserted Island

Post-shipwreck, you find yourself on a deserted tropical island, where there are no phones, and no boss—it's everyone's dream! Time to assemble the staples of your Robinson Crusoe life.

FIND WATER Assuming you don't have any medical emergency, your first priority will be finding safe drinking water. Birds and other wildlife seek water in the morning and evening, so follow them. Also, set up a catchment system: Form large leaves into gutters to direct rainfall into coconut shells. This nifty setup maximizes the amount of water gathered, and also provides storage.

BUILD YOUR CRIB Bamboo and palm are the resources of choice; use the bamboo for structure and the palm fronds for roofing and walls. Lash things together with limber vines, or twist coconut-husk fibers into rope.

STOCK YOUR FRIDGE Shop the tide pools for edibles, especially mussels, clams, snails, crabs, and small fish trapped by the outgoing tide.

GET COOKING Next, you need a fire. Use bamboo shavings for tinder, and a split piece of bamboo as a fire saw to spark up a blaze. You're set . . . for now.

133 Make Rope with an Improvised Vise

Sometimes you need another pair of hands—like, say, when you're trying to twist vines together into a rope. You can make a vise by cutting down a sapling about 15 centimetres in diameter roughly 60 centimetres above the ground. Split the stump downward through the center with an axe or machete. Pry open the jaws of the split with a wedge, and insert the vines you wish to twist into rope. Remove the wedge to secure them. If there's not enough pressure to hold the vines in place, put a rope around the stump just below the object, insert a stick as illustrated, and twist it to tighten the rope.

134 Craft a Raft

If you decide to leave your island, either to move to another one or to get out into the shipping lanes where you might be rescued, you'll need a raft.

FIND RAW MATERIAL Beachcombing might reveal buoys, pallets, plastic containers, or other buoyant materials that have washed ashore. As for wood, bamboo works great, but beware of waterlogged wood—it won't float.

FASHION YOUR FLOAT Use the material you gathered to make a platform. Lash everything together with rope and scavenged fishing nets, incorporating several crossbeams to keep the structure stable. Lash a vertical pole to the end of the raft to serve as a rudder for directional control. Before leaving the island, check the raft's seaworthiness by letting it float for a couple days.

135 Know When Your Raft's Close to Land

In those epic seafaring movies, sailors usually hear a "Land ho!" when they're nearing shore. But if you're on an improvised raft all by yourself without a nice view from a crow's nest, how do you know when you're getting close to land? A hump on the horizon may be land—or it might be clouds. To know the difference, use all your senses.

SMELL You might pick up the scent of foliage or, better yet, the smoke from a shoreside fire.

SIGHT Watch for shore-loving seabirds like gulls. At night, watch for lights in the distance.

SOUND Listen for the distant sound of surf crashing on a shore, or perhaps (if you're really lucky) the hum of human activity.

TOUCH Feel for the wave patterns and current, which change as the water flows around a land mass.

DISASTER

136 Be Ready for Disaster

A tidal wave washes hundreds of people out to sea in an instant. A hurricane doubles a region's homeless population overnight. A tornado knocks out a city's power grid. None of us is safe from nature's whims. But educating yourself on what to do in various situations can make a disaster less disastrous.

MAKE PLANS Know the kinds of trouble that are likely to arise in your area and think about how you and your family should respond to those situations. Pick out the spots that will be the safest refuge for each scenario, and make sure everyone knows emergency numbers, including the number of a trusted relative or friend who lives in another state.

HOLE UP AT HOME Your dwelling may be the safest place to ride out danger, so make sure it's always stocked with an at-home emergency kit. Have a bug-out bag packed in case you have to take off in a hurry.

PLOT YOUR ESCAPE When it comes to hurricanes and floods, your best chance may be to evacuate safely. As soon as there's a hint of trouble, start monitoring local reports and plan the safest, swiftest way out.

RELY ON YOURSELF After a disaster, electricity and running water may be slow to return. Prepare yourself to live without them. It could save your life.

KNOW THE NUMBERS
Disasters

14,802 Deaths from the 2003 heatwave in France—more than any other European nation.

75 Percentage of Ukraine's wheat crop destroyed in the heatwave of 2003.

3.7 TO 4 MILLION People who died in China's Great Flood of 1931.

524 METRES Tallest wave ever recorded, during Alaska's 1958 Lituya Bay mega tsunami.

42 MILLION Litres of crude oil spilled during the Exxon Valdez crisis.

6.6 MILLION Number of people exposed to dangerous levels of radiation from the Chernobyl power-plant accident.

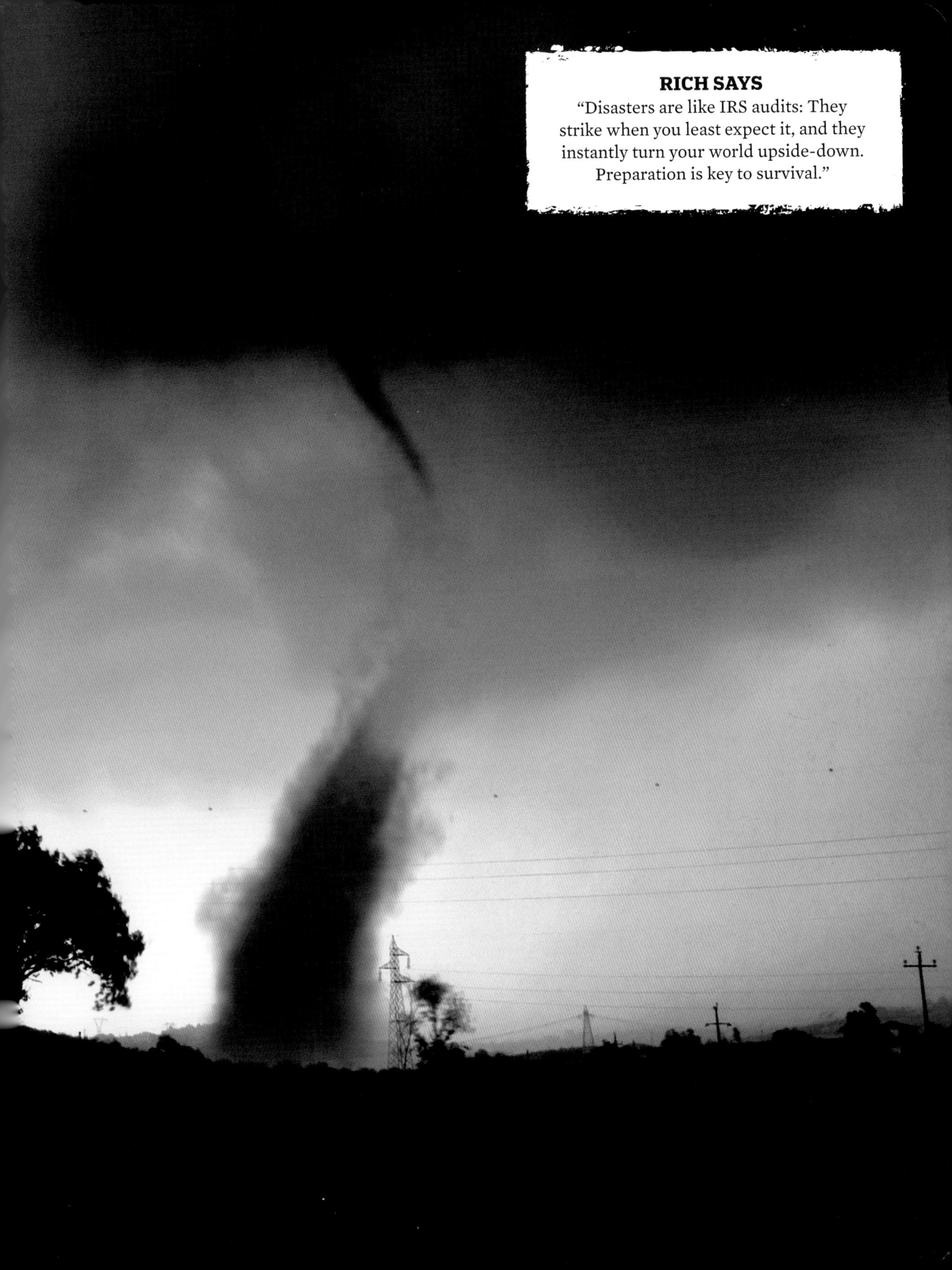

RICH SAYS

"Disasters are like IRS audits: They strike when you least expect it, and they instantly turn your world upside-down. Preparation is key to survival."

RICH SAYS

"They call it a 'finger of God' for good reason. You'd best be on good terms with the man upstairs if you cross paths with a violent storm like this one."

137 Spot Tornado Warning Signs

Is that shape on the horizon an innocent cloud—or a deadly tornado? As you scan the skies, keep an eye out for these telltale signs:

SUPERCELL Look out for a thunderhead with a hard-edged, cauliflower look. This is a supercell: a dangerous formation with interior winds of up to 275 kmh.

WALL CLOUD These have clearly defined edges and look dense and, well, sort of like a wall.

GREEN TINGE A sickly green hue in the sky can mean that a tornado is starting to take shape.

FUNNEL CLOUD A needle-like formation descending from a cloud's base indicates cyclonic activity. When a funnel cloud touches ground, it becomes a tornado. Fortunately, most funnel clouds never touch down.

STRANGE SOUNDS Listen up for sounds similar to swarming bees or a waterfall—that may be an approaching twister you're hearing. If your ears pop, there's been a drop in air pressure, which is another danger sign.

Green Tinge

Wall Cloud

138 Judge Where a Tornado Is Heading

If you're on the ground staring down a tornado, you can usually tell whether it's moving to your left or right. But if a tornado looks like it's standing still, you're right in its path—and you need to get out, quick.

Tornadoes often move southwest to northeast, so use a compass or a car's navigation system to avoid driving in the same direction. Of course, nothing beats the eyeball test. If you see a tornado, drive at a right angle to its path. Don't try driving directly away from the twister—that'll put you exactly in the line of danger. There's an excellent chance that the tornado will overtake you, because twisters are difficult—sometimes downright impossible—to outrun.

139 ASSESS AND RESPOND
Stay Safe in a Tornado

In a Shelter

In a Car

In the Open

A twister can touch down in the blink of an eye, so it's tough to know where you'll be or how bad the storm will get. Here's advice on staying safe in three likely situations, from a tornado that's hypothetical to one that's about to hit.

TORNADO THREAT Highly Possible

- Gather needed supplies.
- Clear shelter of hazards.
- Monitor broadcasts for details.
- Watch conditions for signs of supercell activities.
- Check in with friends and family members, and share plans and location information.

- Avoid back roads and unfamiliar places.
- Head for home or a designated shelter. If the weather becomes severe, pull over until it improves.
- Avoid using hazard lights, which may distract motorists.
- Monitor broadcasts.

- If you're camping, stay close to home base.
- Watch for tornadic signs in the southwestern sky.
- Stash your gear in your vehicle.
- Stay in groups.
- Contact a responsible person back home and fill him or her in on your situation and location.

TORNADO THREAT On the Ground

- Do not open doors or windows.
- Move to the basement or storm cellar if you have one, or to an interior room.
- Have a mattress or other padding ready to pull over your head.
- Prepare to move to a sturdier storm shelter if an evacuation warning is issued.

- Pull off the road and locate the tornado.
- If you can see a funnel, determine its direction.
- If you're in the tornado's path, drive immediately away at a right angle to its path.

- Stay out of tents or makeshift structures, which may collapse.
- Seek a low-lying area in which to ride out the storm.
- If you're in the tornado's path, move quickly to a ravine as far away from the path as possible.
- Keep low to avoid flying debris.

TORNADO THREAT Coming Right at You

- Get into a bathtub or other fixture that's firmly adhered to the floor.
- Pull a mattress over your body to protect yourself from falling debris.
- Lock arms with others.
- Stay low and avoid the temptation to watch or film the tornado.

- Get out of the car.
- Find a low-lying area and lie flat with your fingers locked together behind your head.
- Do not go under an overpass, as the winds will increase there.
- If there's a large boulder, put your hands behind your head and crouch on the side that has some protection from the wind.

- Resist the temptation to watch what's going on. You need to focus on being a survivor, not a witness.
- Lie facedown with hands protecting your head in a low-lying area until the storm has passed.
- Look for a sturdy object like a boulder, and put it between you and the twister.

KNOW THE NUMBERS
Tornadoes

1,500 Number of tornadoes that occur annually worldwide.

80 Number of tornadoes that happen in Canada every year.

28 Number of people killed in 1912's Regina Cyclone, which was Canada's deadliest tornado on record, injuring an additional 300 people and causing over $4.5 million in damages.

1987 Year Edmonton was hit with one of Canada's strongest tornadoes, an F4. The second deadliest tornado in Canadian history, it killed 27 people and injured 253.

352 KM Longest recorded damage track of a tornado.

1.5 M Shortest damage track.

482 KMH Fastest wind speeds recorded in a tornado.

1.6 KM Farthest a person has ever been flung by a tornado.

3 HOURS, 29 MINUTES Longest-lived tornado on record.

491 KM The farthest confirmed distance an object was carried by a tornado. It was a cancelled check.

15 TONS Weight of the heaviest item flung by a tornado: a piece of factory machinery.

140 Reinforce Garage Doors in a Windstorm

Battening down the hatches to prepare for a storm? Don't forget the garage. Double-wide garage doors are a weak spot in a windstorm, as high winds can cause these broad, flexible doors to bow inward and fall off their tracks. And that makes your garage, car, and home vulnerable to greater damage.

You could invest in a wind-resistant door, or reinforce the current door yourself with a kit that allows you to brace your door and still use it. But if a high-wind advisory has just been issued and you have to act fast, you can board up your garage door with wooden planks, just as you would your home's windows. Add horizontal and vertical bracing onto each panel of the door. If you have an automatic garage-door opener, disable it to avoid accidental damage from someone trying to open the door while it's boarded up.

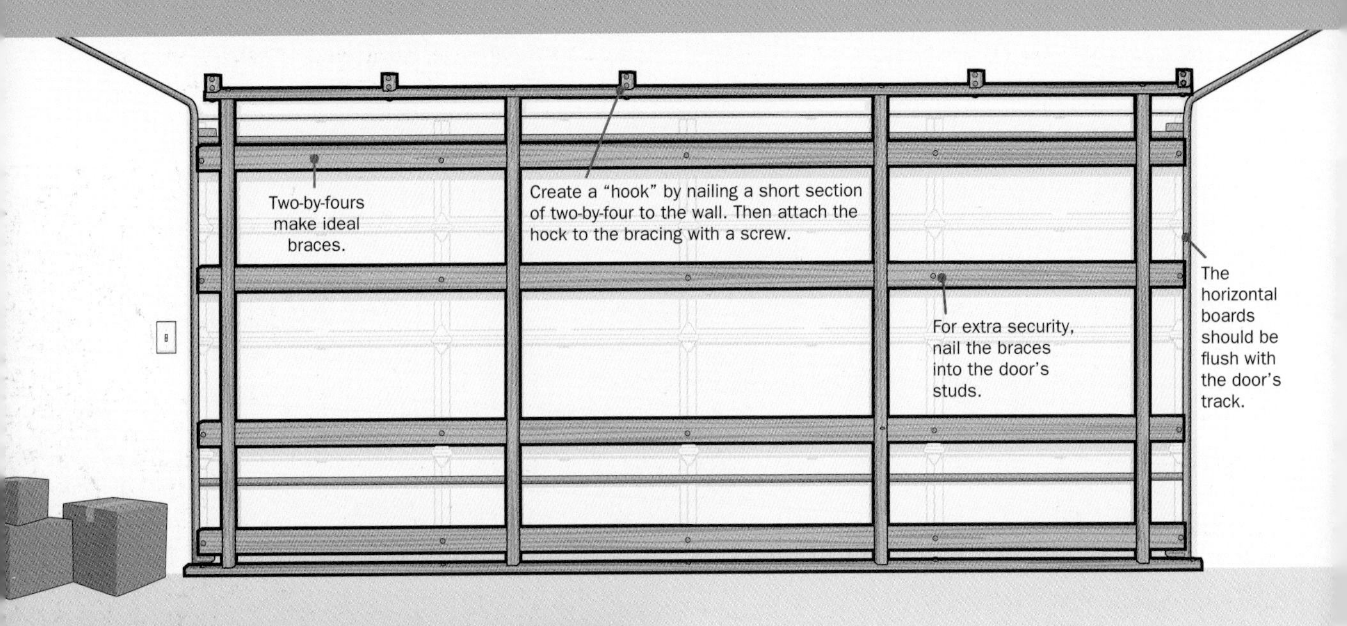

141 Deal with a Downed Power Line in a Car

If a power line falls on your car and disables it while you're inside, you'll have to take action.

PUT OUT AN SOS The safest thing to do is remain in your vehicle and phone for help.

JUMP FREE If you must leave the vehicle because of fire or some other danger, avoid touching any portion of your car's metal frame. The greatest peril comes from touching the car and the ground at the same time, since electricity could travel through you into the ground, causing injury or death. Jump as far away from the car as you can, landing with feet together.

SHUFFLE OFF TO SAFETY Keep both feet in contact with each other and the ground as you move off. Avoid pools of water, which conduct electricity.

142 Tree-Proof Your Home

Large, mature trees can increase the value of your property—unless they crash into your house. Prune weak, damaged, or dead limbs, and consider these other steps to protect your home from tree damage.

CULL THE HERD The best way to tree-proof your home is to remove all trees from your yard that could reach your house if they were to fall.

PLANT DEFENSIVELY Remember that young saplings planted today will grow up to become big trees that might pose a danger to your house. So plant strategically, picking spots where trees won't threaten your home, your neighbor's house, and external features like power lines and propane tanks. Don't plant brittle species that are prone to breakage, such as elm, willow, box elder, poplar, and silver maple. Where ice storms are a possibility, don't plant trees that hold their leaves late into the fall. The weight of ice on leaves can bring down limbs or entire trees.

MAKE NICE WITH THE NEIGHBORS If the tree that's looming over your house belongs to your neighbors, use diplomacy to persuade them to remove the tree. That task will be easier if you can convince them that the tree is a danger to their own house as well.

143

STEP-BY-STEP

Buck a Downed Tree

When severe weather hits, downed trees follow. Make like a lumberjack and use the proper technique to cut up a tree on the ground—a process called *bucking*.

STEP ONE Remove all major branches, then brace the underside of the tree with wood to keep it stable and off the ground.

STEP TWO Standing uphill from the tree, start by cutting the underside of the trunk about one-third of the way through with a chainsaw. Then come back to the top side and finish the cut so it runs all the way through the trunk.

STEP THREE Gravity should pull that trunk section off the tree, but if your saw gets stuck in the cut, shut it off right away. Drive a wedge into the cut to loosen the tension, and then remove the saw.

144 CHECKLIST
Prepare Your House for a Hurricane

If a hurricane is forecast, stay glued to weather reports, and if evacuation is advised, go. But if you have the all-clear to stick it out, ready yourself and your home.

- [ ] Stock up on nonperishable foods, prescriptions, and hygiene essentials.
- [ ] Cover windows with plywood. Use wood screws, not nails, anchored into exterior walls.
- [ ] Lash down (or stow indoors) anything from your yard that might become a flying projectile in a storm.
- [ ] Assess which trees might be blown onto the house. Trim limbs that seem vulnerable, and avoid rooms under big trees once the storm starts.
- [ ] Know how to turn off the gas, water, and electricity in case you're instructed to do so.
- [ ] While the faucets are still flowing, fill up bathtubs, sinks, and buckets so you have an emergency supply if the water is cut off or contaminated by the storm.
- [ ] Shelter in an interior room away from windows. Take a radio—preferably a battery-operated or wind-up one—to keep up with news of the storm.
- [ ] For fire safety, set the bases of your emergency candles in a dish filled with water.
- [ ] Store valuables as high as possible—ideally in the attic. That's also a great place to stash an axe, which will prove useful if you need to break through to your roof to escape rising water.
- [ ] Don't be fooled into thinking the storm is over just because the weather becomes calm. Remain in shelter until after the eye passes, the storm renews its fury, and then gradually moves away.

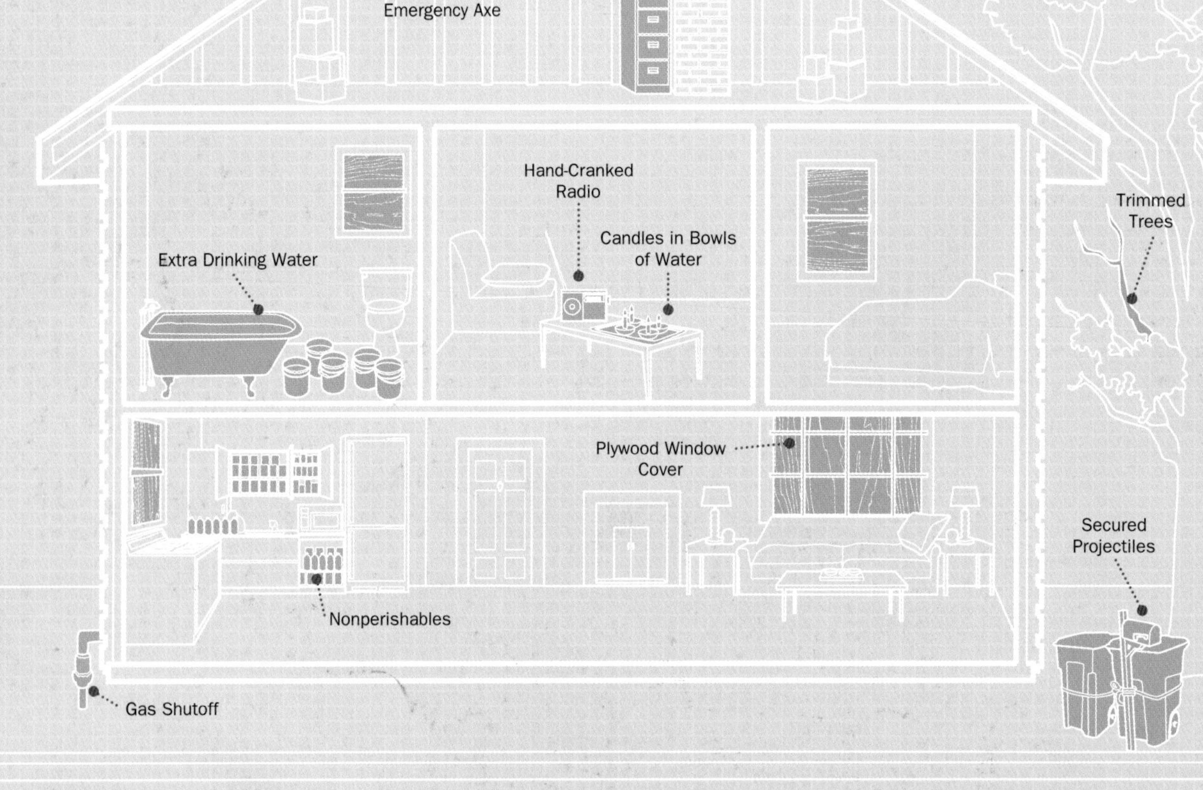

145 Build a Dike

If floodwaters are threatening your home, use sandbags to create a dike.

PICK A SPOT Build the dike on the side of your yard from which water will be flowing. Don't erect the dike against a wall: The weight of the sandbags might compromise the building's structure.

FILL THE BAGS Put the first scoop of sand just inside the bag's mouth to hold it open, then fill it halfway full before tying off the top.

BUILD THE BARRIER Friction between sandbags and the ground holds the dike in place, so remove slippery substances like leaves. If you're going to build your dike more than a metre high, increase its stability by placing the bottom row of bags in a shallow trench that's about 15 centimetres deep and 60 centimetres wide. Stagger the position of bags as you stack them, as if you were laying bricks. As a rule of thumb, the width of the dike at the bottom should be two or three times the overall height.

146 Make DIY Flood Protection

If you're caught without sandbags and an inundation is imminent, it's time to improvise. First off, be aware that you don't have to use sand to build your fortifications—dirt or small gravel will do in a pinch. Fill up pillowcases, tie off T-shirts and pants, or even use socks if need be. If you're building a fortification to protect your home, you can try piling up furniture as an armature, then filling in the gaps with your improvised sandbags. It doesn't have to be pretty; it just has to divert water.

147 CASE STUDY: WIND GONE WILD
Survive a Heck of a Hurricane

With Hurricane Katrina bearing down on his Gautier, Mississippi, home, Armand Charest decided to ignore the weather experts advising evacuation. Instead, he and his wife prepared to ride out the storm—much as they had ridden out previous hurricanes.

As the warnings grew more urgent, the Charests decided to take shelter with neighbors whose house was at a higher elevation. They brought along emergency food and water supplies to add to the essentials already at the home, such as a generator and extra gas in jerry cans. Once the power went out, they used a battery-powered TV to keep track of the storm's progress.

As the winds picked up and the storm surge began rising, the Charests and their hosts began rethinking their decision to stay. When the waters reached the tires of the vehicles parked in the front yard, they moved them across the street to the higher ground of a neighbor's driveway. The one remaining vehicle, which was parked in the garage, was already floating in the floodwaters by the time they got back. Adding to their woes, the car's gas tank leaked, filling the house with fumes. To ventilate the house, they knocked out some of the plywood window covers and opened the windows wide. That, of course, exposed the interior of the house to the wind and rain of the storm.

Once the water level inside rose to their waists, Charest and his host swam out to a boat and tethered it to a column on the front porch in case they had to leave quickly. They spent the next several hours keeping dangerous floating debris, like propane tanks, away from the exterior of the house. As soon as the winds died down, they removed the remaining window reinforcements in an effort to better ventilate the house.

As the waters receded, Charest and his host managed to start one of the trucks across the street. They drove to Charest's home to discover it intact but flood damaged. He contacted family members farther north, who caravanned down to rescue the survivors. But their troubles weren't over: They had to decide whether to cross a bridge that had been damaged when a crane broke from its moorings. They opted to take their chances and go over the bridge, which held up—a harrowing yet happy end to the ordeal.

POST ASSESSMENT
Wind Gone Wild

In August 2005, the Charest family and their friends chose to ride out Hurricane Katrina rather than evacuate. But as floodwaters continued to rise, they regretted their decision to stay behind.

Prior to leaving his home, Armand Charest took precautions to make it hurricane resistant. He boarded up windows and exterior doors and covered all interior furnishings with plastic.

He put together disaster supplies to last through the chaos of the first 72 hours.

The Charests accepted an invitation to ride out the storm with friends whose house was at a higher elevation. Several other neighbors also were invited, providing safety in numbers.

As the floodwaters rose, they moved their cars to higher ground across the street.

They moored a boat to the porch in case they had to make a fast escape.

They worked to keep dangerous floating debris, like propane tanks, away from the house.

Like so many others, Charest ignored warnings to evacuate as Hurricane Katrina approached.

He didn't prepare and place sandbags, which might have countered the storm surge.

Charest and his friend left a car parked in the garage, which spilled gas into the water and filled the house with fumes, forcing them to knock out the plywood protection they'd put on the windows.

The survivors chose to drive across a bridge even though a floating crane had damaged it. They made it—but their decision to trust infrastructure that was compromised could have given their survival story a tragic ending.

148

CHECKLIST

Make a Life Raft from Household Items

Home sweet home isn't so sweet when it's full of mucky water—especially when you are low on supplies and don't know if assistance is on the way. Since your furnishings aren't helping you much (who needs a hutch full of china plates if there's no food to eat off them?), get creative and turn one of them into a life raft. You can simply float away on one of these larger items, or secure several together with rope.

- ▢ Mattress
- ▢ Air compression tank
- ▢ Dining room table
- ▢ Lawn chair cushions
- ▢ Plastic trash cans
- ▢ Ice chest
- ▢ Children's float toys
- ▢ Plastic swimming pool
- ▢ Fiberglass bathtub
- ▢ Spare tire
- ▢ Large plastic tub
- ▢ Collection of smaller plastic jugs and bottles held together under a platform of boards

RICH SAYS

"Unless you're a fish who loves contaminated filth, you'd better get to high ground."

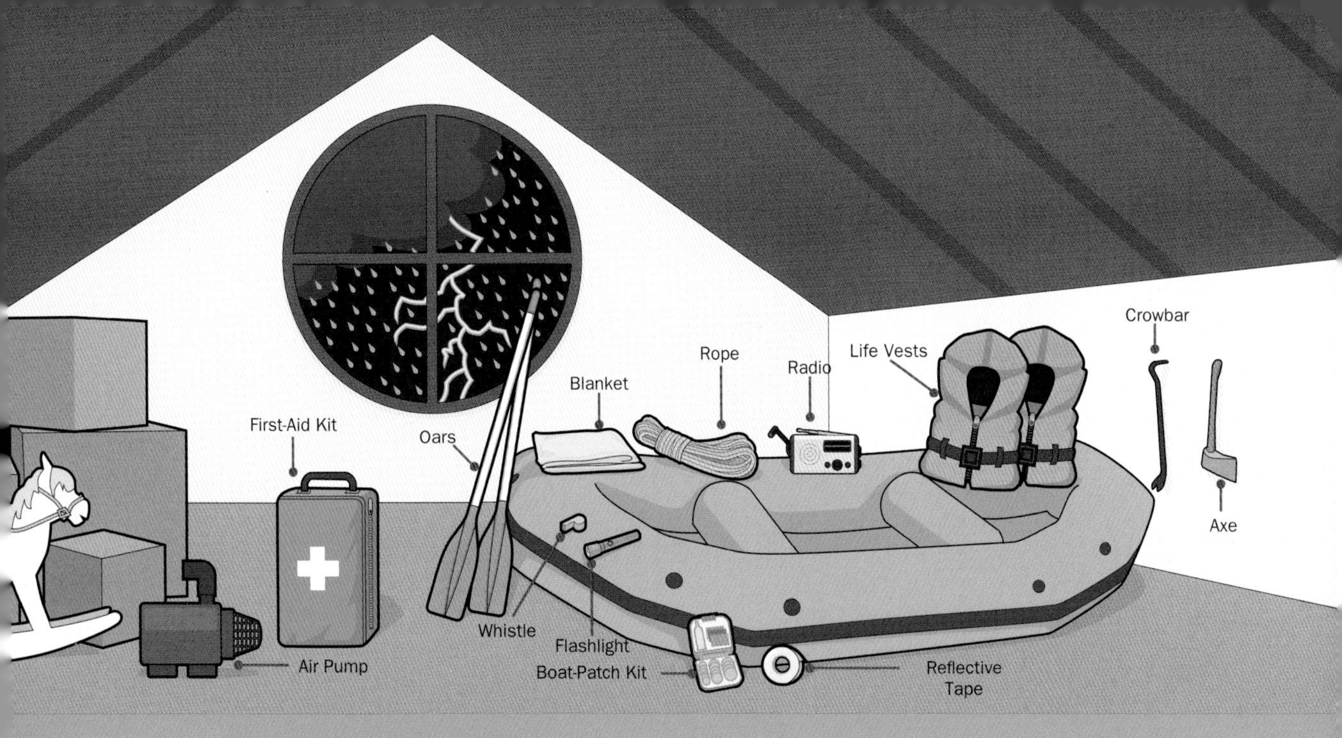

149 Turn Your Attic into an Ark

You don't need to gather up a pair of every animal, but if you live in a flood zone, be prepared for rising waters. We've all seen scary images of homes flooded to their eaves, so learn from those lessons and keep your attic stocked as your getaway point. Equip an inflatable raft with vital supplies, including an air pump, flotation devices, a first-aid kit, and flares. Don't forget a patch kit for your raft.

If you have an exit point to the outside world through your attic, great. Otherwise, store an axe or a crowbar up there so you can break through the roof and escape if floodwaters keep rising.

150 Make Waterproof Matches

When it comes to matches, waterproof ones are best, especially in dire circumstances like a flood. Since they're much more expensive than their pedestrian cousins, you might want to make your own.

USE THE CANDLE TECHNIQUE Burn a candle long enough for a pool of wax to form around the wick. Blow it out, then dip the head of your match into the wet wax, about 3 millimetres up the stick. Remove the matchstick and allow the wax to dry, pinching it closed to form a water-tight seal.

DEPLOY THE NAIL POLISH PLOY Coat your matches with clear nail polish to waterproof them. Dip the head of the match and a bit of the matchstick itself into the polish, then rest the match on a counter with the head hanging off the edge to dry.

TRY THE TURPENTINE TRICK The easiest way to waterproof your matches is simply to drop them in turpentine. Allow the matches to soak for five minutes before placing them on newspaper to dry. After twenty minutes or so, you'll have waterproof matches that will last several months.

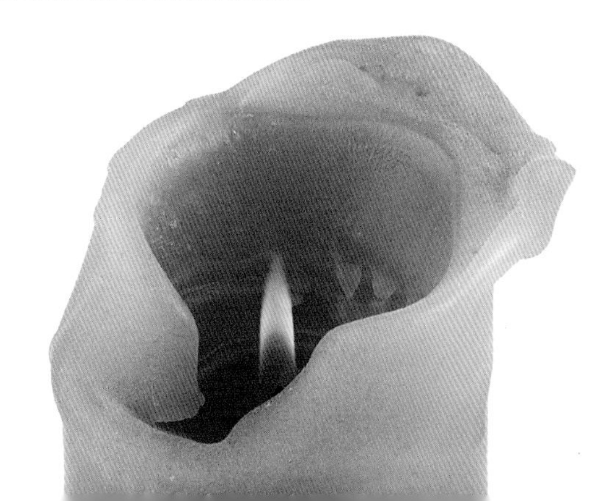

151 Paddle Through Floodwaters

A canoe can be a great way to navigate or escape floodwaters. But there's a huge difference between fighting your way out of a hazard-filled flood zone and paddling down a lazy river.

SIT FOR STABILITY Place yourself slightly behind the middle of the boat with your weight low and centered.

TRY TO STAY DRY You know that floodwater is full of nasty stuff, so do your very best to stay out of it. No trailing your fingers in the water on this trip!

AVOID HIDDEN OBSTACLES Avoid swirls on the water's surface, since they may indicate a submerged object. In a big flood, you might encounter overfalls, areas where water crosses a highway or other submerged feature. Overfalls often hide whirlpools and rapids, so steer away from them if you can.

PADDLE AWAY To steer the canoe through the current as straight as possible, stroke powerfully on alternating sides. Or use a strong J-stroke, turning and pushing the blade slightly outward at the end of the stroke to better control your speed and course.

152 Drive Safely on Flooded Roads

Every year, people lose their lives when their vehicles get washed away as they try to drive on flooded roads.

STUDY THE NUMBERS A measly 15 centimetres of water will cause most cars to lose control and possibly stall. Double that amount, and most cars just give up and float away. At 60 centimetres of rushing water, vehicles are at risk of being swept away (even trucks and four-wheel drives). If flood waters start swirling around your vehicle, abandon it—and save your life.

DON'T HEAD INTO THE UNKNOWN Beneath the water, pavement might be ripped away, leaving a hole that could swallow your vehicle. The rule for driving through water is simple: If you can't see the road surface or its line markings, take a detour.

153 Dig Your Truck Out of the Mud

Sure, getting your vehicle stuck in the mud can ruin your day. But when you're in a disaster (like, say, a major flood), and your escape mobile starts spinning its wheels in the dirt, this annoyance can escalate to a possibly deadly situation. Here's how to free your ride:

TAKE YOUR FOOT OFF THE GAS You don't want to dig deeper ruts and toss around the remaining solid ground under the wheels, so quit stomping the gas.

GO BACK AND FORTH Put the car in reverse and then drive forward; the wheels may pick up enough traction to move forward. Try it a few times.

KICK OUT YOUR PASSENGERS Have anyone in the car get out while you drive forward.

DIG A DITCH Using whatever tool you have on hand, hollow out a hole in the mud in front of each tire. Give each hole a slightly upward slope, then drive forward very gently and, with any luck, up the incline.

IMPROVISE GRIP Search your vehicle and the surrounding environment for branches, wooden planks, or blankets, and lay them immediately in front of the wheels. Then gently drive over these objects onto firmer ground.

154 Live Through a Flash Flood

You're exploring a canyon when all of a sudden the air rumbles like a subwoofer. Then you see it: a wall of water churning with felled trees and boulders. And it's headed your way.

KNOW THE AREA Avoid this hair-raising situation by staying away from flood-prone zones that are in the path of natural drainage areas like riverbeds or canyons. If you're on the coast, beware of storm surges during tropical storms and hurricanes.

HIGH TAIL IT TO HIGH GROUND To escape a flash flood, leave everything behind and run for high ground as fast as you can. If the water starts to rise around you, climb a tree or scramble onto a large rock—anything that will get you higher.

RIDE IT OUT If you end up in the flow, keep your head and upper body safe at all costs. Point your feet downstream and try to deflect—or better yet, steer clear of—obstructions like rocks and trees.

GET A GRIP You won't be able to fight the current, but you may be able to gradually work your way toward the edge of the flood so you can catch hold of a tree or bush and pull yourself out of the water.

HOLE UP AT HOME If a flash flood hits your house, arm yourself with essentials such as food, water, a battery-operated radio, and matches and candles and head for the upper floors. Unless your home's foundation is threatened and is on the verge of collapse, stay put until the waters recede.

155

STEP-BY-STEP

Rescue Someone Caught in a Flood

The fast current of a flash flood is one of its biggest dangers. But if someone is trapped by a flash flood—clinging to a tree branch or perched on the roof of a car—try using that speed to your advantage.

STEP ONE Tie a rescue rope to a solid object (a tree, for example) to anchor it against the weight of the victim and the flowing water's immense pressure.

STEP TWO Coil the rescue rope and throw it upstream of the person you're rescuing, allowing the current to carry the line to the victim. Instruct that person to tie the rope around his or her waist.

STEP THREE Once secured to the rope, the victim can leave his or her perch and work toward the shore.

156 Return Home Safely After a Flood

After the all-clear sounds, you'll want to rush back home and assess the damage. But even once the waters recede, you may still be in danger. Follow these basic guidelines to stay safe.

CHECK OUT STRUCTURAL INTEGRITY If your foundation or roof looks damaged, wait for an inspector to check out your home's stability before you go back inside.

AVOID OPEN FLAMES There may be gas leaks, and after all you've been through, you probably don't want to deal with an explosion as well. So if the lights are out, don't light a candle.

HANDLE ELECTRICITY Turn off the power at the main circuit breaker or fuse box with something nonconductive, such as a broom or a rolled-up rubber mat. Wearing rubber gloves is also smart.

KEEP APPLIANCES OFF Have an electrician check out anything electrical or motorized that got wet.

DRAIN THE BASEMENT SLOWLY Emptying a flooded basement all at once can damage your home's stability. Drain a third of the water volume per day.

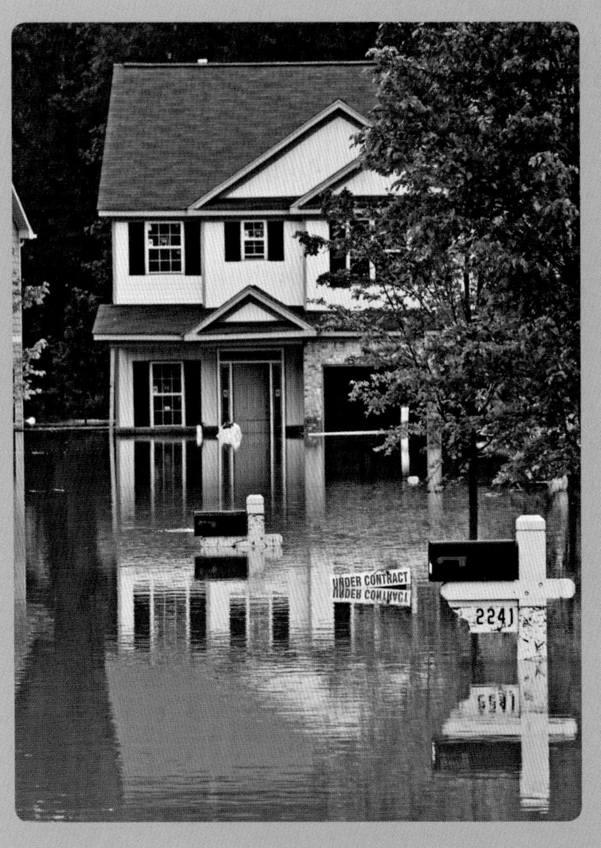

157 Live Through Lightning

The shocking truth about lightning is that a discharge can travel 220,000 kmh, and the bolt's temperature can reach 30,000° C. Yikes! But if you're caught in a lightning storm, there are a few steps you can take to save your bacon—or, more accurately, to keep yourself from turning into bacon.

LISTEN FOR TROUBLE BREWING Sometimes lightning strikes without warning, but often there's a big, rumbling tip-off: the sound of thunder. As a storm approaches, thunder lags behind lightning about eight seconds for each kilometre of distance. If you spot lightning, and the sound of thunder reaches you sixteen seconds later, the strike was about 2 km away. That might sound reassuring, but it's not. A storm can move close to 13 km between strikes, so you're definitely in the danger zone.

SEEK SHELTER Safe shelters include substantial buildings and vehicles, which can act as a Faraday cage (a metallic enclosure that blocks electromagnetic fields). If you can't take shelter, at least head to low ground. Try to avoid water, open fields, and metal objects—especially tall ones like flagpoles. As for trees, standing by a lone tree is a no-no, but sheltering in a stand of trees will up your odds of survival.

SPREAD OUT There's usually safety in numbers—but not in this case. So spread out from your friends. As delightful as they are, they're also energy conductors.

LOSE THE BLING At the first signs of thunder and lightning, remove metal and jewelry from your body.

HEED THE FINAL WARNING If your hair stands on end or you hear crackling noises, place your feet together, duck your head, and crouch low with your hands on your knees.

GET LOW If you have one, put an insulating layer like a blanket on the ground, then crouch on it, keeping your hands off the ground to help the strike flow over your body rather than through it. This position is tough to maintain, so think of it as a last-resort move when a strike seems imminent.

158 STEP-BY-STEP Install Lightning Rods on Your Roof

A lightning bolt is as dangerous to your home as it is deadly to your body. Luckily, a lightning rod can protect that home from strikes—and the electrical shortages and fires that come with them. So buy some lightning rod kits at a home-maintenance store and install them on your roof.

STEP ONE Measure your perimeter to figure out how many poles you need. For every 30 metres of your home's perimeter, you'll need one rod.

STEP TWO Walk around your house, looking for good places to put grounding plates. (Every rod you install will require a grounding plate.) You'll want to put them at opposite corners of the house, if possible.

STEP THREE For each grounding plate, dig a hole 1 metre deep and 30 centimetres larger in diameter than the plate. Make sure the holes are at least 60 centimetres away from the external wall.

STEP FOUR Climb up onto your roof and, above each grounding plate, place a lightning rod at the roof's edge. The rods should be 6 metres away from each other and within 60 centimetres of the roof's edge.

STEP FIVE Using a power drill, make holes in the exterior wall for the clamp that will hold the lightning rod to the roof.

STEP SIX Place the rod in the clamp and secure it to the exterior wall with screws.

STEP SEVEN Connect the conductor cable to the lightning rod, then run it down the exterior wall to the grounding plate below. Every metre, use cable clamps to attach the cable to the wall.

STEP EIGHT Attach the conductor cable to the ground plate and secure it by tightening the screws on the support clamp. Finally, cover the plate with dirt.

159 Help Someone Struck by Lightning

Contrary to popular belief (and millions of cartoons), lightning victims usually aren't badly burned. You're more likely to be grappling with these symptoms:

A STOPPED HEART The primary cause of death in lightning-strike victims is cardiac arrest. It's also common for the strike to damage lungs, so a victim may stop breathing. If you know CPR, chest compressions are the way to go.

PARALYSIS The victim may not be able to move or speak, due to an acute form of paralysis that's unique to lightning strikes—and thankfully temporary. Do your best to keep him or her reassured and warm until medical assistance arrives.

MISSING CLOTHES A strike can blow off your clothes. A blanket will help with warmth—and modesty.

160 Survive a Wildfire

During a wildfire, the most dangerous places to be are uphill or downwind from the flames. Speaking of wind, if it's blowing toward the fire, run into the wind. But if it's behind the fire, you need to move away even faster—that fire will be coming on quick.

If told to evacuate, do so. But if you're trapped at home, stay inside where the structure will protect you. Move to a central room, away from exterior walls. Close the doors to cut down on air circulation, which can feed flames.

If you're caught out in the open, move to an area that has already burned over. Avoid canyons and other natural chimneys. Get into a river or lake, if possible. Look for breaks in the trees, which could mean breaks in the firestorm. If you're near a road, lie facedown along the road or in a ditch or depression on the uphill side. Cover up with anything that provides a shield against the heat.

161 Prevent a Forest Fire

Smokey the Bear doesn't like it when your campfire gets away from you—especially if it torches the forest.

PICK A SPOT THAT HAS BURNED BEFORE The safest spot to build a fire is in an existing fire pit, since surrounding flammable materials have already burned.

START FROM SCRATCH If you have to build a fresh fire base, look for a site that's at least 5 metres from bushes, dry grasses, and other flammable objects. Avoid overhead foliage, too. Clear a spot 3 metres in diameter, removing twigs, leaves, and anything else that can burn. Dig a pit in the soil 30 cm deep. Circle the pit with rocks. When you're done with the fire, pour water on it or use dirt to smother the embers.

162 Protect Your Home from Wildfires

Firescaping is landscaping designed to keep your house from going up in smoke. Always a good investment, eh?

PLANT WISELY Start by choosing the right kind of trees to plant. Conifers contain flammable, sometimes explosive, oils and resins. Trees with leaves are usually a safer bet. Protect structures with fire-resistant, high-moisture vegetation like ice plant. Use a drip-irrigation system to water trees and shrubs year-round. Or use non-flammable ground cover such as mulch and gravel.

TRIM YOUR TREES Make sure to maintain the trees within 9 metres of your home by trimming dead or low-hanging branches, which will be the first to light up. While you're keeping dry wood away from the house, make sure your woodpile is off at a distance, too.

COVER UP Cover external vents with a fine mesh screen to keep embers from blowing in. Consider installing chimney caps, which keep embers from a wildfire out—and those from your fireplace in.

Store firewood away from your home.

Avoid planting conifers.

Cover earth with mulch, gravel, or high-moisture plants.

Grow fire-resistant plants near your house.

Keep plants moist with drip irrigation.

Clear away low-hanging branches and deadwood near your home.

Install a spark arrester on your chimney.

Cover external vents with fine metal screens.

DO THIS, NOT THAT

Caught in a Car

DO roll up windows and close vents if you're trapped in your car. Park as far away from trees as possible. Turn off the engine, lie down on the floor, and, if you have something to cover yourself, use it.

DON'T leave your vehicle and try to run away on foot. Fight-or-flight instincts will make you want to do otherwise. But trust me, you're a slowpoke compared to a raging fire.

163 CASE STUDY: WHEN THINGS GET HOT
Withstand a Firestorm

On October 25, 2003, Jacqueline Lloyd noticed a plume of smoke rising from a hill near her family's farm outside San Diego, California. Fires were not uncommon in the area, but usually firefighters' helicopters quickly arrived to quench them with water. When a half hour passed and Lloyd did not hear the reassuring sound of the copters, she decided to call emergency services.

The dispatcher told her that the fire had been reported, so she shouldn't worry about it. But Lloyd continued to monitor the emergency-band scanner she'd bought for just such an occasion. She and her husband also kept watch from the roof of the house. Several hours later, they saw that the fire was spreading in all four directions.

At that point they had to decide if they should trust that firefighters would extinguish the blaze before it reached them, or if they should pack up their 18-month-old child and various animals and flee to a relative's house on the other side of town. When the dispatcher announced a high-wind forecast on the scanner, Lloyd and her husband knew things would get worse. Santa Ana winds were blowing the flames toward their house.

During the next hour, the Lloyds packed irreplaceable mementos like home movies and photo albums. They loaded everything in the car, along with their pets. But as they tried to load their horses into their trailers, the animals panicked. By that stage, a wall of fire was roaring toward the barn, so the Lloyds turned the horses loose to follow their own instincts. Jacqueline Lloyd drove off with her daughter and pets, leaving her husband behind to run through the house one last time, using a video recorder to document their belongings for insurance purposes.

With her daughter tucked into the car seat beside her, she raced through winding roads rimmed with fire and choked with dense smoke. They arrived at the agreed-upon rendezvous point: her mother-in-law's home at the bottom of the canyon, where other family members had also evacuated. The fire was fast approaching, but no one could see it clearly because of the canyon walls. Then her husband arrived with terrifying news: The fire had jumped the road less than a kilometreaway. This finally convinced the family to leave the area.

Despite the fact that they waited until the last moment to evacuate, Lloyd and her family all survived the fire. What's more, their animals (including the horses left behind) made it through as well. Their mother-in-law's ranch house burned to the ground, and the Lloyds lost part of their home, their outbuildings, and their barn. They were lucky, though: More than 2,000 residences burned in the blaze. Fourteen residents and one firefighter were killed, and 120 people were hurt.

POST ASSESSMENT
When Things Get Hot

When a hunter lost in the California mountains built a signal fire, he got everyone's attention, all right. His fire spread until it destroyed thousands of homes and killed 15 people. Jacqueline Lloyd and her family narrowly escaped the inferno.

Jacqueline Lloyd spotted the fire while it was still small and called 911 to report it.

The Lloyds had purchased a fire scanner, and used it to monitor dispatches and keep up-to-date on the latest conditions.

They understood the weather conditions and the impact they were having on the fire.

Once the horses balked, the Lloyds released them rather than wasting time trying to coax them into trailers.

Jacqueline and her husband set a rendezvous point in case they had to separate.

When the Lloyds and other family members arrived at the rendezvous point, they stayed together and monitored emergency reports.

When the fire jumped the road extremely close, the Lloyds convinced everyone to evacuate.

Although the Lloyds felt threatened, they put off evacuating since no official order had been issued.

When they realized they had to leave, they spent much of their time packing nonessential items and keepsakes.

Despite having been through a previous fire, the Lloyds did not have an evacuation plan.

Their desire to protect their horses put them in danger as they tried to evacuate the animals.

They nearly stayed too long in both locations, waiting until the fire was physically upon them before racing away.

The Lloyds spent a lot of time documenting possessions for insurance purposes rather than focusing on saving their own lives.

164 Survive a Volcanic Eruption

When the earth blows its top, the dangers include fiery lava bombs lobbed by the eruption, a tide of molten rock, and the toxic fumes of pyroclastic gas flows.

HIT THE ROAD, JACK The best place to be is far away. Distance is the best protection against the hellfire and fury of a volcano, so be ready to evacuate when the warning is issued.

TAKE SHELTER If you can't put space between you and the eruption, find shelter and cross your fingers. A house can provide protection from ash and falling debris, but then again, it could catch on fire. So if you shelter inside, be ready to hustle out fast. Taking shelter inside a vehicle also might protect against some dangers. Since things that flow go downhill, wherever you hole up, make sure it's not in a low-lying area.

165 Cope with Ash

Volcanic ash isn't soft and fluffy. Nope, that ash is composed of tiny jagged pieces of rock and glass: hard, abrasive, and corrosive. Because it destroys engines when it's sucked into the intake, volcanic ash can halt air travel and hamper ground transportation for hundreds of kilometres around an eruption. But if you live close to an active volcano, your problems just might be more immediate.

TAKE COVER During ash fall, stay inside—especially if you have a respiratory ailment. Close doors, windows, vents, and chimney flues. Monitor radio and TV broadcasts about the situation.

WEAR LAYERS When outside, wear long sleeves and pants. Breathe through a dust mask, or hold a damp cloth over your nose and mouth. Use goggles or wear eyeglasses instead of contact lenses.

START SHOVELING Ash accumulations can pile deep on roofs, requiring shovel work to prevent them from collapsing. Make sure you clear rain gutters as well.

BE CAREFUL ON THE ROAD To prevent engine damage, avoid driving. If you must, keep your speed down and bear in mind that some roads may be impassable until snowplows clear them.

166 Assess a Lava Field

Even if you're pretty sure it has cooled and hardened, it's better to detour around a lava field—because if you're wrong, you're toast. Literally.

TREAD LIGHTLY If you must cross, try to ensure that the lava has totally hardened. You can't always tell from looking, because molten lava might be flowing below a thin crust that can fool you. As you make your way forward, probe the ground ahead with a stick.

DO A SNIFF TEST Pay attention to air quality. Sulfur dioxide gases indicate flowing lava beneath you. This gives you two reasons to get away: Not only is the ground unstable, but also that gas is toxic.

HEED YOUR FEET If the soles of your boots start to melt, the flow is too hot to cross. And if the ground feels at all mushy, that means it's too unstable to cross.

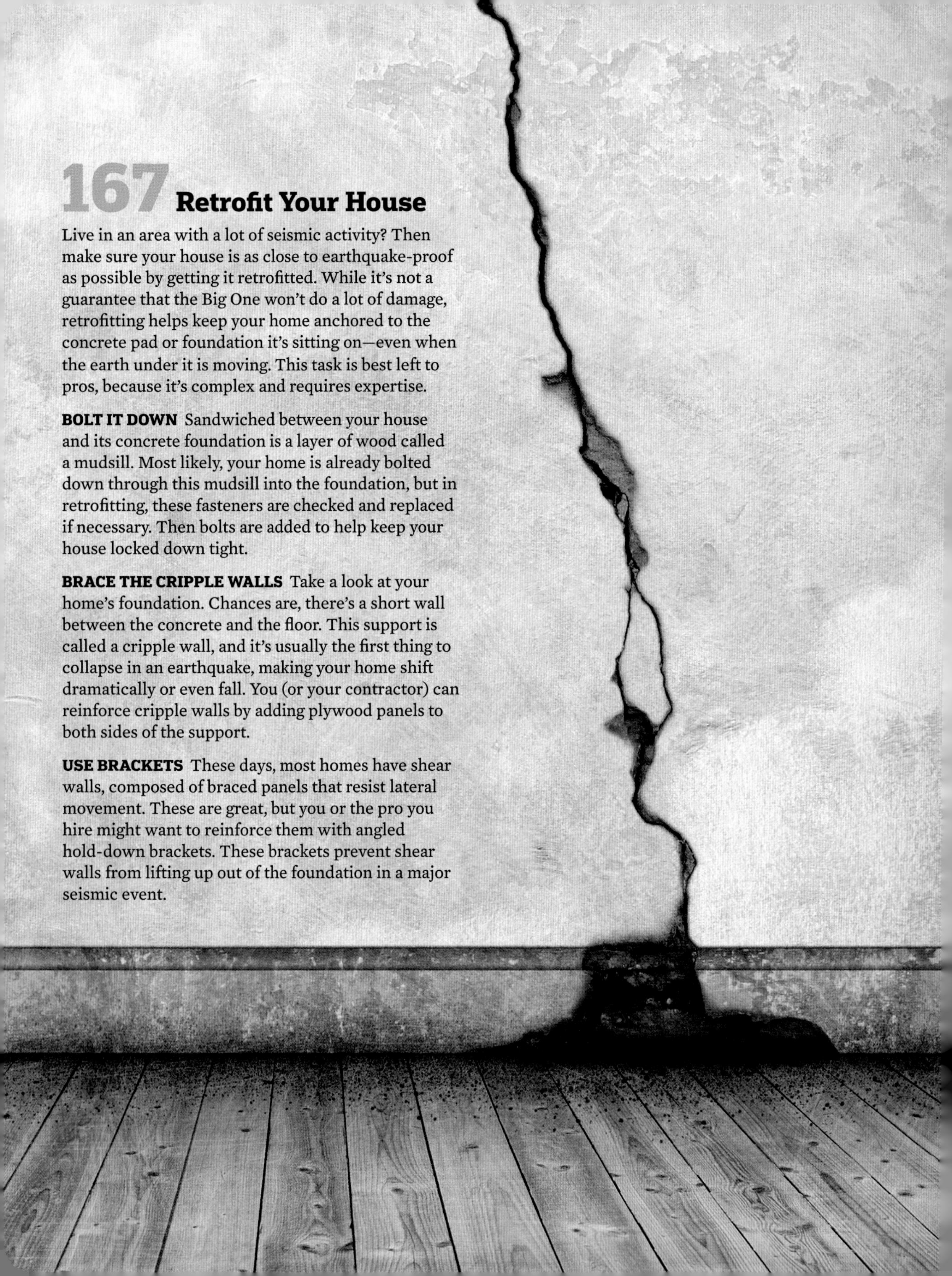

167 Retrofit Your House

Live in an area with a lot of seismic activity? Then make sure your house is as close to earthquake-proof as possible by getting it retrofitted. While it's not a guarantee that the Big One won't do a lot of damage, retrofitting helps keep your home anchored to the concrete pad or foundation it's sitting on—even when the earth under it is moving. This task is best left to pros, because it's complex and requires expertise.

BOLT IT DOWN Sandwiched between your house and its concrete foundation is a layer of wood called a mudsill. Most likely, your home is already bolted down through this mudsill into the foundation, but in retrofitting, these fasteners are checked and replaced if necessary. Then bolts are added to help keep your house locked down tight.

BRACE THE CRIPPLE WALLS Take a look at your home's foundation. Chances are, there's a short wall between the concrete and the floor. This support is called a cripple wall, and it's usually the first thing to collapse in an earthquake, making your home shift dramatically or even fall. You (or your contractor) can reinforce cripple walls by adding plywood panels to both sides of the support.

USE BRACKETS These days, most homes have shear walls, composed of braced panels that resist lateral movement. These are great, but you or the pro you hire might want to reinforce them with angled hold-down brackets. These brackets prevent shear walls from lifting up out of the foundation in a major seismic event.

168 Keep Household Items Steady in a Quake

When there's a whole lot of shakin' going on, there could be a whole lot of falling. And smashing. And crashing. Here's how to keep your home and its contents from tumbling down around or on you in an earthquake. (All the items mentioned here are readily available in home-furnishing and hardware stores.)

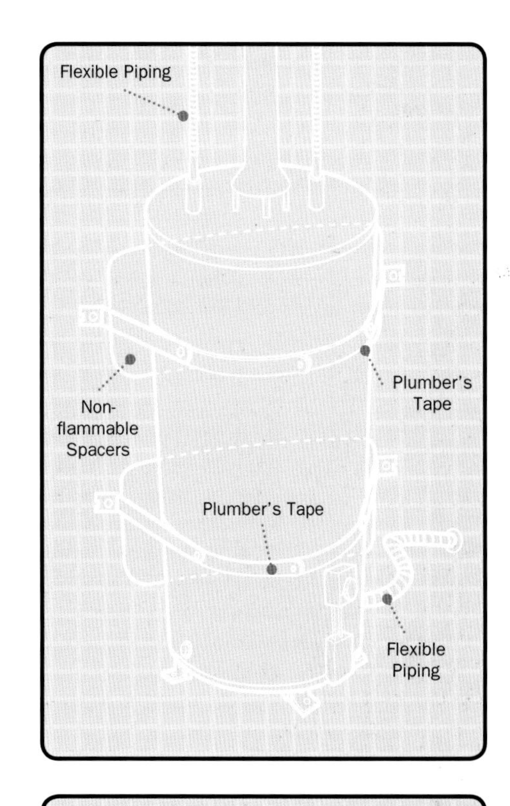

BATTEN DOWN THE BIG STUFF Strap water heaters to the wall with perforated metal strips known as plumber's tape. Make sure that all piping is flexible rather than rigid, and insert a nonflammable spacer between the heater and the wall. For refrigerators and large appliances, use an L-bracket to bolt the top to the wall. To secure your fridge's bottom to the floor, use pronged Z-clips.

MAKE SURE FURNITURE IS FIXED IN PLACE Secure large objects such as cabinets, bookcases, and hutches to the wall using L-brackets or furniture-securing kits. Equip all cabinets with latches to keep their contents from spilling out.

STOP THE SHATTERING Apply clear polyester sheets to help keep windows and mirrors from breaking. You can pick some up at a home-supply store.

BEWARE OF WALL HANGINGS Place heavier ornamental items like mirrors or paintings only on walls well away from beds and seating areas. Don't count on a hook and nail to hold them in place—use wall anchors instead.

REARRANGE DISPLAYS Move heavy objects to lower shelves so they'll do less damage if they're shaken loose. Place objects with low centers of gravity, like fishbowls and vases, on nonstick mats to help keep them in place.

SWEAT THE SMALL STUFF Apply earthquake putty to the bottom of small items so they won't move.

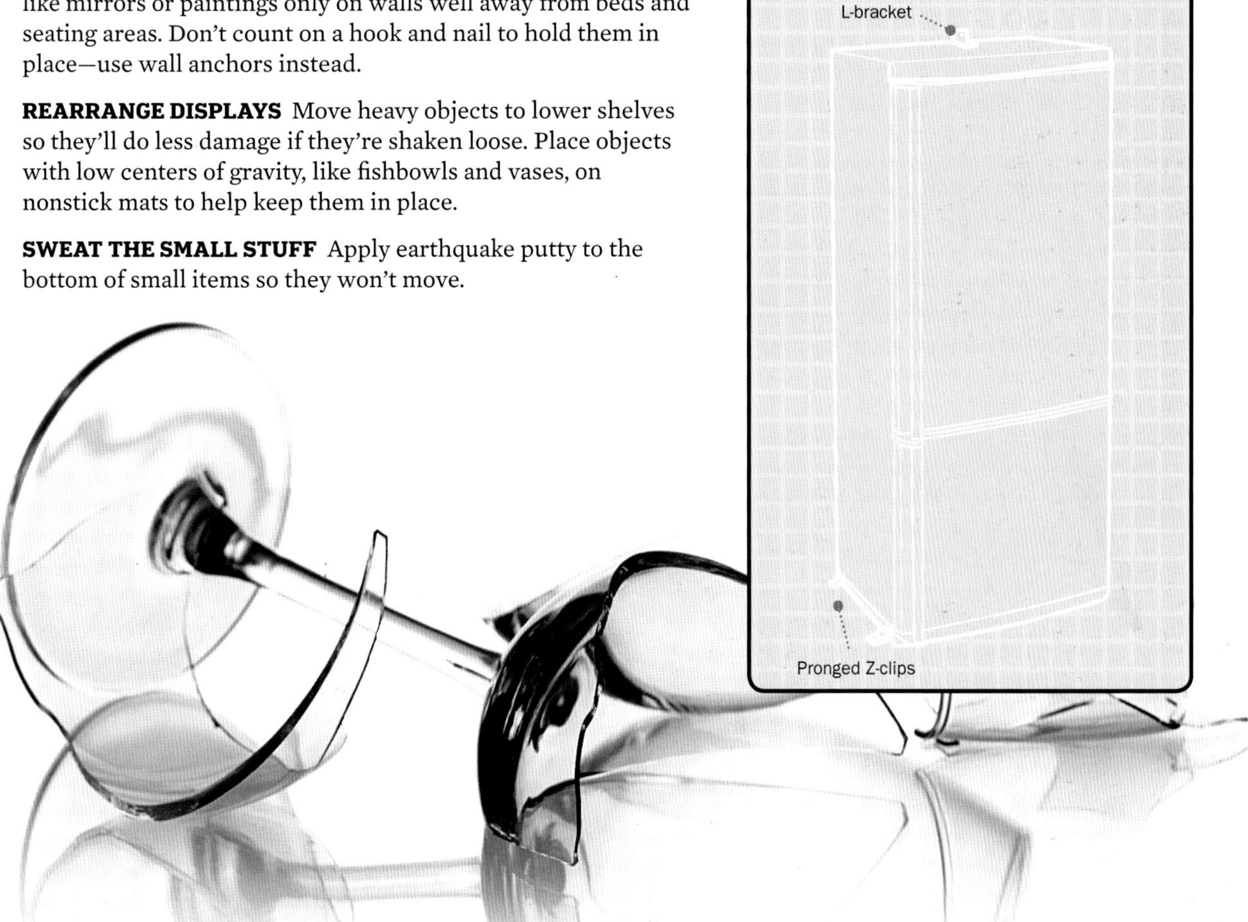

169 Know Earthquake Hot Spots

Earthquakes—they're just one of the many ways our planet reminds us who's boss. But out of the 500,000 tremors that occur every year, we only feel about 100,000. Every so often, though, one will cause extreme loss of life and structural damage. Luckily, we know where such disasters are likely to go down:

PACIFIC RING OF FIRE This is, bar none, the deadliest earthquake territory. More than 80 percent of the world's worst quakes occur on this horseshoe-shape fault system, which stretches up the west side of the Americas, across to Asia, and down into Oceania. Its Liquine-Ofqui fault in Chile created the largest earthquake on record—a 9.5 in 1970.

ALPIDE BELT This volatile swath of earth extends from Java to Sumatra, up into the Himalayas, and through the Mediterranean into the Atlantic. It's the second most dangerous quake zone in the world and features Turkey's North and Eastern Anatolian faults and the Chaman fault in Afghanistan and Pakistan.

CAYMAN TRENCH This system of fault lines exists between the North American and Caribbean plates, stretching from the Caribbean islands to Guatemala. Here you'll find the Enriquillo-Plantain Garden fault zone, which has caused five major earthquakes in Hispaniola and Jamaica since 1692.

ANYONE'S GUESS Most earthquakes occur where the edges of tectonic plates converge, but some occur well within a plate. These intraplate quakes often cause more damage, as buildings are not retrofitted. Take, for instance, Missouri's New Madrid fault system, which famously caused 1,000 earthquakes in one year (1811–1812).

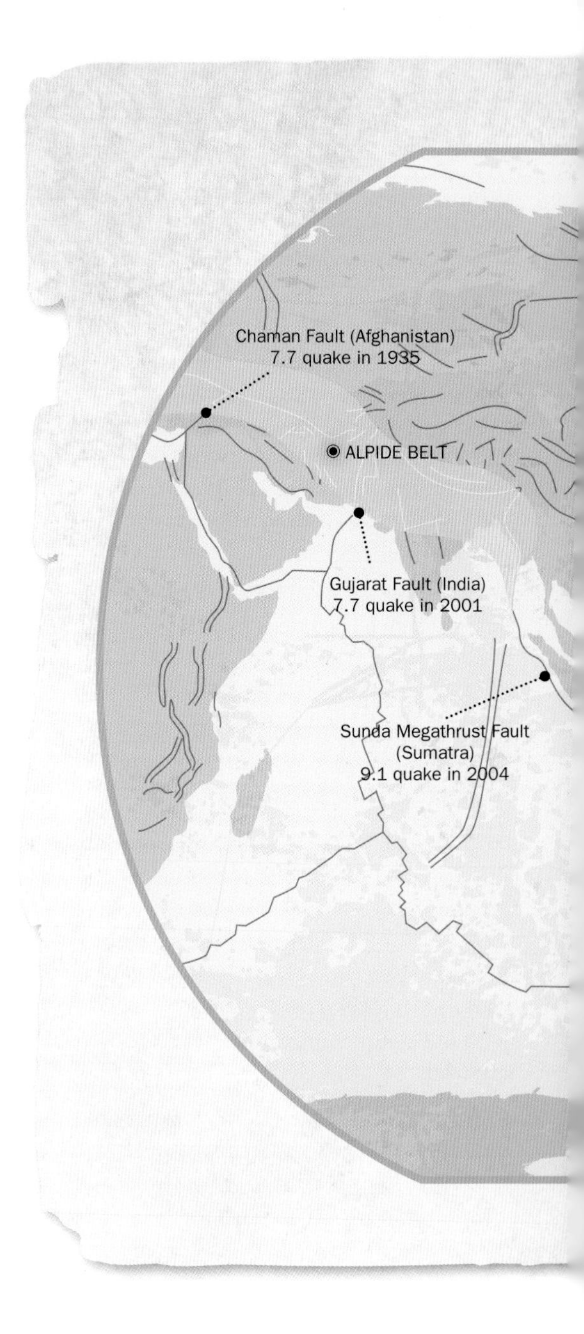

170 Understand Fault Activity

The plates making up our planet's topmost crust are in a constant game of push and shove. Often those plates get stuck together along fault lines, where they store up tension. Eventually, though, something has to give, and the pent-up energy radiates in seismic waves that we feel up above. That's an earthquake.

An earthquake's magnitude is affected by many factors. In general, the longer the fault line, the larger the quake. Tremors that occur fewer than 70 kilometres underground are deemed "shallow" quakes, and they're more likely to cause dramatic effects on land. Lastly, there are three main types of faults along which earthquakes occur . . . and some create worse quakes than others.

What determines an earthquake's intensity? That has much to do with the population density of an affected area, as well as the area's geology: Places with loose soil and rocks are more prone to sliding. Of course, the better a community prepares itself through retrofitting and smart construction, the better off it will be.

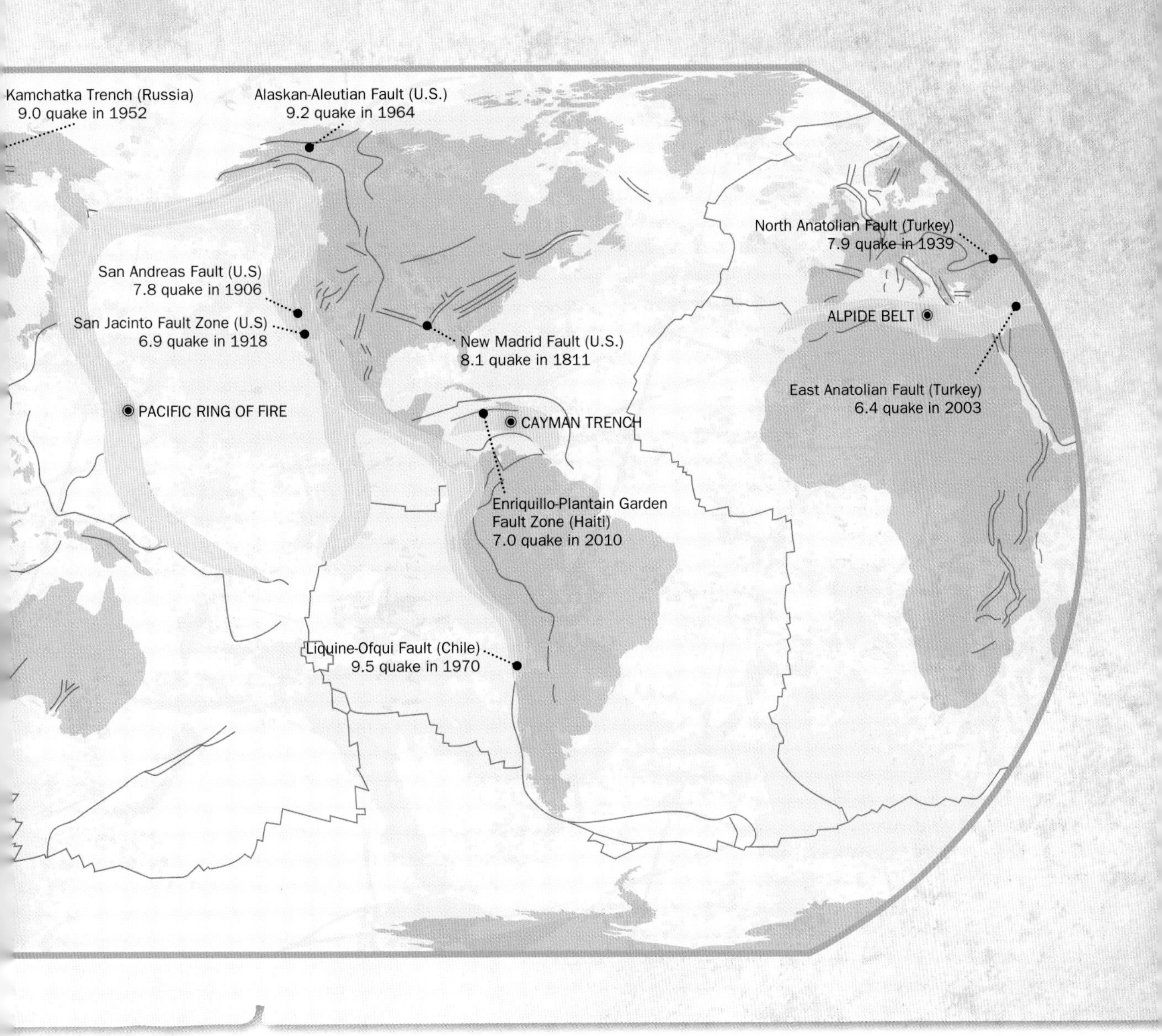

NORMAL FAULTS are also called divergent faults. When pieces of land on opposite sides of a fault pull away from each other, tremors of up to 7.0 magnitude result.

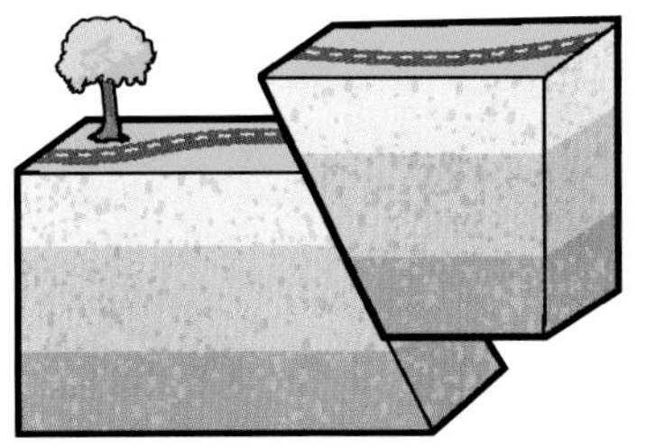

REVERSE FAULTS exist where opposite sides push against one another. Reverse faults are the most deadly, creating earthquakes that hit 8.0 on the Richter scale.

STRIKE-SLIP FAULTS occur where the sides move laterally against each other. Left-lateral faults displace land on the left, while right-lateral faults displace on the right.

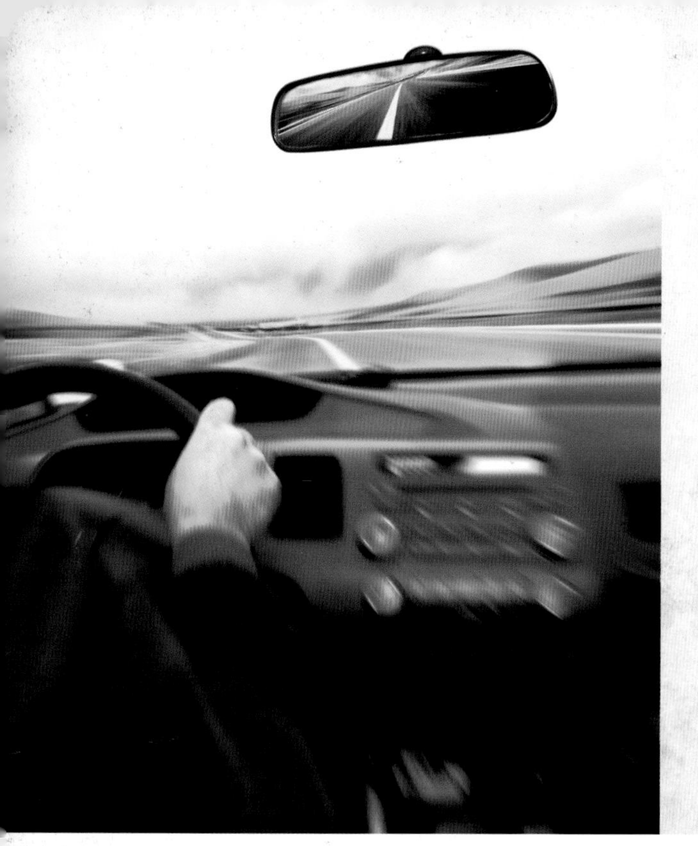

171 Ride Out a Quake in a Car

You probably know the drill: If you're inside a building when an earthquake hits, stay there. If you're outside, get into a clearing. But what if you're driving?

STOP FOR THE SHAKING There are two hazards if an earthquake strikes when you're driving: other drivers and falling objects. Pull over in an area free of things that might fall on your car, such as telephone poles, street lights, and, yes, even overpasses. The more open the area, the safer it is.

DEAL WITH INFRASTRUCTURE If you're on a bridge, take the next exit off it. And if you're stuck under that overpass, get out of your car and lie flat beside it. Should the structure collapse, it will crush your car, but not to the ground—which will hopefully leave a safe zone immediately surrounding the vehicle.

HEAD HOME There may be aftershocks, so don't hurry off. Listen to the radio for updates that may affect your route, and expect accidents and damage.

172 Weather an Earthquake

A surprising number of people—including those in quake-prone regions, who should take a keen interest in the topic—don't know what to do when the shaking starts. But a little foresight could save your life.

TAKE COVER Assess every room you spend time in and pick the spot that's likely to be safest in a quake. For instance, if your office has a sturdy desk, you might want to follow the classic "duck, cover, and hold" advice by diving under the desk and holding on to its legs. Stay there until the shaking stops.

DO GEOMETRY Nothing sturdy enough to protect you from falling rubble (which could include fragments of the ceiling)? Use the "triangle of life" tactic and crouch beside a large, stable piece of furniture that could deflect debris. Or cover your face and head, and stoop in an inside corner of the building that's away from possible falling objects.

GET CLEAR If you're outside when a quake hits, head to an open space that's away from structures, streetlights, and overhead wires. The area of highest risk is directly outside buildings.

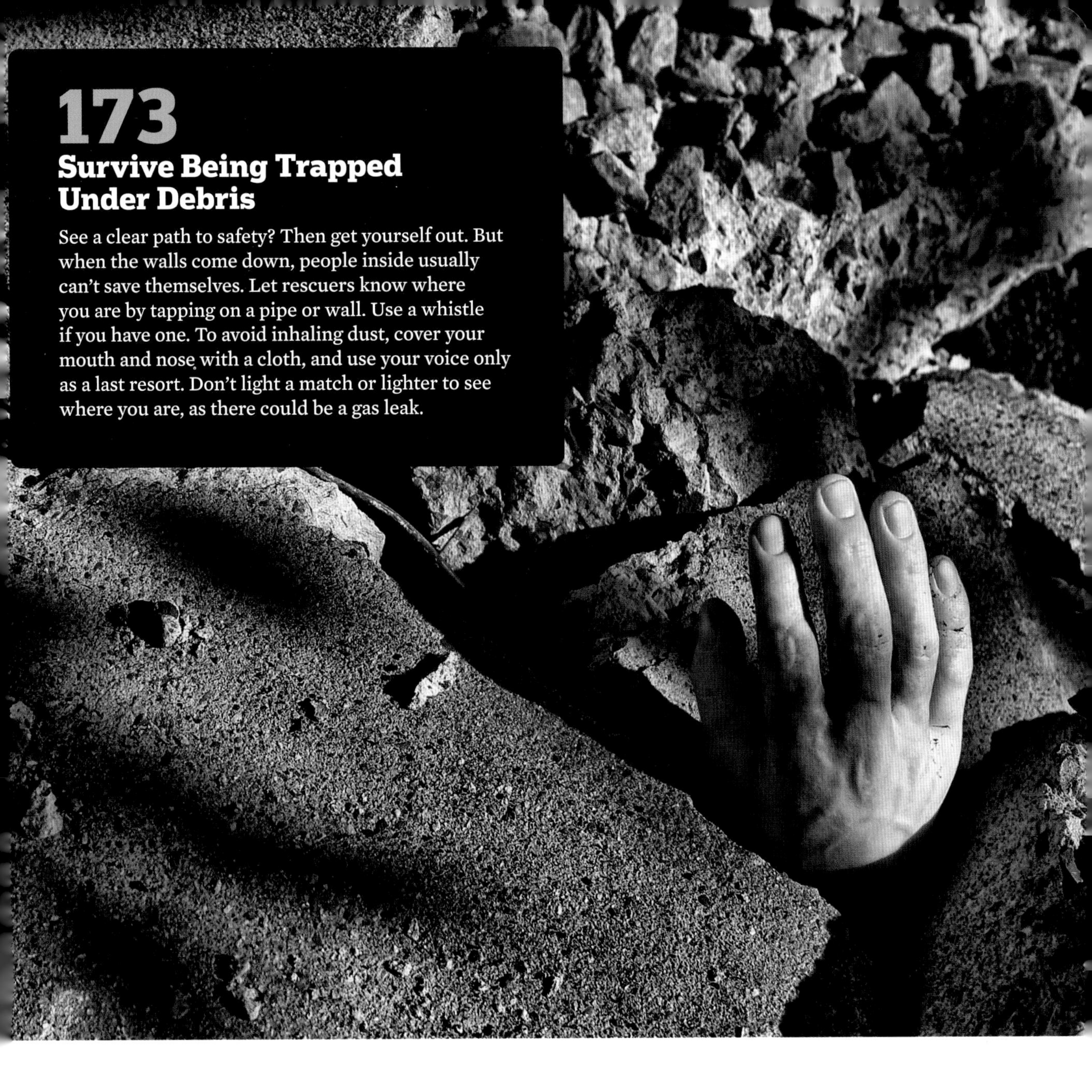

173 Survive Being Trapped Under Debris

See a clear path to safety? Then get yourself out. But when the walls come down, people inside usually can't save themselves. Let rescuers know where you are by tapping on a pipe or wall. Use a whistle if you have one. To avoid inhaling dust, cover your mouth and nose with a cloth, and use your voice only as a last resort. Don't light a match or lighter to see where you are, as there could be a gas leak.

174 Take Action After an Earthquake

Surviving the shake doesn't mean you're out of the woods. What you do immediately after an earthquake is just as important as what you do during one.

PREVENT FIRE If the building you're in appears to be structurally sound, open doors and windows to ventilate gas fumes or dust. Avoid using any gas or electrical appliances, since the greatest danger after an earthquake is fire.

PROTECT YOURSELF Before you go running out into the street, put on boots or shoes with heavy soles, and find a pair of sturdy gloves to wear. Both will help you avoid sharp objects and potential electrical hazards.

MAKE AN ESCAPE If you're leaving a multistory building, be aware that stairwells may shift. Descend slowly so you can be sure of your footing, and don't run: It could disturb and weaken the stairs further.

THIS HAPPENED TO ME!
Tsunami Race

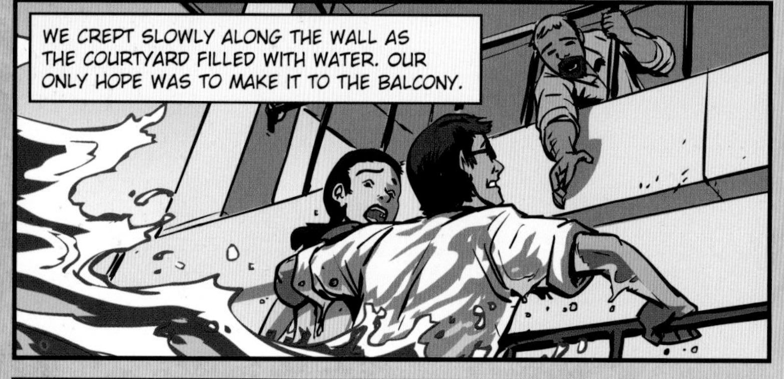

175 Know Tsunami Warning Signs

A tsunami can travel through deep water at more than 965 kilometres per hour, crossing an ocean in less than a day. And it won't calm down when it hits shore: Shallower water actually makes it taller. Here's how to tell if a big wave is headed your way.

A MAJOR SHAKE-UP An earthquake in a coastal region is an obvious warning sign. If you live near the earthquake, seek out high ground. Even if the earthquake is across the ocean, monitor broadcasts for warnings—tsunamis can travel long distances.

ANTSY ANIMALS Look out for changes in animal behavior. Scientists believe critters pick up on the earth's vibrations before we do, so if they're nervous, it may be for good reason.

RECEDING WATER The first part of a tsunami to reach land is the drawback trough, which causes coastal waters to recede, exposing normally submerged areas. If you spot a drawback, you've got about five minutes before the big wave hits.

176 Brace for a Big Wave

It's not just earthquakes that cause tsunamis: Volcanic activity, landslides, or impact from space objects can all set one off. And since the biggest tsunamis are as tall as 30 metres, you'll want to get at least that high above sea level. Anytime you're in a coastal area, think about where you would go in a big-wave emergency.

PLOT YOUR ESCAPE Do a little recon to identify escape routes to high ground. Plan on following designated tsunami evacuation routes (if they're established in your area) or simply heading inland and uphill as quickly as possible.

STAY TUNED Keep your ear tuned to the radio and TV for warnings. Evacuate immediately upon receiving notice of an impending tsunami.

GET THE HECK OUT Unless you have a death wish, don't go to the beach to watch the waves come ashore. Immediately meet up with your loved ones and head for high ground.

177 Survive Being Swept Away in a Tsunami

Getting caught up in a tsunami is like being trapped in a raging river with rapids and falls—only worse. You're caught in a wild maelstrom, along with a floating junkyard full of jagged metal, nail-studded lumber, raw sewage, twisted vehicles, panic-stricken animals, and dead bodies. How are you going to survive that?

AVOID THE FACE The greatest force of a wave is in its breaking face. This churning mass also carries the majority of pulverizing debris. If you're going to get swept away, at least try to hold on to something secure until this deadly part of the wave passes.

SCRAMBLE TO THE TOP After the dreaded face, there'll be several waves. With them come the thing that makes tsunamis deadly and the thing that gives you a fighting chance: debris, and lots of it. Fight and claw your way on top of anything that floats and cling to it for dear life. If the next waves get higher than the first wave, drag yourself to a higher point.

GET BACK TO LAND In a tsunami, you're either going inland with the initial surge or being dragged out to sea. If it's the latter, keep the shore in sight and swim parallel to it as you would do to escape a rip current. Float as much as possible, and use energy-efficient strokes like the backstroke to get back to solid ground.

178 Deal with a Tsunami at Sea

Strange but true: One of the safest places to be during an earthquake-triggered tsunami is on a boat in deep water. A quake beneath the ocean floor produces a powerful energy impulse that races horizontally through the water, but in the deep ocean that energy flows through without disturbing the surface. It's when that energy meets the shallows that the water rises up into a wave.

If you're on a boat in a harbor and you learn that a tsunami is coming, either immediately head for deeper water or abandon the boat and get to high ground. If you're on your way to deep water and the first wave catches you, steer the boat up the wave and apply maximum throttle to climb the swell. Keep heading for deeper water until the entire event has passed.

179 Know When Mud Might Flow

Mudslides occur when sloping ground becomes so saturated with water that the soil loses its grip and gravity takes over. Then you get to deal with a filthy deluge that can destroy your property and put your life at risk. Be smart and heed these warning signs:

KNOW THE STORY Mudslides are recurring events that happen where they've happened before. Contact local authorities to learn the geographical history of your area, including any fires that have destroyed vegetation (which often leads to soil erosion) or construction that has altered water flow.

AVOID EXTREME INCLINES Steep slopes that are close to the edge of a mountain range or valleys are bad news. If you can, simply live somewhere else that's less vulnerable.

WATCH THE WATER Pay attention to changes in the patterns of storm-water drainage on slopes. If there's a river or stream nearby, sudden changes in water level—or a change in color from clear to brown—could indicate an impending slide.

MIND THE GAPS Cracks in pavement and walls pulling away from buildings indicate that the land is moving—which means it may be vulnerable to mudslides. This is also true if cracks appear in your house's foundation, or if doors and windows start to stick in their frames.

LOOK FOR CROOKED STUFF Trees or telephone poles that are starting to lean aren't charming quirks. They mean the soil is eroding, and you should watch out.

180 Make It Through a Mudslide

Mudslides can be spawned by earthquakes, volcanic eruptions, storms that dump a lot of water quickly, or just plain old erosion. However they start, they're pretty much always a dirty bad time.

STAY AWAKE Most mudslide-related deaths occur at night, when people are asleep. If the rain is coming down hard and flooding and slides are predicted, put on a pot of coffee and continue to monitor weather and evacuation reports.

LISTEN FOR THE RUMBLE Massive amounts of soil, water, and debris don't just come crashing down silently. If you hear a rumbling sound emanating from up the hill, evacuate immediately.

GET OUT OF THE SLIDE'S PATH Sometimes there's not enough time to evacuate. If you get caught in a mudslide, the best you can do is try to move out of its way. If it's too late for that, curl into a tight ball and fold your arms over your head for protection.

181

STEP-BY-STEP

Save Your Home from Mudslides

To prevent your dream home from turning into a muddy nightmare, take these steps.

STEP ONE If you suspect your house may be in a slide zone, have a geological assessment done. Better yet, do that before you buy the home.

STEP TWO Think about the drainage on your property. If your home or yard often floods, use gravity to direct the flow of water away from your foundation. Dig a trench 30 to 60 centimetres deep and equally wide, and line it with compacted limestone.

STEP THREE Build a vertical retaining wall, which acts as a buffer and prevents land from sliding all the way down a hillside—taking your home with it. A good rule of thumb is to build a system of walls no more than 60 centimetres high, staggered down the hillside. Be sure to provide drainage behind the walls; otherwise the soil will erode and destabilize them.

STEP FOUR Topsoil needs strongly rooted vegetation to keep it in place. Begin with a solid carpeting of sod, followed by trees and faster-growing shrubs such as privets or decorative perennials like roses.

KNOW THE NUMBERS

Mudslides

300 SQUARE KM Largest area covered by a mudslide.

2.792 TRILLION LITRES Largest volume of mud from a single slide in modern times.

23,000 Largest confirmed mudslide death toll, caused by a 1985 slide in Colombia.

30,000 Largest estimated death toll for a single mudslide, which happened in Venezuela in 1999.

$1.79 BILLION TO $3.5 BILLION Estimated damages from 1999's Vargas, Venezuela, mudslide.

MORE THAN 90 Percentage of mudslides triggered by heavy rainfall.

35 Percentage of mudslides influenced by human activities such as building and scrub-clearing.

210 Average number of yearly landslide events that impact human beings.

50 TO 80 KILOMETRES PER HOUR Average speed of a mudslide.

320 KILOMETRES PER HOUR Fastest recorded speed of a mudslide.

182 Know You're in Avalanche Country

When a layer of snow breaks loose upslope and roars down the mountain at 320 kmh, it buries everything in its path. To avoid becoming a human popsicle, learn to recognize the danger signs.

WATCH THE WEATHER Avalanche risks increase after a heavy snowfall. The most precarious time of all is when snowy weather is followed by warm weather or rain—and then cold, snowy conditions return.

MEASURE THE SLOPE Most avalanches occur when the slope is 30 to 45 degrees, but even slopes of 25 to 60 degrees can slide if the conditions are right (or, from your perspective, very wrong).

SEEK THE SUN Snow is most volatile on slopes that face away from the sun during winter, so try to plan a route that keeps you off them.

STEP AROUND MOUNDS Watch out for areas where the wind has piled snow high (especially at the tops of mountains, gullies, and canyons).

RECOGNIZE BAD SNOW Don't tread on snow that makes a hollow sound when you step on it or on snow that looks like large, sparkly crystals instead of powder—this is deadly stuff called depth hoar.

LOOK FOR WRECKAGE Snow debris and broken trees are signs of previous avalanches, so be especially wary of these trouble spots.

BEWARE OF CHUTES Vegetation and boulders act as anchors for snowpack. If there are no trees or rocks on a slope, then it's a big amusement-park slide for snow—and this is one ride you don't want to be on.

WATCH FOR TRIGGERS A loud noise or tumbles taken by skiers or snowboarders can activate avalanches. Be wary if you see any of these catalysts.

STAY SAFE Some avalanches strike with no warning, so err on the safe side. If you're hiking, stick to ridgelines, windward hillsides, dense forests, or low-angle slopes. If you're skiing, stay on groomed trails.

183 Assess Incline

We all know that most avalanches start on slopes with an angle of 30 to 45 degrees, so these are the ones to avoid at all costs. But how do you figure out the angle?

If you're an avid mountaineer, you might want to invest in an inclinometer—a reasonably priced tool that measures the slope exactly. If you're not a backcountry hiker, skier, or hunter, that's probably overkill. Instead, tie a small weight to a string (one of the cords on your parka will do), dangle it to touch the snow's surface, and eyeball the slope's angle: A right angle is 90 degrees, so half of that is a dangerous 45-degree angle, and if you see that, you'd better move it. High-school geometry does come in handy after all.

184 Recognize Avalanche Types

Understanding the conditions that cause avalanches will help you avoid them—and trust me, you definitely want to avoid them.

SLAB AVALANCHES These bad boys account for more than 90 percent of avalanche fatalities. Slab avalanches don't generate from a single point, which might allow a skier or hiker to move laterally out of the way. Instead, an entire sheet of snow—sometimes a massively wide one—gives way at once. Slab avalanches happen when a thick layer of dense snow settles on top of looser snow.

LOOSE-SNOW SLIDES Also called sluffs, these are the least dangerous avalanche types, but they often injure skiers and snowboarders by causing them to change course and head into dangerous terrain. Sluffs occur in cold, dry conditions, when the snow is powdery and lacks cohesion.

WET AVALANCHES These avalanches tend to move slower than dry avalanches, but they present just as much danger. When temperatures are at or above freezing for a period of days, the surface snow melts and saturates the layers beneath it, making it prone to sliding. To check for wet-avalanche conditions, pick up a handful of snow and squeeze. If your glove gets very wet, it's best to take a different route.

RICH SAYS
"The best solution in a survival situation is to attract the attention of someone who can rescue you."

185 Ride Out an Avalanche

Caught in an avalanche? Well, that's plain bad luck. Use skiing (or even surfing) moves to try to ride on top of the snow, and attempt to maneuver toward the edge of the slide. If the snow is moving slowly, try to catch hold of a tree without getting creamed by it. In a fast-moving slide that knocks you off your feet, swim in the snow and try to avoid hitting stationary obstacles.

186 Get Rescued from an Avalanche

Being buried under the snow is not an enviable position. But it doesn't have to be a fatal one.

REACT QUICKLY Once the snow stops moving, it turns from a fluid medium to a cement-like consistency. So try to work your way to the surface as the slide slows.

SEEK THE SURFACE If possible, shove one arm toward the surface and move it around to create an air shaft. Use your hands to carve out a breathing space. Work methodically to avoid exhaustion.

DON'T SHOUT RANDOMLY Conserve your breath until you hear rescuers above you.

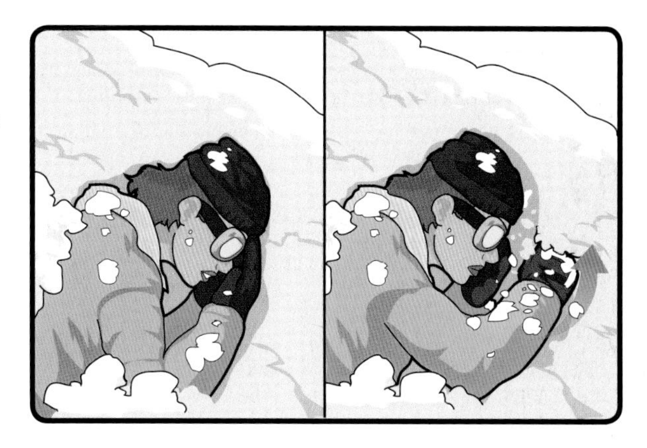

187 Know Which Way Is Up

You might be able to dig out after an avalanche has tumbled and rolled you—but only if you know which direction is up. If the snow layer above you is relatively thin, light might shine through, so go toward that. If you're too deep for light to be your guide, clear a space near your mouth and spit. Watch the direction in which gravity pulls the spit, and head the other way.

188 Strap On an Avalanche Beacon

If you're crazy enough to spend time in unstable snowscapes, you might want to invest in an avalanche beacon. Turn the unit on, set it to transmit, and strap it around your waist and over a shoulder under your outer layer of clothing. Let others know your plans prior to heading out. If you end up buried in a snowslide, rescuers will pick up your signal and know where to start digging.

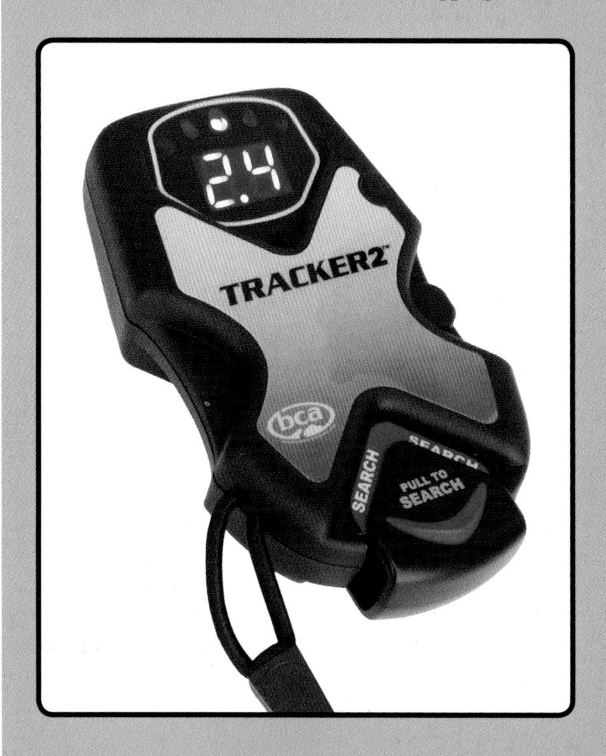

189 Walk in a Whiteout

I have a friend who got lost between his house and barn because the snow was falling so fast that he couldn't see the ground—much less the 30 metres between the two structures. He survived getting lost in a whiteout. I hope you're as lucky.

RESPECT THE STORM Forget winter wonderland: A whiteout is a horror show. You can't imagine how disorienting it is until you're in one. So only venture out as a last resort—say, if you have to get to emergency gear, clear the hood of your car to keep it visible to rescuers, or help someone who is stranded a short distance away.

TIE YOURSELF TO HOME BASE One way to keep from getting totally lost in a whiteout is to tie one end of a long rope to your starting point and the other end around your waist. The rope doesn't help you reach your destination, but it will help you get back. (If you know a blizzard is coming, and you anticipate needing to travel back and forth between buildings, tie a rope between them before the snow starts.)

PROTECT YOUR FACE Cover your mouth and nose to shield them from the wind and snow. Heck, go ahead and cover your eyes, too, since you're definitely not using them to see.

190 Drive in a Blizzard

Driving in a snowstorm is like trying to steer with a pillowcase over your head. It's bad enough during daylight, but it gets really hairy at night when you turn on your headlights, since every snowflake reflects the light back into your eyes. And it's not only you: Everybody else out there is blind, too.

If a snowstorm escalates, pull to the side of the road. Reduce your beams to parking lights to aid your own vision, and use emergency flashers to help others see you. Above all, stay inside the vehicle so that you don't get hit by another car. When the weather does clear up and you think it's safe to drive away, clear snow out of your brake lights (so other drivers can see you) and off the top of the car (so the snow doesn't tumble down and impede visibility). Chances are you'll also need to dig out your wheels to gain traction and get moving. Experienced winter drivers carry a shovel, as well as kitty litter or long pieces of wood. Lay these items down on the snow or ice in front of your wheels to help increase traction.

191 Deal with Being Snowbound in a Car

If you're stuck in a blizzard, a vehicle can protect you from wind and snow, and its visibility ups the odds that a search crew will find you. But in bitter cold, your car can feel like a freezer, because metal and glass offer no insulation. The solution is the same as the problem: snow.

PILE IT ON If you are driving in snowy conditions, keep a shovel in the trunk. A quarter-metre of snow piled on the car's roof and trunk will turn it into a cozy-ish snow cave.

HEAT THINGS UP Wear all the clothing you have in the car and run the heater in short bursts. Just don't use it constantly (you'll run out of gas), and clear snow from the exhaust pipe periodically to prevent carbon monoxide poisoning. If you happen to have a candle, light it up—it'll deliver an amazing amount of warmth.

STAY VISIBLE Keep snow off the car's hood so searchers can spot the color contrast from the air. Tying a colored strip of cloth to your vehicle's antenna can also get you rescued more quickly.

KEEP MOVING Exercise every so often inside the car to keep your circulation going. This will also keep you from falling asleep—which can be deadly if it's cold enough.

192 Ride Out a Blizzard at Home

Once a blizzard hits, all you can do is sit tight; there's no skipping out to the grocery for supplies when visibility is zero. Get your act together while the clouds are still gathering.

STOCK UP Make sure your at-home survival kit is well loaded with the usual essentials, plus extra blankets, sleeping bags, and heavy coats and other warm clothing.

WATCH YOUR WATER Severe cold can freeze pipes, leaving you without water to drink or the ability to flush a toilet more than one last time. Store water in containers where it won't freeze.

REDECORATE STRATEGICALLY Hang quilts over windows for extra insulation. In the daytime, keep your curtains and blinds open to allow sunlight to warm up your home. At night, keep them shut to trap heat inside.

STAY WARM A storm might tear down power lines, and without electricity you can't operate a furnace. So get a generator or stock up on fuel for a wood-burning stove or fireplace. And if you're not on your own, huddle with others in a small room to combine and maximize your body heat. It's not pervy: It's survival.

193 Prevent Carbon Monoxide Poisoning

If you're snowed in without power, you'll have to improvise ways to cook and stay warm. Be careful, though, or you'll face a whole new problem: poisoning from carbon monoxide (CO).

CHECK THE METER Install a carbon monoxide detector in your home. It will alert you if levels of this odorless gas ever get dangerously high.

PREVENT THE PROBLEM Never bring a charcoal grill indoors for any reason. Even operating a propane lantern or stove indoors can raise the CO concentration to a dangerous level. Space heaters are notorious killers, especially when they're left running after everyone goes to bed.

KNOW THE SYMPTOMS Watch for common signs such as vertigo, fatigue, and headaches, as well as odd behavior. If more than one person in the house is experiencing these symptoms, you've got a problem.

BREATHE BETTER If you suspect that someone has been poisoned by CO, get everyone outdoors immediately and open the windows and doors to allow ventilation. For mild cases, fresh air is sufficient treatment. For serious cases, hyperbaric treatment at a medical facility may be needed.

FIX THE PROBLEM Discover the cause of the high concentration of CO and have the situation remedied. Call the fire department to test for safety.

194

STEP-BY-STEP
Store Food During a Blizzard

There's one upside to losing power in the winter: the ease with which you can store perishable food items. Essentially, the world is your freezer.

STEP ONE If there's a decent amount of snow covering the ground, dig yourself a cubby.

STEP TWO Direct contact with snow can damage meats and vegetables, and unpackaged food is also susceptible to hungry scavengers looking for an easy meal. It's best to put all perishable items into individual plastic bags to reduce odors that might attract animals.

STEP THREE Store the packaged items in a wooden box or trunk (even a small side table with a latching door will work) and bury this item in the snow. You may end up losing a piece of furniture, but you'll prolong your food stores—and that trade-off is well worth the sacrifice.

195

STEP-BY-STEP
Clear a Heavy Snow

Folks who live in snow country know the value of a strong roof. A 2-centimetre layer of snow weighs approximately 20 kilos per square metre—and that can really add up. Sure, a little bit of snow can help insulate your home, but too much poses a hazard and should be removed.

STEP ONE Use an appropriate shovel with a longer handle for hard-to-reach areas. Start by clearing the apex of the roof, which will help you maintain a secure footing, and then work toward the edges.

STEP TWO Keep your gutters clear to avoid standing water—it will freeze in the cold, potentially causing structural damage to your home.

STEP THREE Don't forget tree branches, which heavy snow and ice can bring down; they may land on your home, a vehicle, a loved one, or a stranger passing by who happens to know a lawyer. Clear snow and ice by brushing it off the ends of limbs with a shovel, then work your way back to the trunk.

196 Protect from Wind Chill

Wind chill factor is a decrease in temperature felt by exposed skin due to the flow of cold air. With any air movement, the wind chill temperature will always be lower than the temperature read on a thermometer. The body loses heat through convection, increasing the risk of frostbite, hypothermia, or even death.

COVER YOUR HEAD Even when dressed in the best cold-weather gear, you lose a lot of body heat through your head, so keep a lid on it.

DRESS IN LAYERS Wear windproof outer layers; the air temperature won't seem as cold. Use a base layer to wick moisture from your skin, so you'll be less vulnerable to heat loss from sweat.

SHIELD YOUR EYES Glasses or goggles deflect wind from your face and keep extreme cold temperatures away from your eyes. If they get irritated and start to water, they will quickly freeze, and you don't want that at all.

COVER YOUR SKIN Use a neck gaiter, scarf, or hat to protect your face and neck. Gloves or mittens will ensure that your digits don't freeze up.

197 Drive in a Hailstorm

Although some people around the world think Canadians still live in igloos, extremely hot summers and the violent thunderstorms associated with them are a common occurrence. Hailstones may not seem scary, but when they exceed the size of softballs they can be deadly.

STOP If you get caught in a violent hail storm turn on your four-way flashers and pull over in a safe spot. Keep your lights on to make yourself more visible to other traffic. Tune in to your radio to stay informed about storm warnings.

FIND SHELTER Try to pull behind a large building or other obstacle that will break the direction the hail is coming from. Finding a covered garage or parking area is ideal. Watch for downed power lines, fallen trees or other debris created by the storm. If the storm is severe, press pillows or rolled-up clothing against windows to prevent breakage or shattering. When the storm has passed, evaluate your vehicle for damage (and restock your cooler with ice) before driving on.

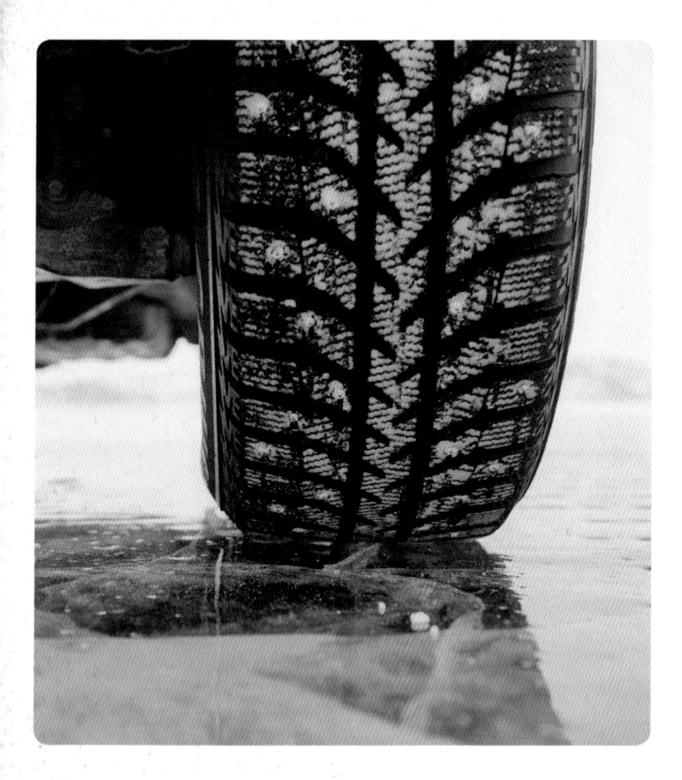

198 Beat Ice on the Cheap

You might be a Canadian if you've ever been late for a hockey game because you were left spinning your tires with no traction at that last stop sign—or took a nasty fall on the ice. Here are cheap ways to beat the ice, whether you're driving or walking.

LITTER A LITTLE Buy two bags of inexpensive kitty litter and throw them in your trunk before the first signs of winter. If you do get in a pickle and can't get traction, simply break open a bag and spread it in front of your tires. Once you get rolling your problems will be solved.

HIT THE MAT The next time you're stuck on ice or crusty snow and rocking your vehicle won't bounce you out of the rut, try taking your vehicle floor mats out and pushing them as far under the front edge of your tires as possible. Your tires will grip the mats and allow you to drive forward.

SCREW IN Don't let melting/freezing snow or ice storms get you down. Visit your local golf shop and purchase some screw-in cleats for your favorite winter shoes or boots. They work just as good as studded tires on your vehicle. You may have to drill small holes in your soles to get them started.

199 STEP-BY-STEP Stop a Train

Your train blows through your stop at lightning speed, and it occurs to you that you're not on the express—you're on a runaway train! What to do?

STEP ONE Locate the emergency brake in your car and pull the cord.

STEP TWO If the train doesn't stop, head toward the engine up front. In each car car, look for the friction brakes, usually controlled by a wheel or lever. Activate these to slow the train's overall speed.

STEP THREE Once in the engine car, push the button labeled "E-brake" or "emergency brake." Lower the throttle handle to decrease speed, then find the dynamic brake handle and move it to "setup"—this will kill the throttle. Wait five seconds and move the brake handle to the highest position. Finally, locate the air-brake handle and move it to 100 percent.

STEP FOUR After you've applied the cockpit's various brakes, use the radio to call for help.

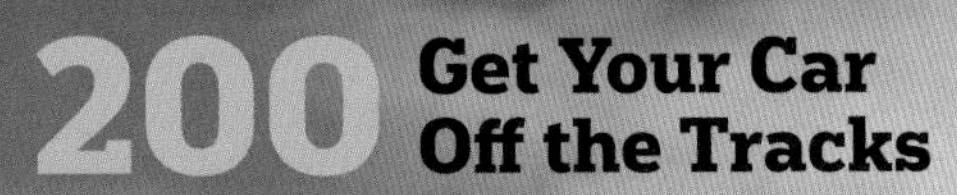

200 Get Your Car Off the Tracks

Car versus train is a matchup that never works out well—especially for the car. So never stop a vehicle on railroad tracks, and never race a train to the crossing. Play the lotto instead: You have a better chance of winning.

If for some reaso, your vehicle gets stuck on the tracks when you are absolutely certain that no train is coming, go ahead and try to push or tow it off. Enlist help for this.

If you get any hint that even a distant train is on the way, is there anything to gain by staying? Let me answer that one for you: Nope! Run like crazy and get at least 60 metres away, because parts of your beloved Camaro are about to become flying shrapnel.

201 Jump from a Moving Train

Unless you're riding an out-of-control train carrying explosives or hazardous materials, you're probably safer riding out a train wreck than attempting to jump while the train is moving. In a worst-case scenario, however, you've gotta do what you've gotta do, so at least prepare yourself for a rough landing.

LOOK BEFORE YOU LEAP Try to miss obvious obstacles, such as platforms, bridge infrastructure, posts, and trees. Aim to hit the ground on a soft, open spot.

ASSUME THE POSITION When you jump, hold your body in a slight crouch, bent at your knees and waist so you can absorb the blow. Keep your feet and knees together and your arms wrapped tightly across your chest, with your chin tucked. Try to hit the ground feet first, then roll with the momentum.

KNOW THE NUMBERS
AIR TRAVEL

1 Number of passengers killed in the first fatal aviation accident. It was in 1908, and Orville Wright piloted.

22 Percentage of airplane fatalities caused by mechanical malfunction.

12 Percentage of fatalities that are entirely weather-related.

1972 Year with the most plane accident deaths.

3,214 Number of fatalities in 1972.

202

Use Your Cell for an Airborne SOS

You aren't supposed to make calls on a cell phone during a commercial flight, because electromagnetic interference from the phone might adversely affect aircraft controls. However, if you can't reach the cockpit to use the radio—or if the radio's down—all bets are off. (That was certainly the case on September 11, 2001, when passengers on United Airlines Flight 93 placed emergency calls after terrorists took control of the plane.) As long as there's a cell tower in range, a mobile phone will work on a plane. The lower the plane's altitude, the greater the chances for a successful connection—and for getting assistance.

203 Contact Air Traffic Control

A quick hop on a small plane seems like a good idea—until the pilot starts clawing at his chest and turning blue.

CALL FOR HELP Make sure the radio is on and place your Mayday call on the frequency that's already set, since that's likely to be the one the local tower uses. If you need to select a frequency, try 121.5 MHz or 243.0 MHz, which air-traffic control usually monitors.

LISTEN CAREFULLY The vast majority of successful landings by nonpilots are assisted by air-traffic controllers. Many are pilots themselves, so they're likely to know how to get you down safely.

204

STEP-BY-STEP

Jump Out of an Airplane

Gravity is a drag, especially when you're falling from an airplane without a parachute. If you're going to jump, use a chute.

STEP ONE Step into the harness so the leg-hole straps encircle your thighs, then bring the top straps over your shoulders and tighten the harness across your chest. Don't touch the ripcord before exiting the plane.

STEP TWO Jump from the airplane any way you can—except in front of an engine. If you think falling's bad, you should see what passing through a propeller or a turbine will do to your day.

STEP THREE Count to three, then pull the rip cord.

STEP FOUR Plan your landing. Steer the parachute by pulling the handles, using the ones on your right to go right and those on your left to head left. Before landing, bend your knees, tuck in your elbows, and lower your chin to your chest. Roll with the landing.

THIS HAPPENED TO ME!
PANIC IN THE AIR

205 CHECKLIST
Salvage a Crash Site

After a plane crash, survivors face the challenge of staying alive until rescuers arrive. Depending on where the plane goes down, salvation might be only minutes away . . . or it could take days or even weeks for rescuers to find you. It's time to get creative.

- ☐ Check the cockpit for the plane's radio. If it works, send out a distress call.
- ☐ Use the fuselage as a shelter—that is, unless fuel has spilled, in which case there's a chance of fire, and you should move at least 30 metres away.
- ☐ If the plane has broken up, put the cabin debris to good use: The carpeting, upholstery, seat cushions, bulkheads, overhead-bin doors, plastic windows, and aluminum can all become useful components of a temporary shelter.
- ☐ Dig through cargo compartments and luggage bins to find clothing, blankets, pillows, food, and water.
- ☐ Look for electrical wires, which you can use to lash together elements of your shelter.
- ☐ Punch a hole in the fuel tank (usually located in the wings of larger aircraft), drain the fuel into a container, and use it to start a fire.
- ☐ Use reflective materials for signal mirrors.
- ☐ Nearly all planes carry advanced medical supplies, including automatic defibrillators. Don't leave those critical items behind.

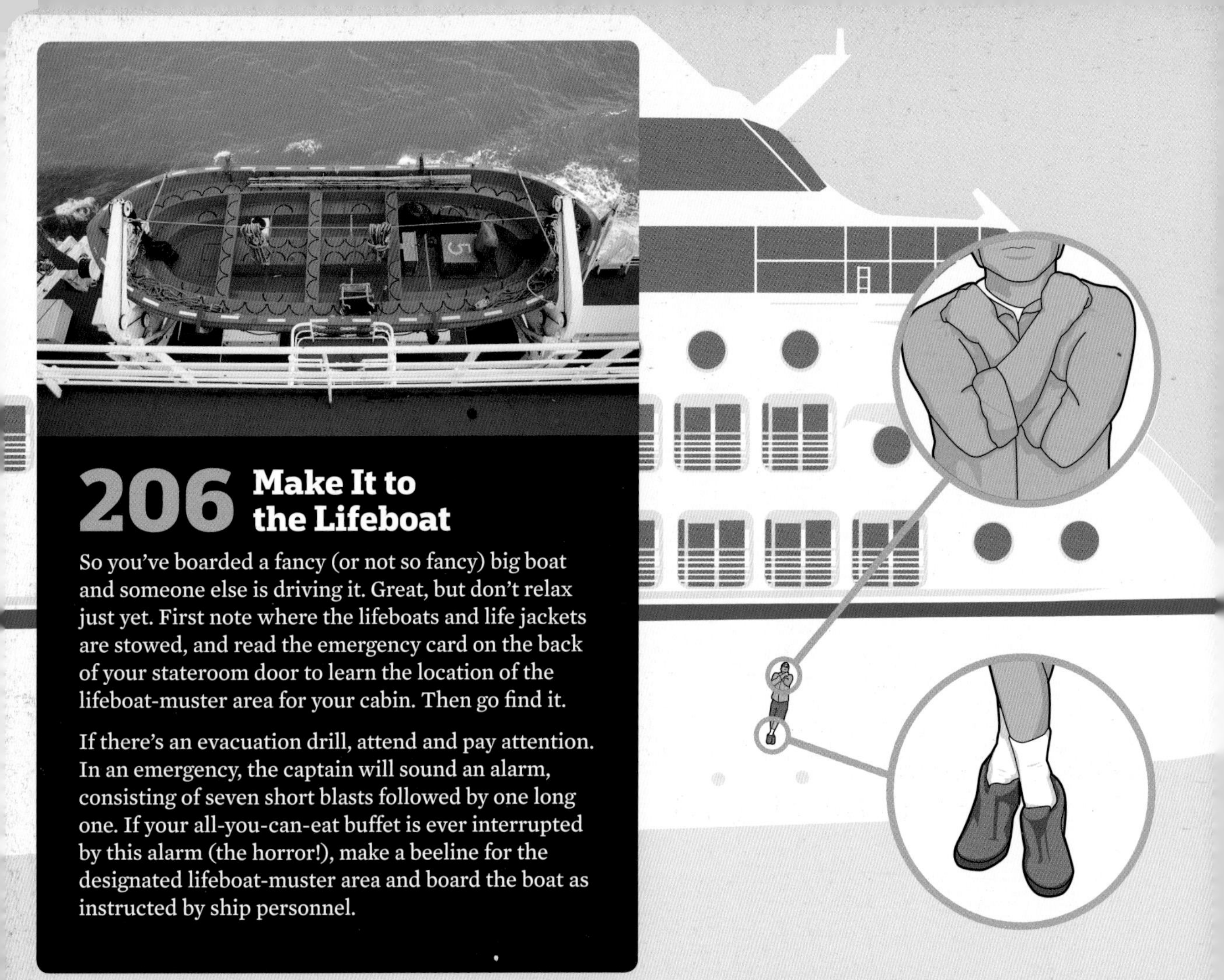

206 Make It to the Lifeboat

So you've boarded a fancy (or not so fancy) big boat and someone else is driving it. Great, but don't relax just yet. First note where the lifeboats and life jackets are stowed, and read the emergency card on the back of your stateroom door to learn the location of the lifeboat-muster area for your cabin. Then go find it.

If there's an evacuation drill, attend and pay attention. In an emergency, the captain will sound an alarm, consisting of seven short blasts followed by one long one. If your all-you-can-eat buffet is ever interrupted by this alarm (the horror!), make a beeline for the designated lifeboat-muster area and board the boat as instructed by ship personnel.

207 STEP-BY-STEP Abandon Ship Safely

Unless you're the captain, you definitely don't want to go down with a sinking ship. But going over the side is no picnic, either. It's difficult to swim in the turbulent water around a sinking vessel. Even still, if ordered to abandon ship, move as fast as you can. Follow these steps to make a safer exit.

STEP ONE You want to be away from the crowd to avoid jostling for position. Move to the railing and prepare to jump. If the ship is rolling to one side, abandon ship from the high side so you aren't crushed by the boat if it capsizes. If you're higher than 5 metres (15 ft) above the water, it's too dangerous. Find a lower position or wait for the ship to sink further.

STEP TWO Cross your arms over your chest and grab your lapels (or the area where they'd be). This position protects your neck and shoulders so that when you hit the water they don't break.

STEP THREE Look for a spot in the water that's free of debris and aim for it. It will take some courage, but when you've picked your spot, don't wait.

STEP FOUR As you leave the rail, cross your feet at the ankles—keeping your legs together will help prevent the force of the impact from causing injury. Take a big breath just before the splash.

STEP FIVE The biggest danger of being close to a sinking ship is getting clobbered by debris falling from the deck, so get yourself well out of the way. Swim at least 30 metres (100 ft) from the ship. Use either a sidestroke or a backstroke to conserve energy while keeping your eyes peeled for obstacles or hazards.

208

STEP-BY-STEP

Swim Through Burning Oil

When ships go under, oil tanks often rupture, releasing fuel that coats the surface of the water. If that film ignites—and when a ship sinks, it almost always does—you have to get through it to safety.

STEP ONE Jump feetfirst through the flames.

STEP TWO Submerge and swim beneath the surface. Don't try to hold your breath too long, as loss of breath tends to cause panic.

STEP THREE When you come up for air, try to look for a clear area. Keep your arms extended over your head, and violently splash the surface with your hands as you emerge to throw the burning oil clear. Take your breath, then immediately dive again.

STEP FOUR Repeat the process until you're clear. If injury prevents you from swimming underwater, swim at the surface while constantly splashing the oil away from you on all sides.

RICH SAYS
"Thousands of chemical and oil spills happen each year due to accidents or natural disasters. Be ready to run, and have a place to go."

209 Deal with a Hazmat Situation

Hazmat situations usually involve noxious gases or explosive materials—hence the word *hazmat*, which is short for "hazardous materials." These events are the real deal, so don't mess around.

STAY INFORMED Tune into radio or TV broadcasts to stay up-to-date on the situation. If you're told to evacuate, do it as quickly as possible. Keep all car windows shut as you flee the scene, and set your air conditioning to recirculate air inside the car.

AVOID THE DANGER ZONE If you're caught outdoors when the hazmat warning is issued, cover your face as completely as possible and maneuver yourself to stay upwind, uphill, and upstream of the hazmat location, preferably at least a kilometre and a half away. Most likely the source will be an industrial facility, a railway, or a major highway.

210 Decontaminate Yourself

If you're unlucky enough to get hazardous materials on your person, better act fast:

STEP ONE Strip off your clothes immediately and don't put them back on until they've been thoroughly laundered. This is no time for modesty—even a few seconds can make a big difference. While you're undressing, avoid touching your eyes, mouth, or nose, because you could be introducing dangerous chemicals into your system.

STEP TWO Rinse every affected area for at least fifteen minutes. If the material is flammable, brush it off before stepping under the showerhead.

STEP THREE If your luck is even worse and you do end up with the bad stuff in your eyes, rinse them out as well, rolling your eyes back and forth under the stream to cleanse as much surface area as possible.

211 STEP-BY-STEP
Seal Your Home During a Chemical Spill

The instant you learn of a hazmat problem nearby, move indoors to limit exposure (unless you're told to evacuate). In especially bad cases, authorities may advise sealing your home. Here's how:

STEP ONE Shut any vents leading to the outside, including the fireplace damper. Turn off all air conditioners, fans, and ventilation systems.

STEP TWO Use plastic sheeting and duct tape to seal windows and doors. You can use aluminum foil or even wax paper to seal around air conditioner vents, kitchen and bathroom exhaust fans, and clothes dryer vents.

STEP THREE Even outlets and light switches let in fumes. Tape them up, too.

STEP FOUR Close and lock exterior doors and windows so that no one can enter or leave after you seal the house.

STEP FIVE Move to an interior room. Once you're inside with all needed supplies, seal off conduits into the room with duct tape, close all interior doors, and place towels at the bottom of doors to limit the air circulation within the house.

212 Get Clear of a Hazardous Spill

Suddenly, a chemical facility in your area starts spewing smoke. Yikes. It's always a good idea to run, but it's also important to know when you're far enough away from the event to be safe. One nifty trick is literally a rule of thumb.

Spot the incident site and extend your arm toward it. Line up your thumb with the site; if you can obscure the entire area with your thumb, then you're at a safe distance for the moment. If your thumb doesn't cover it and the wind is blowing in your direction, then start sprinting: You need more distance between yourself and that toxic inferno, stat.

213 STEP-BY-STEP
Don a Gas Mask

Few things are more terrifying than a chemical or biological attack. Learning how to quickly don a gas mask and ensure a proper seal could be the difference between life and death. In an attack, you'll likely only have seconds to reach your mask and put it on, so practice until it's second nature.

STEP ONE With your thumbs on the inside of the mask, hold it by the sides. Insert your chin first, then pull the mask over your face and remove your thumbs.

STEP TWO Holding the mask in place with one hand, pull the straps over your head as far as possible, then tighten them from the top down. The mask should fit snugly and not move when you shake your head.

STEP THREE Place the palm of your hand over the filter or air intake, and breathe deeply until the mask seals tightly to your face.

STEP FOUR Remove your hand from the filter and breathe normally. Then get to safety as quickly as possible—the gas mask's canister has a limited capacity, and the clock is ticking.

KNOW THE NUMBERS
Pandemic

200 TO 500 MILLION Most people killed by a single disease, smallpox, over history.

100 MILLION Most people killed in a single outbreak of a disease, the flu pandemic of 1918.

95 PERCENT Highest mortality rate in a pandemic outbreak—the pneunomic plague of the 1890s.

33.3 MILLION Number of people infected with HIV.

150 MILLION Estimated death toll from a feared H5N1 flu pandemic.

2 PERCENT Odds a new tuberculosis infection will be drug resistant.

2 WEEKS Time it takes for an airborne virus to spread throughout the world population.

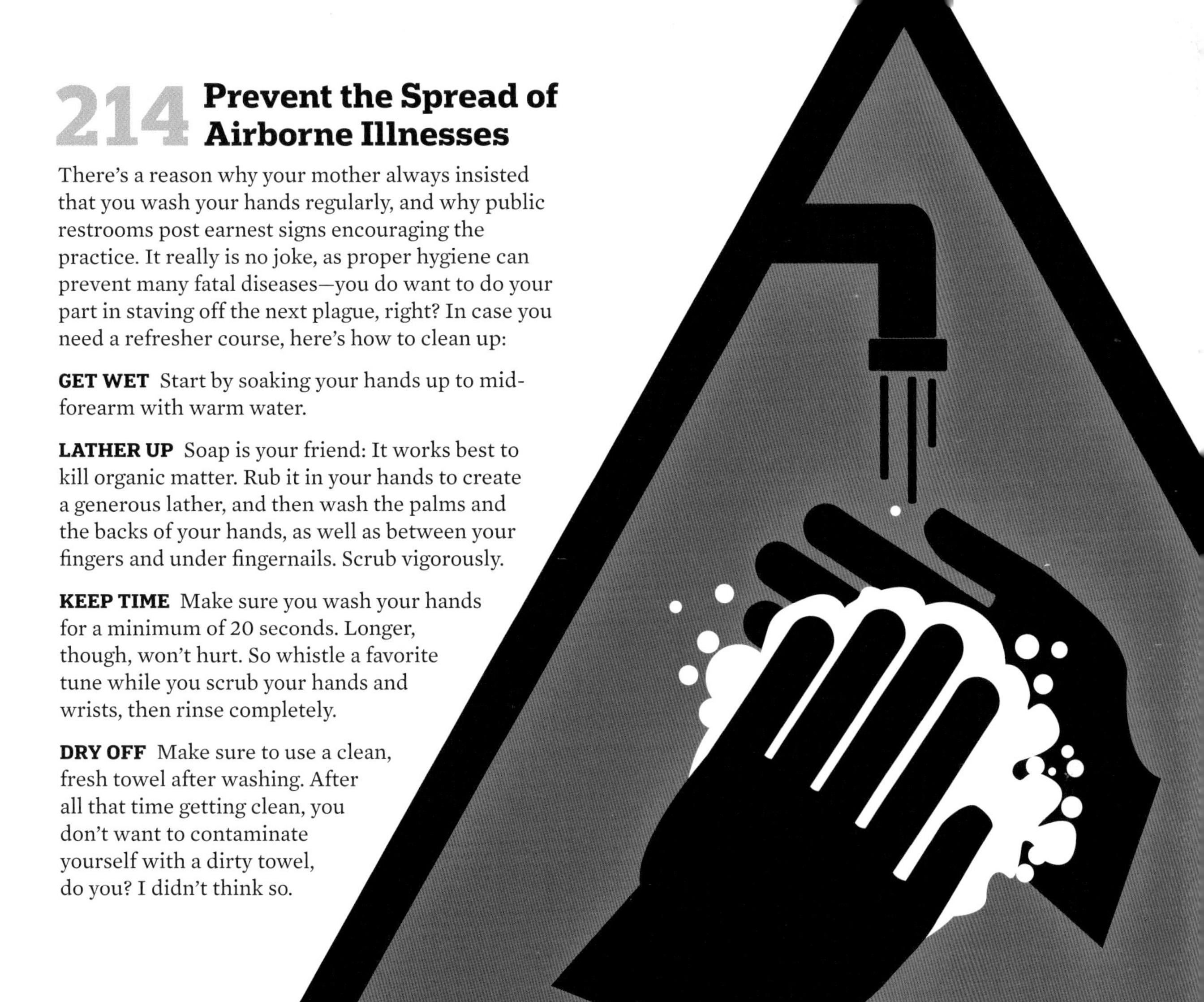

214 Prevent the Spread of Airborne Illnesses

There's a reason why your mother always insisted that you wash your hands regularly, and why public restrooms post earnest signs encouraging the practice. It really is no joke, as proper hygiene can prevent many fatal diseases—you do want to do your part in staving off the next plague, right? In case you need a refresher course, here's how to clean up:

GET WET Start by soaking your hands up to mid-forearm with warm water.

LATHER UP Soap is your friend: It works best to kill organic matter. Rub it in your hands to create a generous lather, and then wash the palms and the backs of your hands, as well as between your fingers and under fingernails. Scrub vigorously.

KEEP TIME Make sure you wash your hands for a minimum of 20 seconds. Longer, though, won't hurt. So whistle a favorite tune while you scrub your hands and wrists, then rinse completely.

DRY OFF Make sure to use a clean, fresh towel after washing. After all that time getting clean, you don't want to contaminate yourself with a dirty towel, do you? I didn't think so.

215 Make a Mosquito Trap

One of Canada's peskiest home invaders is the mosquito. They can carry disease, and besides that, they're just plain annoying. But the chemical repellants can be downright toxic. Here's a more natural option to try.

First, cut a 2-liter plastic bottle in half, setting the top half aside for later. Mix 50 g brown sugar into 200 ml warm water, and let cool. When it's cold, pour it into the bottom half of the bottle. Add a gram of yeast (no need to mix, it'll make carbon dioxide all by itself).

Place the top of your bottle upside down into the other half of the bottle, forming a tight-fitting funnnel top. Then, wrap the entire bottle with something black, minus the top, and put in some corner of your house or camper.

The carbon dioxide generated by the mixture attracts mosquitoes that fly through the funnel of the bottle and into the trap, unable to escape. It won't take long to see how many mosquitoes die inside the bottle.

216 Improvise Shelter During Nuclear Fallout

When all hell finally breaks loose and a mushroom cloud takes shape in the sky, you need to take cover. The most important principle is to get as much mass between you and the radioactive dust, which can go through walls and roofs, as possible.

If you have a basement, you're in luck. Pick the corner with the highest soil level outside, and push a heavy table into it. Then grab anything that's available and start heaping it on top—books, bricks, water containers, food stores, anything with high mass. Push large furniture up against all exposed sides of the table, leaving yourself a small entrance. Then get inside, seal it off, and wait it out, only coming out when absolutely necessary.

217 Bunk Up in a Bunker

You remember the Cold War, when the threat of nuclear battle loomed large and we all readied bunkers in our backyards? Well, contrary to popular belief, that war never ended. Every day countries add to their arsenal of nuclear arms. So if you didn't build that bunker then, build it now. Here's how.

PILE IT ON The goal is to protect against radiation's rays, so the more mass, the better. Construct the roof of steel, concrete, rock, soil, and wood layers, and build your bunker at least a metre underground.

TRICK IT OUT You're going to be down there for a while; an optimistic estimate is ten days. That means you'll need several amenities, such as a chemical toilet (which deodorizes waste) and a septic tank, an air pump and a filter, a periscope, and a Geiger counter, which will help you monitor radiation levels.

STOCK IT UP You'll need food, water, medical, and hygiene supplies for all the occupants, plus clothing and bedding. All in all, figure on 3.75 litres of water per day per person, and gather canned and dehydrated foods (just remember, you need water to hydrate them). Keep a radio and extra batteries so you can keep up with what's going on above ground, and bring a few books and games to fend off boredom.

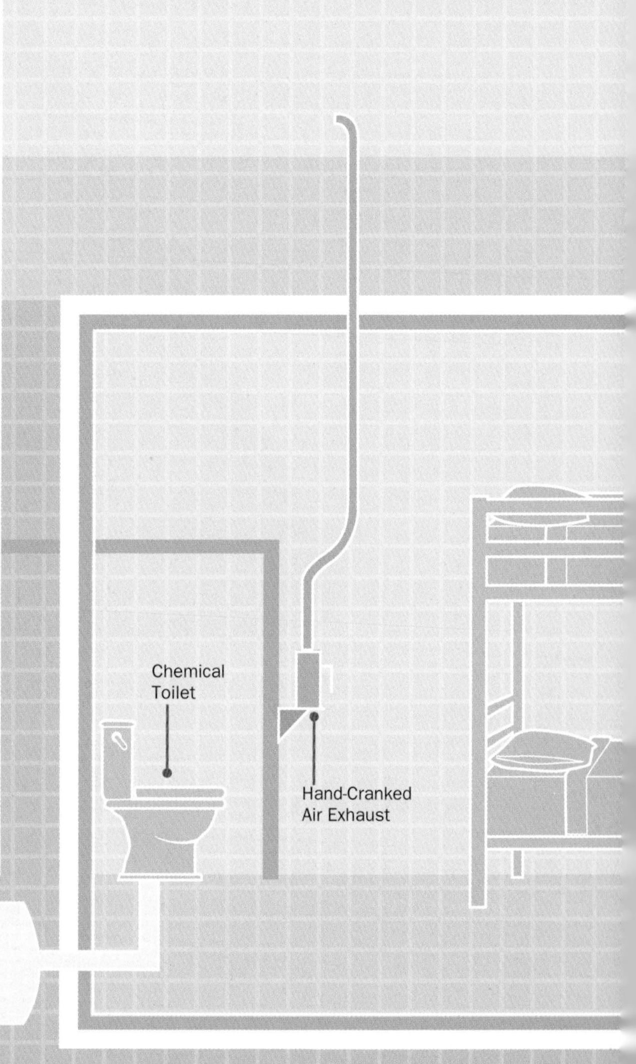

RICH SAYS

"Ask yourself, 'How did my great-granddaddy live?' That's how you'll live after a nuclear event. It's an instantaneous journey into the Third World."

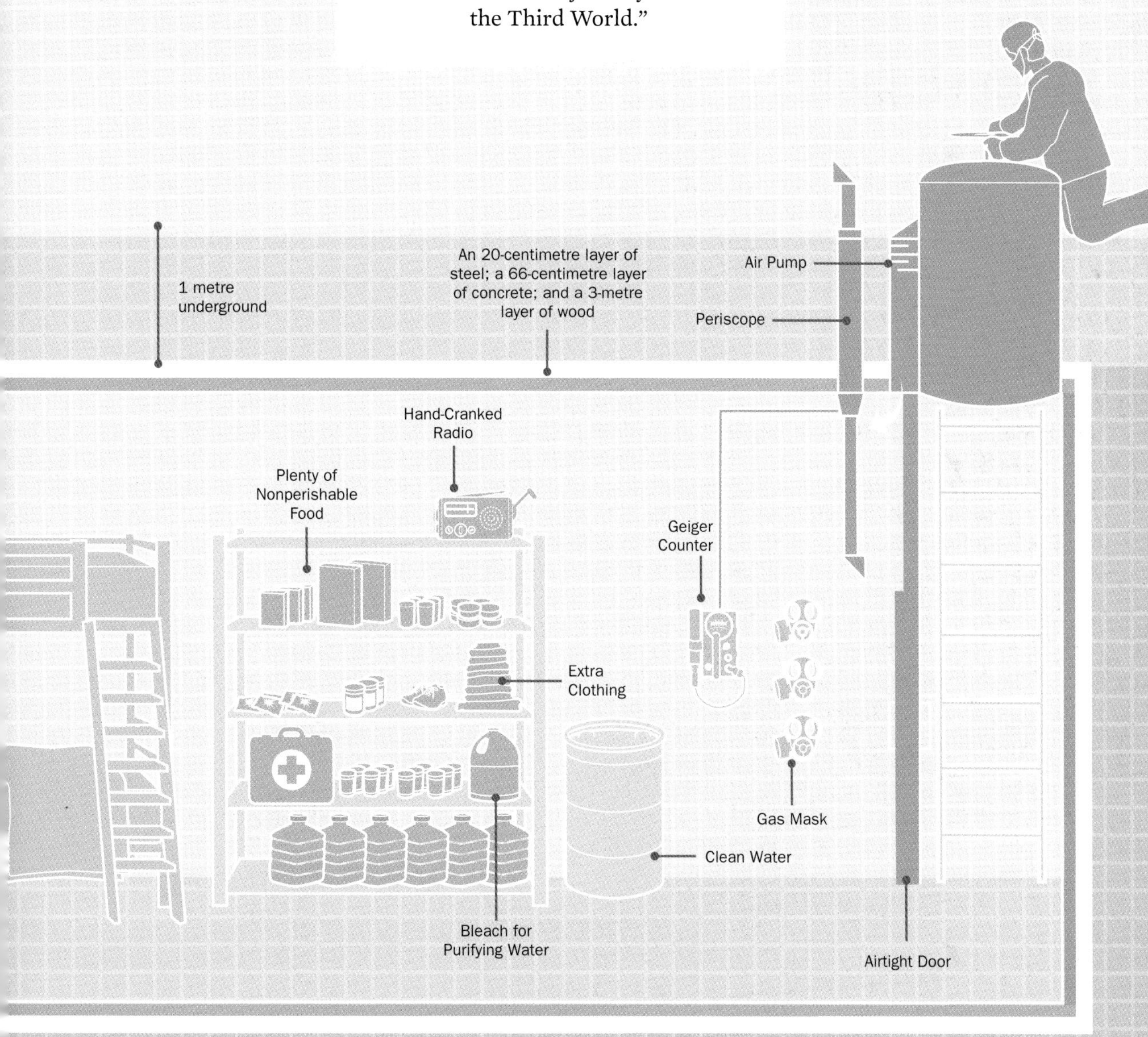

218 ASSESS AND RESPOND
Understand Radiation

Simply put, radiation is bad. We're all exposed to various levels of it throughout our lives, and our bodies know how to cope with these daily doses. But a nuclear event is hardly an everyday occurrence, and the radiation it silently releases can have devastating effects on the human body. Here's a range of radiation levels and examples of each, along with what ills to expect.

LOW LEVELS

0 to 1,000 microsieverts (μSv): With an exposure this minor, you can expect no symptoms nor any increased cancer risk.

0.1 μSv Dose obtained from eating a banana.

0.4 μSv Natural radiation level in the human body.

1 μSv Amount absorbed by using a computer monitor for one year.

10 μSv Average dose received each day from a normal environment.

40 μSv Dose during a flight from Los Angeles to New York City.

100 μSv Amount absorbed during one chest X-ray.

250 μSv Maximum amount of radiation release permitted per nuclear power plant per year.

1,000 μSv Maximum exposure level for the general public.

MODERATE LEVELS

100 to 1,000 millisieverts (mSv): You'll have no immediate symptoms, but you may have health problems later.

100 mSv Annual dose at which lifetime cancer risk increases.

250 mSv Maximum dose for U.S. radiation workers in life-saving emergency operations.

400 mSv Highest hourly rate at Japan's Fukushima Daiichi power plant during the disaster in 2011.

500 mSv Amount of radiation exposure that triggers a reduction in blood cell count. Fortunately, you'd return to normal after a few days.

1,000 mSv Amount of radiation that surfaced in the water hourly outside the Fukushima No. 2 reactor during the disaster.

HIGH LEVELS

2,000-plus millisieverts (mSv): Extreme exposure may prove fatal, and you'll have a higher risk of health issues later in life.

2,000 mSv Level at which severe radiation poisoning occurs. Recovery is likely with treatment and evacuation.

5,000 mSv Magnitude of dose required to kill half of those people exposed within one month.

10,000 mSv Fatal dose.

50,000 mSv Ten-minute exposure to the Chernobyl reactor core after meltdown.

100,000 mSv Level that causes death within mere hours.

Some parts of the body are more vulnerable to radiation exposure than others. Here are your likely trouble spots, should you be exposed.

THYROID Radioactive iodine can build up here, leading to cancers. Children's thyroid glands are especially at risk.

SKIN Exposure can cause extreme redness and irritation.

LUNGS If you inhale radioactive material, your lungs are likely to undergo DNA damage.

STOMACH AND INTESTINES Ingesting contaminated foods or liquids puts your digestive system at risk.

REPRODUCTIVE ORGANS High doses of radiation often lead to sterility. In pregnant women, exposure to radiation has resulted in birth defects.

BONE MARROW If you're exposed, radioactive elements can mutate your bone marrow, leading to leukemia and other immune system diseases.

219 Anticipate Radiation's Lasting Effects

A onetime exposure to radiation is bad enough, but to make matters worse, this stuff can really stick around, lasting from eight days to more than a billion years. So if a radioactive event happens near you, know that you could be at risk long after the news coverage stops.

WATCH WHAT YOU EAT Animals are the most sensitive to exposure, and guess what: You're an animal. Chances are, you also eat animals and their products—such as beef, milk, and eggs. And many of those creatures eat grasses, which radioactive particles may coat. Avoid eating locally cultivated animal products following a nuclear event, especially if your government issues warnings. You may wish to stock up on potassium iodide tablets, which may prevent thyroid damage. It's best to purchase them prior to an emergency, as demand will quickly outstrip supply.

CONSIDER THE WATER Immediately after a nuclear event, authorities will be testing the local waters to see if they're safe to drink or bathe in, and if fish and seafood is okay to eat. This is when that emergency water stock I've been talking about comes in handy. Use it until you hear that the coast is clear.

THINK BEFORE YOU STAY Depending on the amount of exposure, land that has been impacted by radioactive fallout can suffer long-term damage, rendering it unusable for agriculture or residence for decades. Just because there's no radioactive material spewing into the atmosphere at the moment doesn't mean that it's safe to plant crops, raise livestock, or live in the area. Take, for instance, the land surrounding Chernobyl: It's still uninhabitable, more than twenty-five years after the nuclear accident.

220 Make it Through a Power Outage

When the lights go out, it's a sure sign the electrons have gone on strike. You never know how long a power outage is going to last, so it's wise to break out the pack of cards and prepare yourself for a long one.

GO OFF-GRID Turn off or unplug all unnecessary or sensitive electric equipment (electric stove, computers, TV, sound systems) so an electrical surge or spike won't damage them when the power is restored.

BE REACHABLE Keep an old-school corded phone on hand; it's likely to work even during a power outage.

DEAL WITH LIGHTS Leave one light switched on so you'll know when the power comes back on. If it's nighttime, use flashlights and candles for illumination.

GO THE EXTRA STEP If someone requires electric-powered life-support equipment, provide a backup power supply in your emergency preparedness plan.

221 Survive a Heat Wave

High temperatures can be worse than insufferable: They can be deadly. To make matters worse, everyone using their air conditioners at once can trigger a power outage. And if you thought a heat wave wasn't fun, try a heat wave without air conditioning. Here's what to do when the mercury rises.

BE SUN SAVVY Open windows on the shaded side of the house. On the sunny side of the house, hang exterior shades to block sun from hitting windows.

PROMOTE CIRCULATION Open the doors and set battery-operated box fans in each entry. They'll expel hot air while drawing cooler air inside.

STAY LOW Remember the old adage about hot air rising? Now's the time that tip comes in handy. Keep to your home's lowest level, where the air is coolest.

GET WET Soak your feet in a basin of water, and wear a damp bandanna around your head. If you have one, fill a spray bottle with water and give yourself a cooling spritz every so often.

DRINK UP Make sure you're getting lots of water, and slow down to reduce perspiration and overheating. Avoid caffeine or alcohol, as they'll just dehydrate you.

UNPLUG IT If your power is on, know that all your household appliances create heat—and that heat really adds up. Unplug computers and lamps with incandescent bulbs, and make meals that don't require heat-generating appliances, such as stoves.

WATCH FOR WARNING SIGNS Know the symptoms of various heat-related illnesses (such as heatstroke and heat exhaustion), and call the authorities if a member of your family displays these signs.

222 Eat Right in a Blackout

A power outage suddenly reduces your stovetop to mere counter space and makes your refrigerator no better for food storage than a pantry. But you've still got to eat.

MIND THE EXPIRATION DATE Open the refrigerator door only when necessary to keep perishables and frozen food fresh. Usually food in the fridge is edible for a day, and food in the freezer for a couple of days.

IMPROVISE A FRIDGE If it looks as if the power outage is going to last a few days or (gulp) a few weeks, you can store your perishable foods in camp coolers or on blocks of ice in the bathtub.

COOK SAFELY Never fire up a BBQ or a hibachi, or start an open fire in the house. Instead, cook outdoors on a propane grill or using a Dutch oven and briquettes. If your fireplace is equipped with an iron-top inset, you can cook on that.

APPLY THE SNIFF TEST Discard unsafe foods that have a foul odor, color, or texture. Even when you're hungry, fuzz growing on the food is a bad sign.

223 Start Your Car with a Screwdriver

If you've ever been stranded in dire straits without your keys, you've probably contemplated hotwiring your car. But if your car was manufactured before the mid-90s, try the screwdriver trick.

Take a flathead screwdriver and cram it into the ignition. It ain't elegant, but with any luck, you'll be able to use the screwdriver to turn the ignition cylinder as if you were using your key. Don't worry too much about damaging the cylinder. If you're in a position where you're jacking your own car, damage is the least of your concerns.

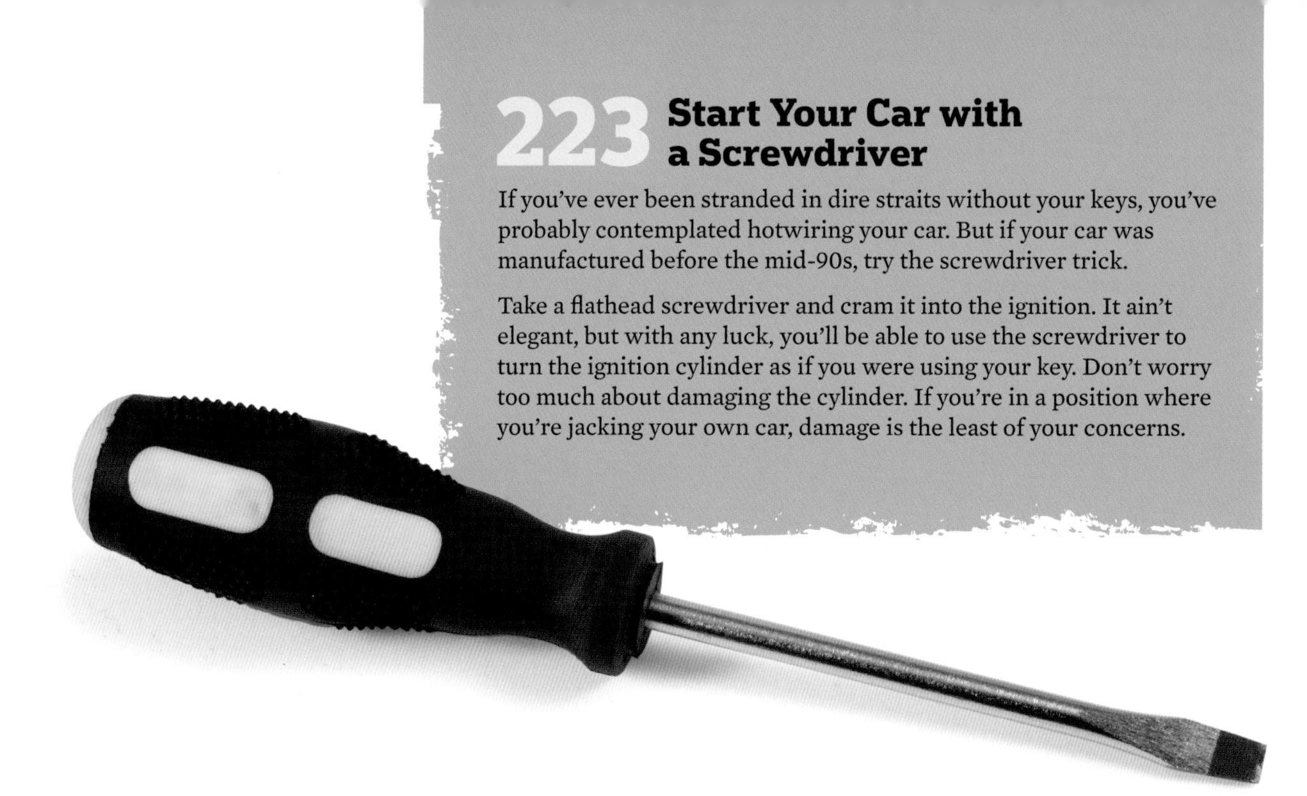

224 Siphon Fuel

Siphoning sucks. But sometimes it's your only option.

SET UP YOUR SIPHON Uncap the gas tank and insert a clear, small-diameter tube that's long enough to reach down to the bottom of the gas tank with enough length left over to reach as far as the ground.

START SUCKING Apply suction to the tube with your mouth. Go easy and don't inhale the fumes. The clear tube (hopefully) lets you see the fuel before you get a mouthful.

GATHER THE GOODS Stop sucking when the fuel has reached your mouth (spit out any inadvertent sips you may have taken), then put the end of the tube into a container that's below the level of the vehicle fuel tank. Gravity will do the rest.

225

STEP-BY-STEP

Charge Your Phone with a Flashlight

Crank it up! In survival situations, crank-charging versions of small electronics are mighty handy (literally). Some flashlights and radios work for hours once you've cranked them into full power. Even cooler, you can convert them into basic generators capable of charging a phone or other small device.

STEP ONE Open the housing of the flashlight and locate the package of button cells, which look like a cylinder.

STEP TWO To charge an external object like a cell phone, cut off the plug end of the charger cord and strip enough of the insulation from the two wires to solder to the corresponding contacts on the button cells.

STEP THREE Turn the flashlight crank to generate power and divert it to your phone.

226 Harness a Car Battery's Power

In survival situations, car batteries can be a godsend. They hold a large charge, and you can recharge them if you have a method for generating current, such as a solar panel. Once you've got it charged, what you do with the car battery is up to you. Here are some ideas.

START A FIRE Mix a small amount of gasoline with tinder and let it rest for a few seconds so the gas fumes can blend with the air above the tinder. Then attach jumper cables to the battery's terminals and strike the positive and negative leads together over the tinder. You'll be rewarded with a spark, and the fumes should ignite immediately.

TURN MASTER WELDER For longer-term use, you can use car batteries to weld. For simple electric welds, connect three car batteries in a series (meaning a connection between positive and negative terminals) with jumper cables. Connect your ground cable to the first battery's positive terminal and the object to weld. Connect your final cable, with a small wire or rod clamped in the opposite end, to the last battery's negative terminal. As you touch the rod to the object you're welding, the three batteries provide 36 volts and plenty of amperage to perform most basic welds. You'll drain your batteries quickly, so have your weld well planned out before you start.

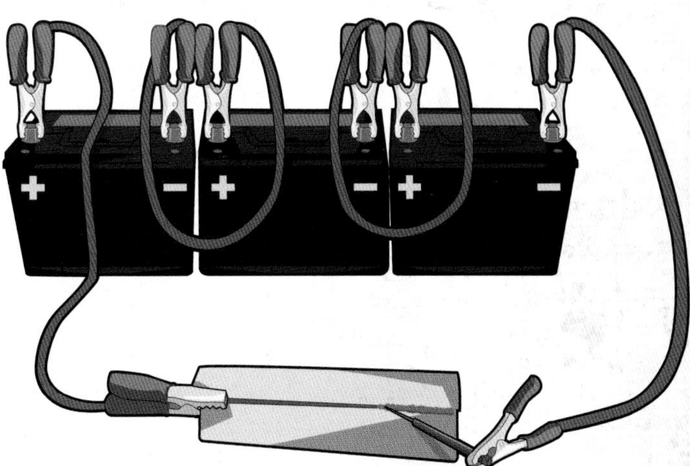

227 STEP-BY-STEP
Harvest Aspirin from Tree Bark

So your homestead is surrounded by looters, you've got a sprained ankle, and you left your aspirin in your other bunker. Good thing certain trees contain salicin, a relative of aspirin, and it's pretty simple to use them to improvise your own painkiller.

STEP ONE Find yourself a willow or poplar tree, which are popular in residential neighborhoods.

STEP TWO The salicin is located in the tree's soft inner bark, between the hard exterior bark and the hardwood. In younger trees, simply pull off the green bark. If you're dealing with an older tree, use a knife to skin the harder stuff. Scrape the interior of the bark until you have a handful of pulp.

STEP THREE If you're in a hurry, chew the bark at once. If you have the time, boil a handful of pulp in water for 10 minutes. Drink a few glasses a day of this tea, and you'll be back on your feet in no time.

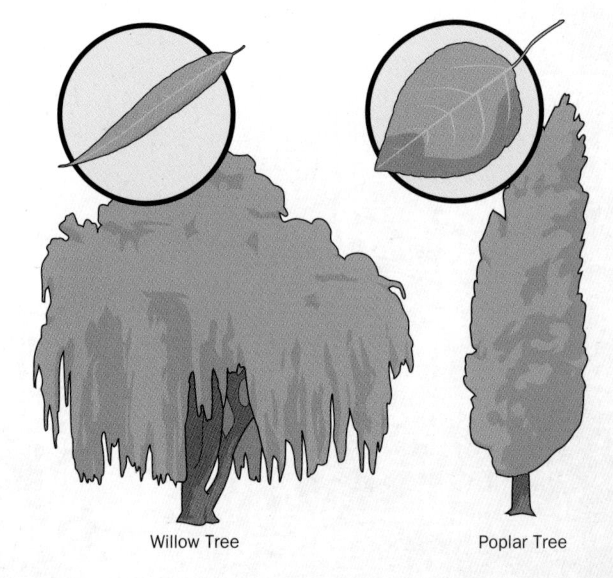

228 STEP-BY-STEP
Catch a Squirrel for Dinner

When civilization ends, your grocery store of choice will likely shutter, and eventually hunger pangs will set in. But take a peek at a tree in a neighborhood or park, and you'll likely see a squirrel. In fact, you'll probably see several. And getting a squirrel out of a tree and into a stew pot is a snap with a squirrel pole.

STEP ONE Start with a sturdy tree branch at least 7.5 centimetres in diameter. Prop this branch against the trunk of the tree where the lower branches grow.

STEP TWO Strip insulation from a computer's coaxial cable or a phone line. (You have tons of it in your home.) Cut the wire into sections 30 60 centimetres in length, then put a loop 5 to 7.5 centimetres in diameter in each section, twisting the wire back around itself so the noose tightens easily.

STEP THREE Anchor the other end of each wire noose to the pole with a nail, ensuring that it's no more than 2.5 centimetres above the pole's surface.

STEP FOUR Place a dozen or more nooses up and down the pole on all sides, which will require squirrels to pass through one or more loops to traverse the pole's length.

STEP FIVE Sit and wait. Squirrels are naturally curious, and they'll eventually explore the pole. When a squirrel runs through a noose, it will fall off the pole and strangle. Then other squirrels will come to investigate—suddenly, you'll find yourself with a feast.

229 Eat Roadkill

In a worst-case scenario, food will be scarce. Roadkill might be an option, but how do you know if that raccoon with rigor mortis is dinner-worthy?

MARK YOUR CALENDAR Actually, rigor mortis isn't all bad. Most animals in rigor are good for at least another day in hot weather, up to three days in cold.

CHECK FOR FRESHNESS Here's where it's helpful to know your area. If the critter wasn't on the side of the road yesterday, well, you know it's fresh. The nose really does know, so if it smells putrid, it is.

LOOK FOR PESTS Flies are usually the first guests at the road pizza party, so seeing them is a good sign. However, if you see eggs already laid on the carcass, or if maggots are feasting, it's best to move on.

EYEBALL THE ORGANS If the poor beast's internal organs have ruptured, find something else to eat.

All clear? Good. Then butcher it as you would a fresh kill (see entry #065), but be extra thorough in the cleaning and preparation. And when it comes to cooking, the longer and hotter, the better.

230 Avoid Hitting a Moose

Moose are found all across Canada, and their populations have been expanding into new habitats. Collisions with moose are often deadly, as their long legs mean they are sent up and through a driver's windshield upon impact. Here are the best ways to avoid making Bullwinkle your hood ornament.

Clean your windshield and lights before driving into moose country. They are dark animals and extremely hard to see at night, so take all the precautions and give yourself every advantage you can.

Most moose are hit between dusk and dawn, when they are most active. Slow down and expect the unexpected when driving in low light and at night. Take heed of any moose-crossing signs. They are there for a reason and are only put up in areas where collisions have been a problem. Be extra alert and watch the periphery of the roadway and ditches.

If you see a moose anywhere near the roadway, hit the brakes. They can be unpredictable creatures, and even though you can see them standing on the side of the road doesn't mean they won't bolt out in front of you without warning.

If you see what you think is someone in dark clothing cycling down the road at night, you might be very wrong. Moose have a silvery-white patch of hair near the top of their legs and when they are trotting down the road or along the ditch, the patches will look like reflectors on bicycle pedals going up and down. In most cases you'd never find a cyclist out at night where you find high densities of moose, so don't let your eyes fool you. And do be prepared to brake.

231 Stash Valuables for Dark Times

In a postapocalyptic world, money won't have value. If you can't eat it, wear it, or use it to accomplish a task, it's probably worthless. Staples that you can barter are worth far more than stock certificates or even gold.

If the planet doesn't sink into a low enough state to wipe out commerce entirely, money and precious metals could come in handy, so stock some. You also might want to hang on to identification, deeds, and insurance documents, just in case society recovers and you need to prove who you are and what you owned before everything went to hell.

232 Scavenge Effectively

A savvy scavenger visualizes how to make use of an object, and then makes it happen.

GET CRAFTY WITH CANS You can make a tin can into a knife or flatten it into a roof shingle.

DECONSTRUCT ROPE A rope can be stripped down to its fibers to make fishing line and snares.

BE SOLEFUL The sole of an old shoe might become a hinge for a shelter door or an oven mitt for picking up that boiling pot from your fire.

233 Fend Off Looters

What's one thing you can count on after a catastrophe? Looters. If the times get truly tough, you'll need to protect yourself from folks who are after your food and gear.

DON'T ATTRACT ATTENTION View yourself and your shelter from a looter's perspective. Make both as inconspicuous as possible. Keep your supplies hidden.

FORTIFY YOUR CAMP Erect sturdy, defensible barricades. Chain-link fencing, sheet metal, and cinder blocks can slow a looter's progress. Have weapons and less-than-lethal deterrents ready throughout the camp.

KEEP WATCH Keep a sharp lookout to spot looters before they spot you. Use alarms set up at various ranges to alert you to the presence of intruders.

234 CHECKLIST Run Bartertown

If you've absorbed the lessons of the *Mad Max* franchise, you're aware that barter is the way to do business in a postapocalyptic world, and, for that matter, in many Third World locales. Keep in mind that immediate usefulness may be irrelevant. Just because you think something's handy doesn't mean it will be a high-value item to someone else. Above all, make sure you don't trade away what you need for your own survival.

Barter items fall into two main categories: essentials and luxuries. Some basic items that might turn out to be hot tickets include the following:

- [ ] Fuel such as gasoline, kerosene, and oil
- [ ] Tools, especially ones that require no power, like hammers, screwdrivers, and saws
- [ ] Fire starters, including matches, lighters, and strikers
- [ ] First-aid supplies such as bandages and prescription medications
- [ ] Ropes, straps, bindings, and duct tape
- [ ] Food and water, especially dry rations like rice, oats, barley, and grains

And these luxury items may start a bidding war:

- [ ] Soaps and detergents
- [ ] Clothing like socks, shoes, undergarments, and climate-specific items
- [ ] Sweets, from prepackaged desserts to candy bars
- [ ] Coffee, tea, and other beverages
- [ ] Salt and sugar
- [ ] Liquor (especially hard spirits), drugs, and painkillers
- [ ] Cigarettes
- [ ] Power sources such as batteries
- [ ] Jewelry and precious metals

Finally, don't forget that you can barter your skills as well. Woodworking, metalsmithing, plumbing, and electrical know-how are all likely to be in demand. Manual labor will also be highly valued, so here's hoping you're handy.

235 Build a Compound

Congratulations on inheriting the land for your hilltop compound. Here's what to think about when constructing your own fortress of survival solitude.

BERM, BABY, BERM Elevation is key for defense. It's tricky for looters or trespassers to get to your place if they have to run up steep inclines. Alternate dirt berms and fencing (concertina wire works great).

DRIVE THIS WAY Keep the entrance and exit simple. A single driveway with a sturdy gate is the way to go here. A cattle guard also provides a solid base to brace your gate closed. Use sturdy metal poles, and your entrance is that much more secure.

LIVE SUSTAINABLY If you want to survive, it's all about living on your own for the long haul. Plant a garden and compost everything. A stand of fruit trees can provide vitamins year-round if you preserve what you don't eat right away. Windmills and solar cells generate electricity, and a barn houses animals. Keep your wells clean, store wood for both heat and cooking, and place a cesspool off the property.

EYE, AYE You've got the vantage point of being on the top of the hill. But having a watchtower or two is a good idea, and install floodlights so you can monitor what's going down on your property.

PLAN FOR DEFENSE If things get really gnarly, a buried school bus makes for a great shelter, and a single escape tunnel is also a good idea. Camouflage and reinforce the exit as well as possible.

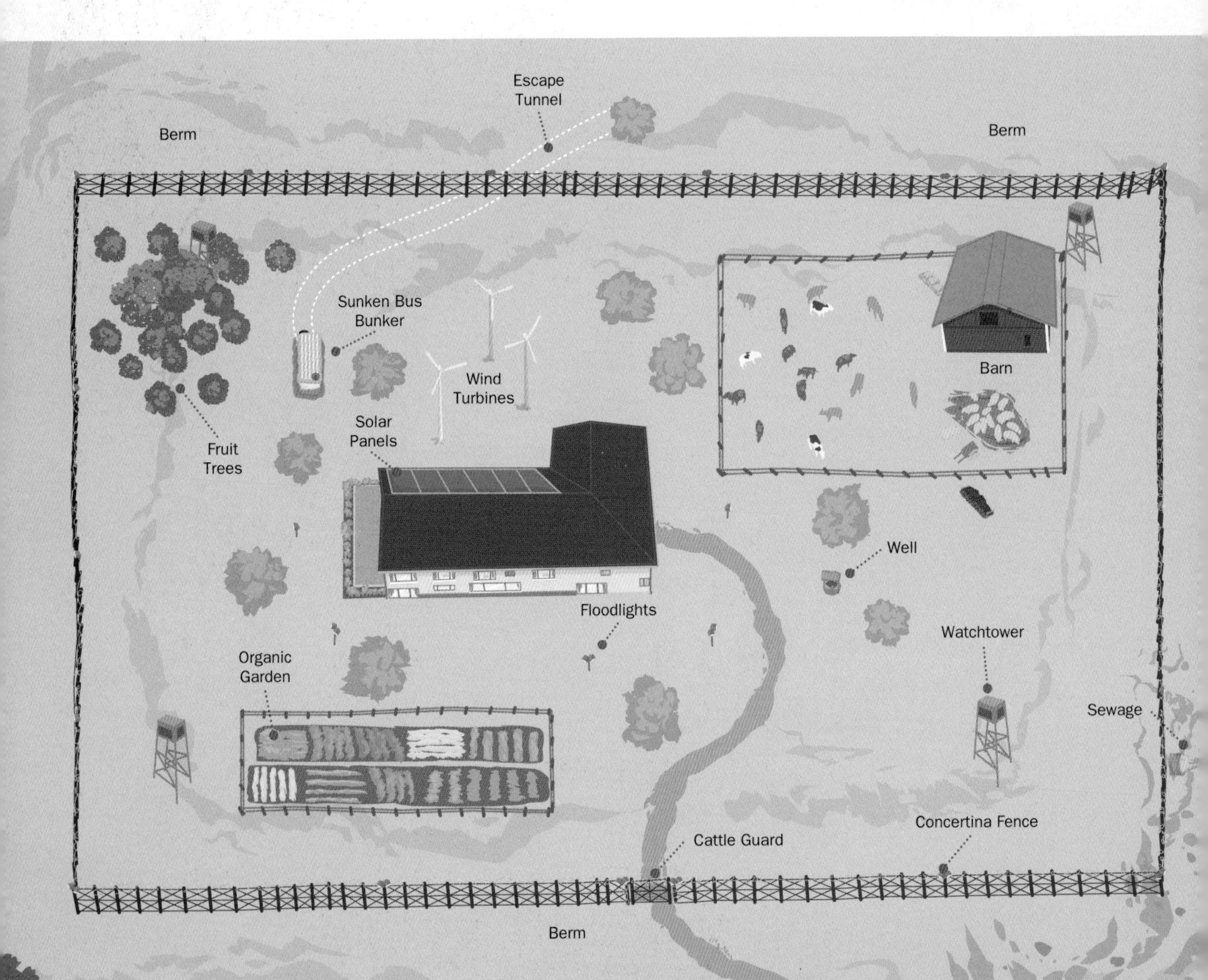

236 STEP-BY-STEP Rig a Hobo Stove

Just because the end is nigh doesn't mean you shouldn't enjoy a properly cooked meal. That's where the simple hobo stove comes to the rescue: It's just an old paint or coffee can (or even a larger metal or tin receptacle, if you have one) and a clothes hanger.

STEP ONE Using tin snips, remove the bottom and top of the can.

STEP TWO Draw a 10-centimetre square about 2.5 cm away from the can's bottom, then use a rotary tool to cut away three sides of the square. Leave the fourth side intact (it doesn't matter which one you choose to be the intact side).

STEP THREE Score the fourth side to serve as a hinge—this door will allow you to add fuel.

STEP FOUR Cut a clothes hanger into two metal rods of equal length. These rods should be long enough to extend across the can's diameter.

STEP FIVE Locate the upper rim of the can. Using your rotary tool, make four holes just below this rim: Two on one side of the can, with about 2.5 cm between them, and two on the opposite side, again with 2.5 cm between them.

STEP SIX Slide the hanger sections through these holes so they traverse the can. Fold any excess over on the outside of the can to hold the rods in place.

STEP SEVEN Punch a few holes above the door, and along the top of the can in the back. There should be six to eight total.

STEP EIGHT Remove the metal rods, fill your stove with twigs and tinder, put the rods back through the slots, and then light it up.

STEP NINE Balance your cooking pot on top of the can and heat up your meal.

237 Improvise Tools

The day some bandit makes off with your tool kit is a bad day indeed. But fear not: You can fashion basic tools out of junk you find lying around.

AXE If you can get your hands on a piece of thick, flat metal (try scrap metal or copper) and a hefty oak or hickory branch that happens to be crooked, you've got the makings of a fine axe. Position the metal at a 90-degree angle at the limb's bent end and wrap lashings around it to hold it in place, then grind the blade against a stone to sharpen it. (If metal's scarce, try shaping an axe head out of stone, granite, or flint.)

SHOVEL Affixing a container to the end of a stick will allow you to scoop up dirt and other stuff that needs carting. Try nailing an old milk crate, a plastic tub, or a large tin can to the end of a broomstick.

BOW SAW With any luck, you still have a wire saw from your basic survival kit in a can—you can use this to make a lightweight bow saw that can cut through saplings and small PVC pipes. First, find a slightly curved stick that's about 1 metre in length and 2.5 centimetres in diameter. Carve notches in the stick's ends and string the wire saw between them, then ease the saw's end rings into the notches.

URBAN

238 Sense Your Surroundings

Many people walk around with their heads stuck where the sun never shines, missing critical signs that can impact their well-being. The most basic urban survival skill is making sure you're not one of those people. Situational awareness is key to getting out of tricky scenarios—or, better yet, avoiding them entirely.

LOOK AROUND YOU When you turn a corner or enter a room, watch out for potential dangers—and possible escape routes. Observe how people are behaving, since that can clue you in to trouble spots you'll want to avoid.

LISTEN TO RUMORS Many will be false, but information from credible sources can help you decide which people or places to avoid.

SENSE DANGER Your nose can alert you to urban danger, be it fire or a gas leak. You'll likely hear a commotion before you see it. And if something looks out of place, it is. Don't investigate. Get away.

KNOW THE NUMBERS

Street Crime

8 P.M. TO 3 A.M. Time frame when most muggings occur.

25 Percent higher likelihood that you'll be mugged in London than in Harlem.

3 Number of mugging-related deaths in New York City each year.

44.5 Percentage of robberies that are confrontational, such as muggings.

90 Percentage of people arrested for robbery who are male.

50 Number of children mugged daily in London, mostly for their cell phones.

5 Age of the youngest mugger on record.

91 Age of the oldest pickpocket on record.

3 Number of people commonly involved in a pickpocket operation: the blocker (obstructs), the grabber (grabs), and the shill (takes the handoff).

115,000 Number of people pickpocketed in Barcelona during a recent one-year period.

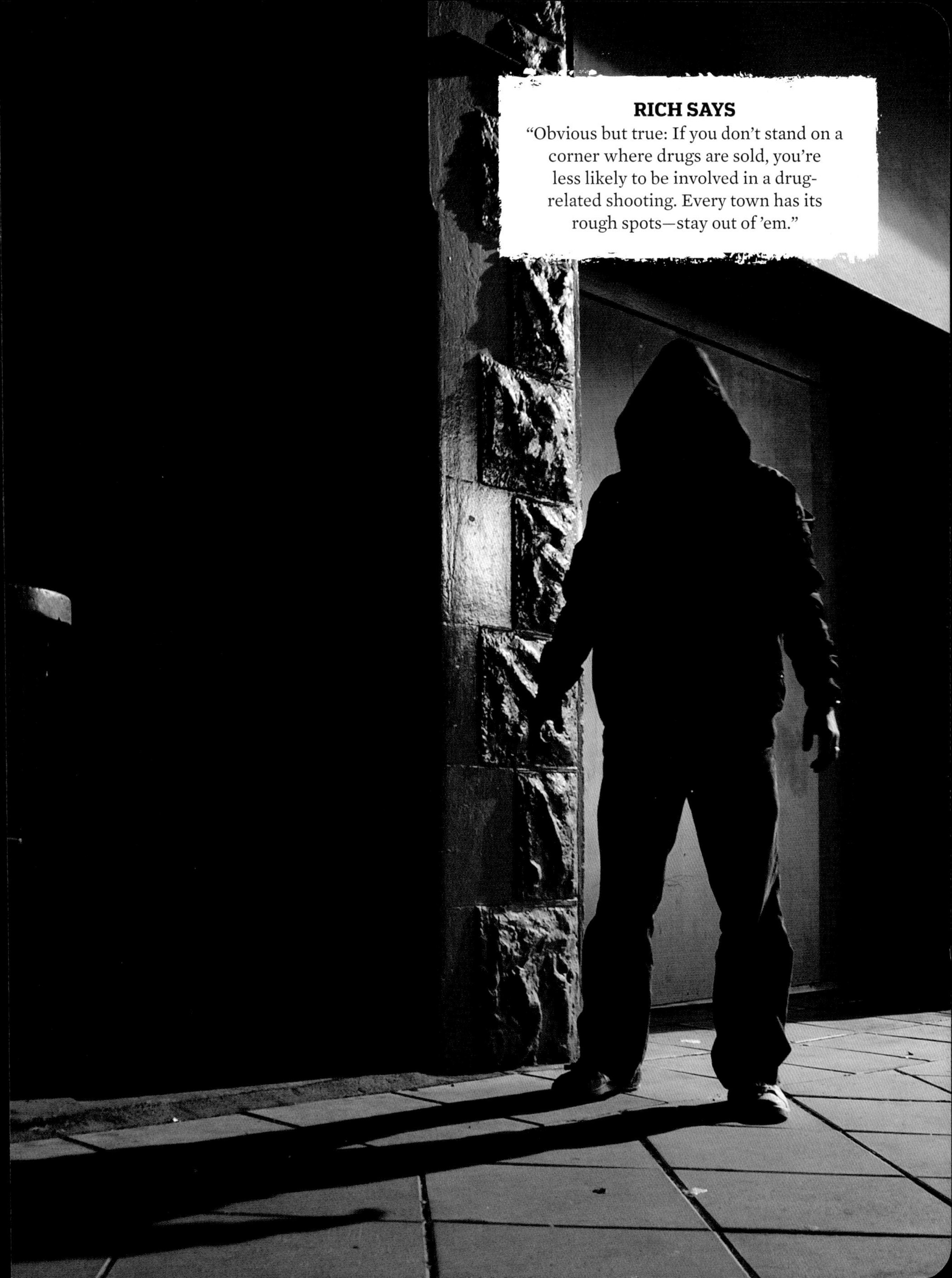
RICH SAYS
“Obvious but true: If you don’t stand on a corner where drugs are sold, you’re less likely to be involved in a drug-related shooting. Every town has its rough spots—stay out of ’em.”

239 Foil a Pickpocket

Alertness is the best defense against light-fingered predators. Pickpockets prefer crowded places like tourist attractions and rush-hour buses where they can move in and out undetected. They often work in pairs or small groups, so be wary of diversions such as a person falling down or causing a commotion. And sure, that street musician sounds great, but he might also have a partner working the crowd. Likewise, never assume a panhandler is alone.

Avoid theft by keeping your wallet in a front pocket rather than a rear one. If a person bumps into you, immediately check your valuables.

240

CHECKLIST

Carry Survival Gear on a Keychain

Fact: You never leave home without your keys. So why not deck out your key ring with small survival basics so they're always at the ready? You can find most of those essentials with key fobs already attached, making it easy to cinch them together. Try to include:

- [ ] A small multitool with pocket knife, screwdriver, and plier extensions.
- [ ] Multiple means of starting a fire. A lighter is easiest, but an ignition striker has a nearly limitless life.
- [ ] A military-grade can opener is small, light, and efficient. Pick up one at your local army surplus store.
- [ ] A mini canister of pepper spray—in case someone tries to get too cozy with you.

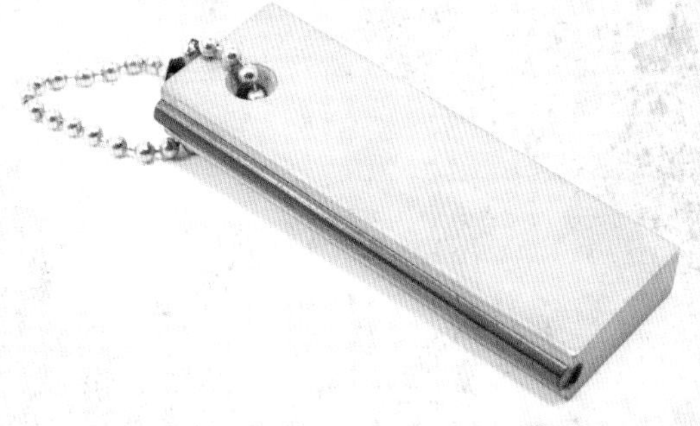

241

Drop a Decoy Wallet

Out of the darkness, some jerk approaches you with a blade or a gun and demands your money. Even if you're broke, this guy isn't going to believe you. He might decide to take you down and search your corpse. To avoid that ugly scenario, carry a drop wallet: a decoy (maybe filled with a few singles or even some play money) that you can toss on the ground as a distraction to keep your assailant busy while you run away. A caution: If you use this tactic, don't let the crook catch up with you. He'll have an attitude about your attempt to trick him.

242 Hit Where It Counts

If someone attacks you, fight back. And don't just flail around blindly—place your blows strategically for maximum impact. If you target fragile areas of your attacker's body and strike with an elbow or a closed fist, you could stun an assailant, buying yourself the time to get out of there. But use this information responsibly: Reserve the more injurious moves for fights that truly require it.

Potentially Deadly

Could Cause Serious Injury

Excruciatingly Painful (Minimal Risk of Death or Serious Injury)

The pain from striking or pressing on any pressure points can be agonizing. Bear in mind: any hit can be lethal if it's powerful enough.

1. Base of Skull
2. Back of Neck
3. Back of Elbow
4. Kidneys
5. Sciatic Nerve
6. Tailbone

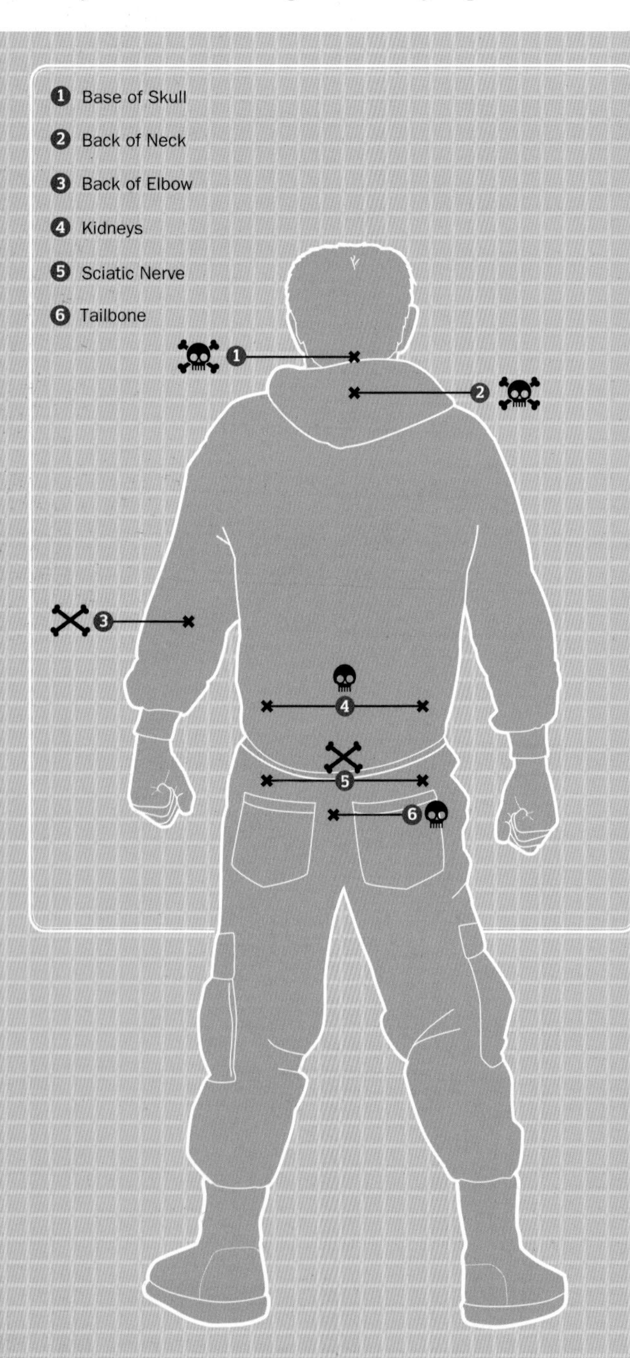

7. Temple
8. Below Ear at Hinge of Jaw
9. Side of Neck (Carotid Artery)
10. Base of Neck Behind Collarbone
11. Base of Throat (Trachea)
12. Front of Shoulder Joint
13. Armpit
14. Solar Plexus
15. Bladder and Abdominal Wall
16. Groin

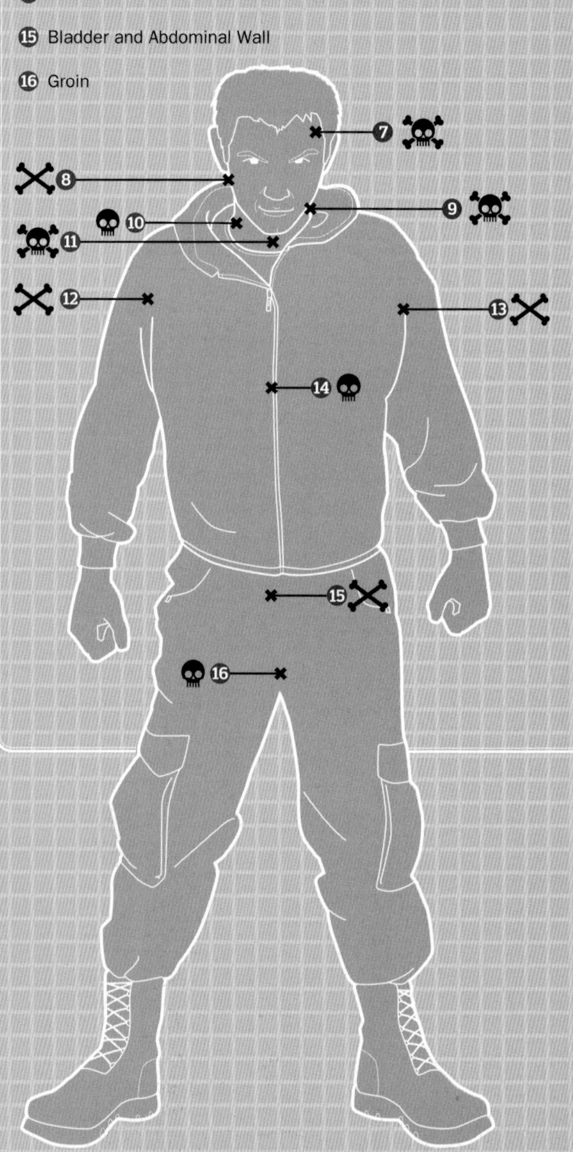

243 Maximize Your Impact

The best way to win a fight is quite often by avoiding it entirely. However, that's not always possible. If you are confronted by an aggressive person, try responding verbally first. The instant someone touches you inappropriately, shout "Back off!" loudly, and push them away if necessary. This serves the dual purpose of not only alerting folks around you that something bad is going down but also letting the aggressor know that you're not easy prey. This may be especially effective for women—many attackers count on womens' social programming to avoid making a fuss.

If you do need to fight back, do so quickly and decisively. You don't want to trade punches or kicks with an attacker, you want to throw your body weight into disabling those critical strike zones right away. When striking the upper part of the body, use the outer edge of your hand (the so-called "knife hand"), a palm strike, or tightly curled fist (see item 246), or jab with your elbow. For the lower part of the body think of striking with your knee rather than kicking with a foot—the attacker can grab your foot and yank you off balance or you can break a toe.

Finally, one thing that the movies actually do get right is the efficacy of the head-butt. Your skull under your forehead is very strong, and most bad guys don't expect to get smashed with it. You might end up with a headache, but the attacker will get a broken nose. You win!

244 Avoid Getting Cornered

In real estate, it's all about location, location, location. And the same thing applies to a street fight. Stay aware of your environment and use it to your advantage.

BARRIERS Duck behind walls and fences to get away from your attacker and to use them as a shield. If the setup allows you to lob rocks or bricks at the bad guy, all the better.

HIGH GROUND Moving upward helps you get a better perspective on the area and avoid being surprised.

CONFINED SPACES Watch out for corners, tight spaces, and dead ends. These are all places you can get trapped.

WALLS Despite usual meaning of "back against a wall," this isn't the worst place to defend. You're assured that no one's sneaking up behind you, and as long as you have room to bolt to the left or right, you're in an okay place.

245 Master Basic Fighting Technique

If a stranger corners you in an alley, there's only one escape route: through your attacker. The best way to protect yourself from injury (and take out your assailant) is to disable him or her. Then get away fast—don't prolong a physical altercation any longer than what's necessary to let you escape.

PARRY You can ward off an incoming blow by thrusting it aside with your arms or legs, a move called *parrying*. Effective blocks follow a circular motion either inward or outward, depending on where the threat is coming from. Use your arms and hands to parry attacks from punches, high kicks, and weapons. Parry with your legs to deflect kicks or low strikes.

PUNCH Bring your fist to waist level, with your elbow pulled back. Step forward with the opposite foot as you punch, landing the blow as your foot hits the ground. Aim for vulnerable targets such as the nose, the throat, or the ultrasensitive solar plexus.

KICK High kicks take lots of practice and finesse, so concentrate on delivering powerful kicks to lower targets. Raise your foot to knee level and thrust the kick forward toward the gut, groin, or knee of your assailant. Step forward and follow through with punches and more kicks. Don't stop until your attacker is disabled or stunned enough for you to make a safe and fast retreat.

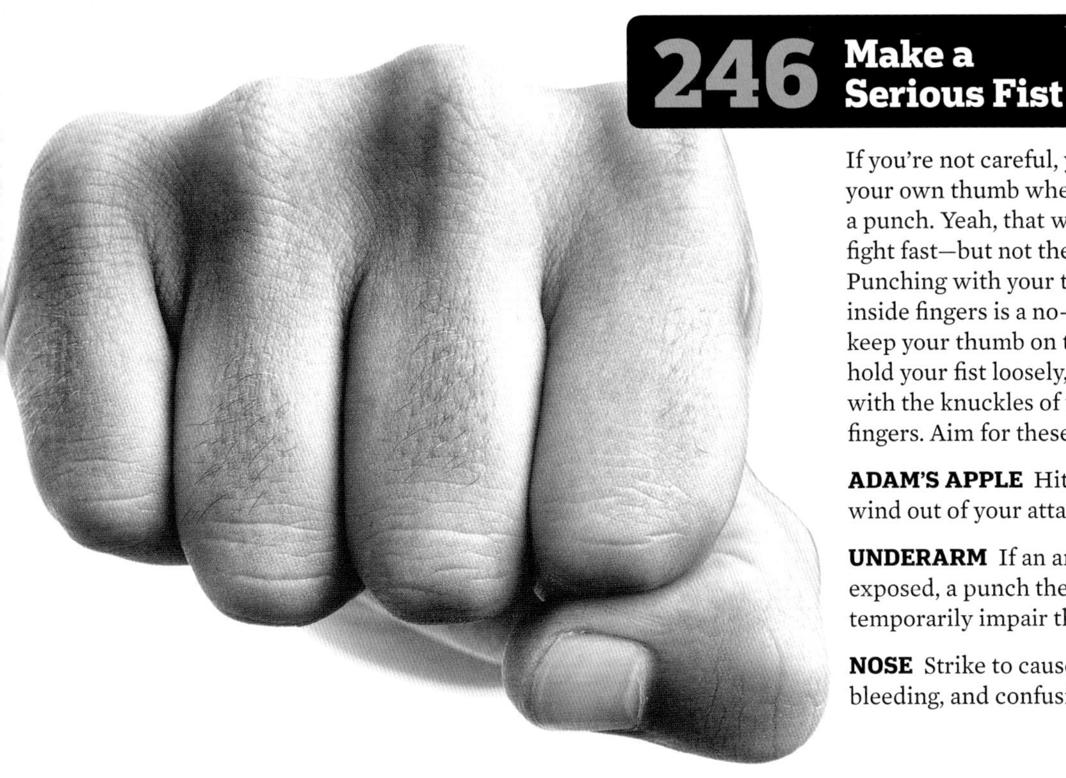

246 Make a Serious Fist

If you're not careful, you can break your own thumb when you throw a punch. Yeah, that would end the fight fast—but not the way you want. Punching with your thumb tucked inside fingers is a no-no. Instead, keep your thumb on the outside, hold your fist loosely, and strike with the knuckles of your first two fingers. Aim for these weak points:

ADAM'S APPLE Hit to knock the wind out of your attacker.

UNDERARM If an armpit is exposed, a punch there can temporarily impair the entire arm.

NOSE Strike to cause whiplash, bleeding, and confusion.

247 Clutch a Roll of Quarters

Want to pack more of a punch? Tightly grip a roll of quarters—the added weight will turn your fist into a more powerful weapon. The solid support inside your closed hand will make your fist feel as if it's made of stone, and also help prevent injury to your hand while you wail on a bad guy.

248 Defend Yourself with Your Keys

A parking lot can be a dangerous place, especially on a dark night. While walking to and from your vehicle, be ready to fend off an attack. Make a weapon by gripping your key ring in your fist with individual keys protruding between your fingers. A slashing blow to an attacker's face (particularly the eyes or throat) causes serious injury. While you're at it, hit the panic button on your key ring: It'll activate your car alarm and hopefully get you rescued.

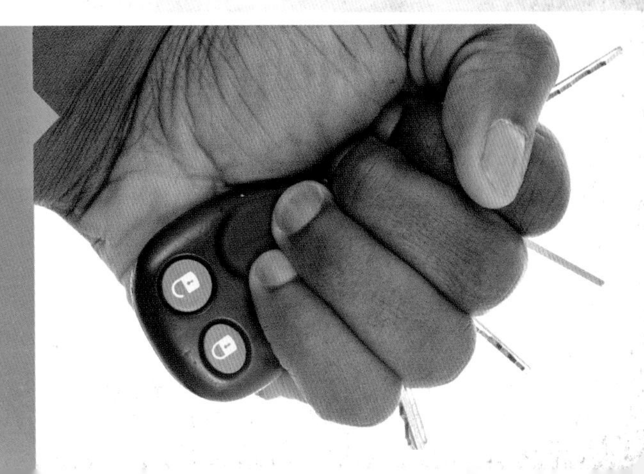

249 Figure Out If Someone Is Armed

If an assailant's packing heat, you want to know about it. Look for these telltale signs:

BEWARE THE BULGE Criminals don't usually holster their weapon. It's often in their waistband or a pocket, causing an unusual bump or a weight that makes clothes hang crooked.

STUDY BODY LANGUAGE Behavior is an important tell. Tip-offs include repeatedly touching a spot where a weapon might be hidden or adjusting something that could be a gun.

TRUST YOUR SPIDEY SENSE A guy who's wearing a trench coat on a hot day may have the flu. Or he may be carrying a gun under that coat.

250 Conceal a Weapon

When choosing a weapon for concealed carry, remember that smaller is easier. If your weapon becomes visible, you'll scare people and possibly make yourself a target. In almost all cases, a permit is required to carry a concealed weapon.

KEEP IT ON YOUR HIP There's a wide range of holsters for your belt, the small of your back, and your shoulder. All of these work well—just as long as you don't remove your jacket.

STASH IT Other options include a day pack, a briefcase, or a purse. The drawbacks are relative inaccessibility and increased risk that you might lose control of your weapon.

DO THIS, NOT THAT
Self-Defense

DO swallow your pride to avoid a brawl. But if you can't get away, fight dirty. You're in it to injure someone and be done with it, not to score sportsmanship points with a referee. If you're fighting fairly, your strategy sucks.

DON'T raise your fists and take a stance like the Karate Kid. You're not here to put on a show, and—unless you actually *are* a black belt—all that fancy footwork could possibly make you more vulnerable to your opponent.

251 Disarm an Attacker

When you're facing an armed assailant, your goal is to escape injury and, above all, to stay alive. Avoid a stare-down that might infuriate your attacker, and always submit to demands for your possessions. But if things reach a point where you have no other choice but to disarm the bad guy or die, surprise your attacker with explosive violence.

AVOID A KNIFE Stay back so your attacker can't slice you, then deploy the Nike defense: Run. If you can't escape, grab the attacker's wrist and angle the blade away.

SNATCH A CLUB Move quickly; it'll reduce your assailant's ability to swing a club. To release his grip, push him back, grab his wrist, and then twist it violently.

GRAB A GUN First, pivot out of the line of fire by turning sideways, rather than facing your attacker head-on. Then gain control of the shooter's wrist with one hand and his gun with your other. Twist the gun away from your body and down to disarm.

THIS HAPPENED TO ME!

Home Invasion

252 CHECKLIST Secure Your Home

Most home invasions start with envy—someone sees something that he or she wants, then plans to steal it. Take these common-sense precautions:

- [ ] Make yourself a less appealing target. Keep valuables in secure locations—such as bank lockboxes—instead of home safes or hiding places.
- [ ] Don't discuss your valuables and material possessions with others.
- [ ] Use only licensed, reputable workers for in-home repairs, and always check their identification.
- [ ] Install motion-activated lights on the exterior of your house. Leave on a few lights while you're out.
- [ ] Keep all windows and doors locked, including garage doors. Opt for additional locking mechanisms, such as deadbolts or locking bars for sliding-glass doors. You can also wedge a cut-off broom handle behind sliding doors and windows.
- [ ] Get a guard dog. Or two.

253 STEP-BY-STEP Handle an Intruder

There are few things more horrifying than being confronted by a stranger who has broken into your home. Here's what to do if the unthinkable happens.

STEP ONE If you hear someone trying to enter, don't investigate: Dial 911. Police recommend using a land line, as the call will be routed to local police rather than state agencies. Stay on the line—the operator will continue to hear what's going on, which can help speed up the dispatch.

STEP TWO Escape. Just about anything is better than being trapped inside with a criminal. Even if you can only make it to the backyard, you can yell for help or try to break through a fence.

STEP THREE If you are trapped, don't resist. Most home invasions are about obtaining property, which isn't as valuable as your life—ever. Give the robbers what they ask for.

STEP FOUR If you can't escape and you own a weapon, consider arming yourself. But make sure you have enough control over the situation to keep the weapon out of the home invader's hands.

254 Wield a Tactical Flashlight

A tactical flashlight is specially designed for use in combat zones, and you can pick one up at a sporting-goods store near you. What's so great about it? It's two weapons in one—which is awfully James Bond. Pretty slick, eh?

SHINE A LIGHT Grip the flashlight with your thumb on the switch button. Raise your fist and switch on the light, aiming directly into your assailant's eyes. That should temporarily blind him.

DELIVER A SMACKDOWN The second weapon is the flashlight's sharply scalloped front edge. Bring it down repeatedly with hammer blows on your attacker's nose and eyes.

255 CHECKLIST Improvise a Weapon

Say you need to defend yourself, but you don't have a gun or can't get to your gun safe quickly. All is not lost, especially since your home is probably chock-full of defensive weapons.

- ☐ Rolling pins, pots, and pans make great clubs.
- ☐ Use knives and forks for a dinner to remember.
- ☐ Blow cayenne pepper into an attacker's eyes.
- ☐ The jagged edge of a broken china plate can be an effective cutting weapon.
- ☐ In a pinch, a broom or mop handle, a fireplace poker, or even a barrage of knickknacks can be pressed into defensive service.
- ☐ Wrap something heavy (such as a brick or a can of soda) in a sock or pillowcase, then swing it to strike from farther away.

256 Make a DIY Alarm

Burglars want to enter silently, burgle quietly, and then leave without a sound. That's why you want a noisy alarm system. If you don't have an in-home security system, you can achieve a similar effect with common household items.

PROTECT OUTSIDE Start in your yard, where a burglar must tread before he or she has a chance to reach your home. Outside motion sensors are commonly used to turn on lights, but up the ante by connecting a sprinkler system to the same sensors. It's one thing to illuminate a burglar: Just imagine his surprise when he's not only lit up but soaked. He's leaving fast—and he's not coming back.

WARN INSIDE Place door chimes on the backs of all interior doors. If the door moves, the bell will let you know that something's up. You can also put bells on door handles or window latches.

SQUEAK AND CREAK Homes often come with natural alarms, and you have the tactical advantage of knowing where the noisy spots are. Don't repair squeaky floorboards or oil your door hinges. If you know the third stair creaks when you step on it, leave it that way. These passive alarms are effective. You'll get used to the noise, but they'll grab your attention if they sound when they shouldn't. The best part? They won't cost you a dime.

257

STEP-BY-STEP

Stash Valuables in a Book

What robber is going to peruse your bookshelf, much less take down a volume and read a passage? None. So transform a book into a safe, pack it with small but valuable items, and put it on a shelf, camouflaged by the classics.

STEP ONE Pick out a hardback that blends in with your books.

STEP TWO Turn ten to twenty pages in and use a clamp to hold those pages to the front cover.

STEP THREE Use puzzle glue (it has a firm hold and dries clear) to bind the outside edge of the remaining pages. Apply a few coats, smoothing out any sloppy areas, until the pages are stuck together.

STEP FOUR Remove the clamp, then put the book in a vice or under a cinder block to keep the pages smooth as they dry. It'll take about 24 hours.

STEP FIVE Open the book, measure and mark the space you intend to cut out from the glued-together pages, and then use a razor blade to hollow them out.

258

STEP-BY-STEP

Build an Outlet Safe

Need a wall safe? Improvise one with this decoy electrical outlet—and hope burglars don't try plugging in anything.

STEP ONE Head to the hardware store and pick up a faceplate, a residential-grade volt receptacle, a cut-in box, and some roofing nails and washers.

STEP TWO Place the cut-in box on the wall where you want your safe and trace around it. Cut the hole with a drywall saw.

STEP THREE Slide the cut-in box into the hole—this is your safe. Fill it up with small valuables.

STEP FOUR The receptacle has two holes, one at its top and one at its bottom. Slide the roofing nails through the washers and then through these holes.

STEP FIVE Attach the receptacle to the box by sliding the nails into the box's top and bottom holes.

STEP SIX Screw the faceplate onto the receptacle.

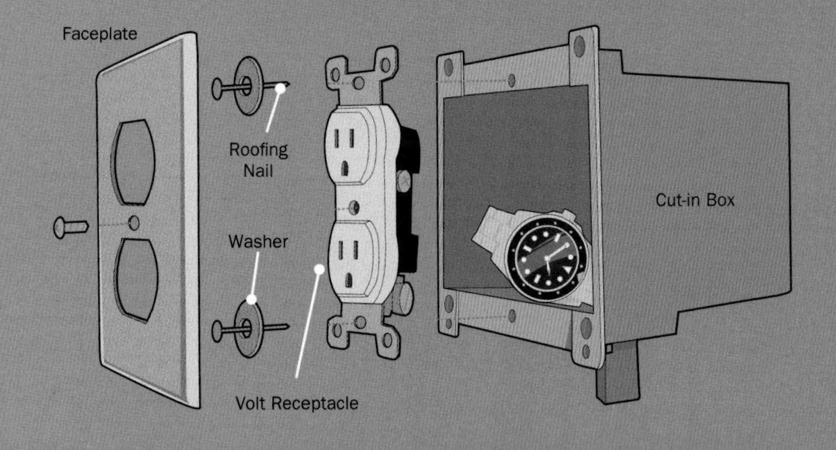

259 Avoid Identity Theft

People want to be you. They also want to use your name, credit cards, identification numbers, and bank accounts to buy things for themselves and have you pay for them. They're identity thieves—and they do business to the tune of billions of dollars a year.

To protect yourself from having your identity stolen, it helps to know how these criminals operate.

TRASH SNOOPERS They rummage through your garbage, looking for papers with credit-card, checking-account, and personal-identification numbers.

SKIMMING When processing your card at a restaurant or store, it's easy to skim your account number from your card's magnetic strip. So use cash instead.

PHISHING On the phone or online, when someone says he or she is from your bank and asks you to verify your account number, don't take the bait.

MAIL REROUTERS Criminals use a change-of-address form to divert your bills to another location so they can steal your account numbers or set up new credit cards without your knowledge.

CLASSIC THEFT Or they might resort to old-fashioned robbery by stealing your wallet or purse and using the information in it.

To protect your identity, burn or shred all discarded papers with any account information, especially anything with government-issued identification numbers. Use an identity-theft service to track activity on your accounts and monitor your statements for charges you didn't make.

260 STEP-BY-STEP Pick a Lock

Have to get through a locked door? Don't let the fact that you don't have the key stand in your way. It's not hard to pick a lock of the pin-and-tumbler variety—that's the kind where pairs of pins hold a cylinder in place. The trick is pushing the pins up one at a time until they're no longer blocking the cylinder's ability to rotate. When all the pins are out of the way, presto: The tumbler turns and you're in.

Ideally, you'll have a tension wrench and a pick from a lock-picking tool set, but you can use bobby pins.

STEP ONE Insert the wrench into the keyhole and determine which way the cylinder rotates to unlock. It'll give a little bit when turned the correct way. Keep applying pressure to the wrench to keep the cylinder held open that fraction of an inch.

STEP TWO Insert the pick into the keyhole above the wrench, and find the pins locking the cylinder in place. Start with the farthest pin, pushing it up until you hear a click—that sound means the pin is out of the way.

STEP THREE Repeat with the rest of the pins until they've all been pushed out of the cylinder.

STEP FOUR Use the wrench or bobby pin to turn the cylinder and open the lock.

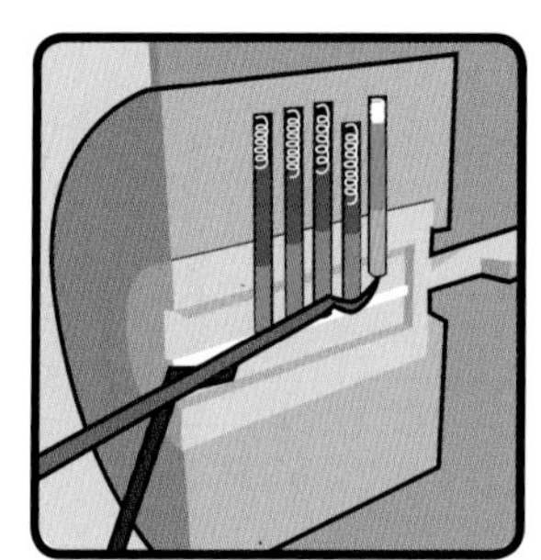

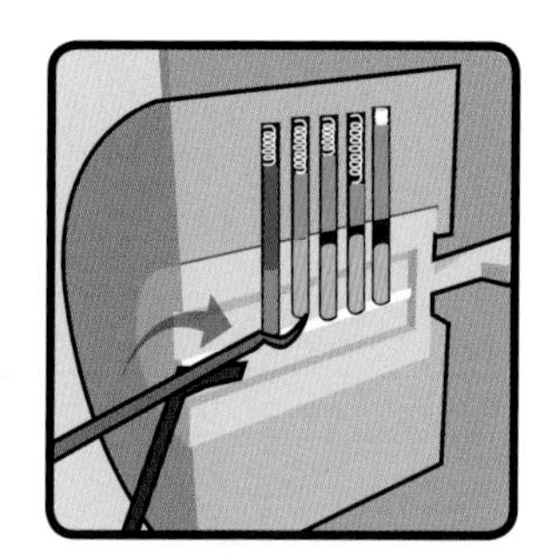

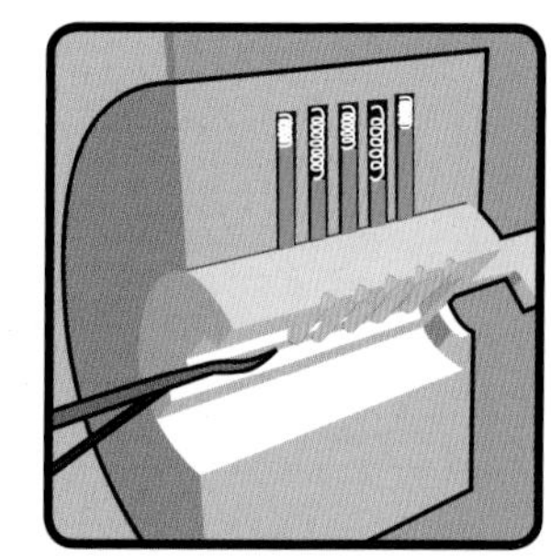

261 Figure Out If Your Home Is Bugged

So you suspect someone is eavesdropping on you, but you can't find the bug. You could buy a bug detector, or you could just do some old-fashioned sleuthing.

CHECK THE WALLS Look behind anything hanging on the wall, like picture frames and mirrors. And scope out vents for small cameras or microphones.

LOOK DOWN Scan for discolored carpeting or inconsistencies in the floor's finish. These could indicate that someone has replaced a section of the floor or carpet to conceal a bug underneath.

FEEL YOUR WAY Don't just rely on your eyes. Use your hands to feel along the backs of objects for recording devices.

PRICK UP YOUR EARS Listen for changes in volume during phone conversations, or unexplained static in radio or television broadcasts. The transmitters of most bugs interfere with broadcast signals.

262 Lose a Tail

You probably know the feeling: The hair stands up on the back of your neck, telling you that someone is following you. If that happens while you're on the road, you need to figure out if you're really being tailed—or if you've been reading too many detective novels.

KNOW THE SCENE Most drivers tail you from your home or office. As you enter your car, scan to see if there are any unfamiliar vehicles nearby and notice if they leave when you do.

DRIVE AS IF YOU'RE LOST In an urban setting, the easiest way to confirm if a car is really on your tail is to make four successive left turns. Someone might make one or two with you, but the chances that someone else is driving in exactly the same square are pretty small.

MIX IT UP Make frequent lane changes and vary your speed, then observe to see if the person is still following you.

MAKE A BEELINE Is that car still riding your bumper? Then you've got a tail all right. Assuming you're not a fugitive, your safest bet is to drive directly to a public place—ideally, a police station.

KEEP COOL You might be tempted to floor it, but you're better served by remaining calm and driving deliberately. Make sure you don't box yourself in at intersections or stoplights, and travel through well-populated areas.

FIND A SAFE SPOT Yes, your home or office may beckon as a sanctuary, but if this person doesn't already know where you live or work, you probably want to keep it that way.

RICH SAYS
"Just because you're paranoid doesn't mean people aren't out to get you."

263 Beware Common Poisons

We all know it's important to keep household cleansers, detergent, and bleach away from children. The same goes for medicines: Pills can look like candy to kids. But do other dangerous substances lurk in your home?

IN THE BATHROOM Beware of nail-polish remover, shampoo, and even mouthwash. In fact, due to their ingredients or alcohol content, the majority of personal-care products can be poisonous if swallowed.

IN THE GARAGE Pesticides, paints, paint thinners and removers, fuel, and oil are all dangerous to inhale or swallow. That's pretty obvious just from the smell, but other substances to watch out for are antifreeze and windshield-washer fluid, which are brightly colored and may have a sweet taste and smell—although they are deadly.

IN THE KITCHEN AND PANTRY It's a fairly well-known fact that raw or undercooked poultry and fish can be a source of foodborne illnesses like salmonella. Less well known is the fact that uncooked beans also warrant caution. Nearly all varieties of beans, especially red kidney beans, contain substances called lectins, which cooking breaks down. But if beans are eaten uncooked, they can cause nausea, vomiting, and diarrhea.

INSIDE ELECTRONICS Many household gadgets run on various batteries, from tiny button-size cells to honking-big D-cells. Batteries contain nasty hydroxides that can be harmful if inhaled and life-threatening if swallowed.

264

STEP-BY-STEP

Save a Poisoning Victim

Helping a poisoning victim can be tricky, since there's no one-size-fits-all solution. But in every case, it's vital to find out what the toxin is and seek help.

STEP ONE Make sure the victim is breathing. If not, call 911 to summon an emergency crew.

STEP TWO Check for any remaining poisonous substance in the victim's mouth. If you find any, wipe it away.

STEP THREE If the victim isn't breathing and you're certified in CPR, begin rescue breathing.

STEP FOUR If the toxin is a household product, check the label for advice, or contact your local poison-control hotline. Do not induce vomiting unless instructed to do so.

STEP FIVE If the victim goes to the emergency room, take the pill bottle or package that contained what was ingested. That will help doctors start proper treatment immediately.

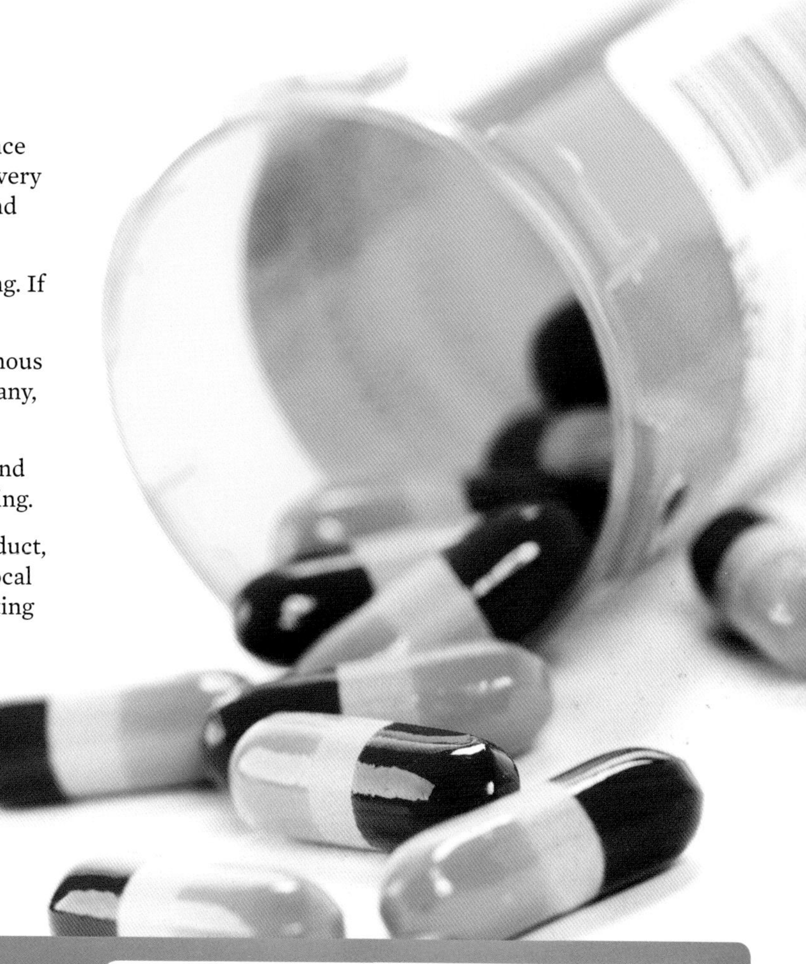

265

Soak Up Poison with Activated Charcoal

Wouldn't it be swell if there were a simple pill to take after accidentally ingesting a common poison? There's no cure-all, but you might try activated charcoal. (No, not the kind of charcoal you use on your grill—this stuff's only available at pharmacies.) A mainstay in many first-aid kits, this light and practically tasteless powder binds with ingested poisons and prevents your body from absorbing them. But before taking it, check with your local poison-control center, as activated charcoal could hurt—not help—if taken in combination with certain toxins.

266 Install Smoke Detectors

Trust me: If a fire ever starts in your home, you'll want to know about it. So make sure there's at least one smoke alarm in every room of your house, except for bathrooms and closets.

SAVE THE DATE Before mounting your smoke detector, write the date of purchase on the alarm. (After eight years pass, swap it out for a new one.)

HANG IT HIGH You know the old adage about smoke rising? It's true. So mount your detector on the ceiling away from windows and doors and at least 4 inches (10 cm) from the wall. Avoid placing one in the path of heat or steam coming from the kitchen or bathroom; otherwise it'll go off all the time.

MOUNT IT RIGHT All smoke detectors come with specific mounting instructions. Most make it easy for you: Installation requires little more than a screwdriver and two screws. Some types are even adhesive.

TEST IT OFTEN You should check your detector once a month to ensure that it's working properly. Simply push the button until you hear a loud noise confirming that all's as it should be. If there's no sound, you've got a dud—replace it.

KEEP BATTERIES FRESH Replace the battery once a year. If it starts making an annoying chirping sound, that's your cue that it's time for new juice.

267 Prevent Electrical Fires in the Home

Crack open one of your walls and you'll find a network of powerful circuits and wires. These keep your lights on and your appliances working—and they can also send your house up in smoke if you're not careful.

WATCH THE LIGHTS If lights are flickering on and off, or if they make noise or give off a smoky odor, you've probably got faulty wiring. Call an electrician. If he or she doesn't spot a problem, you've got poltergeists—or an incompetent electrician.

VISIT YOUR FUSE BOX Every home's got at least one—it's often hidden behind a panel in the basement or garage. Check for signs of trouble, like circuit breakers or fuses with multiple wires crammed into individual terminals, since those are likely to blow. While you're there, scan for signs of corrosion and smoky residue. Take a look to ensure that wires aren't precariously spliced and that the insulation around them appears to be in good shape.

PICK THE RIGHT PLUGS Try to use electrical sockets and plugs that are grounded—they provide protection against electrocution. (In the United States, look for models that have three prongs—most modern appliances do.) If your home doesn't have grounded outlets, have an electrician install them.

CHECK FOR PESTS Rodents love to gnaw on wires and cables, chewing through crucial insulation that prevents the electrical current from sparking. Every now and then, head to your attic, basement, garage, and any crawl spaces you have. Check wiring to make sure it's intact. If not, get it replaced—and call an exterminator, while you're at it.

RICH SAYS
"A basic rule of combustion: If it can burn, it will. Try not to get cremated until you're already dead."

268 Make Your Home Fire-Safe

Home fires are scary stuff, but they're largely preventable. Follow these guidelines and fret no more.

WATCH APPLIANCES Keep appliances such as toaster ovens, coffeemakers, fans, and space heaters away from water sources and flammable materials. Unplug them when they're not in use. As for water heaters, furnaces, and dryers, clean their vents regularly and check that the ignition systems or pilot lights are operating correctly.

BEWARE THE GAS If your home runs on natural gas, check the system for loose fittings, malfunctioning pilot lights, or nearby flammable materials. If you smell even a whiff of gas, have a professional come in to check for a leak.

KEEP A TIDY HEARTH If you have a working fireplace, have your chimney inspected and cleaned once a year by a pro. Keep glass fireplace doors or a mesh screen in front of your hearth; they'll prevent sparks from setting the rug or floor on fire.

COOK SMART What Mama told you was true: Never leave a stove burner unattended—even if it's just to grab a ringing phone or catch some of the big game. Most house fires are started by unattended stovetops. You don't want to be another sad statistic, do you?

269 ASSESS AND RESPOND
Fight a Fire

Not all fires start the same way, so why would they all be extinguished the same way? You should know the best tactics for fighting each class of fire (especially those that are most likely to happen in your home) and always have the correct extinguishers on hand.

	TYPE OF FIRE	RESPONSE
	**COMMON COMBUSTIBLES** Class A fires are the most common household fires and the easiest to extinguish. They usually involve flammable materials such as wood, paper, clothing, and some plastics.	You can use plain old water to douse these flames. Smothering or a CO_2 extinguisher may also work in a pinch.
	**FLAMMABLE LIQUIDS AND GASES** Another common household fire, class B fires spring from combustible liquids and gases such as motor oil, gasoline, or common solvents. Water can spread these fires rather than extinguish them.	Spray a CO_2 extinguisher to remove crucial oxygen from the fire. You can also throw a wet blanket over the flames.
	**ELECTRICAL** Electrical fires ignite and burn in live electrical equipment such as computers, fax machines, household appliances, and wall outlets. These are doubly dangerous, as they can also deliver a shock.	A class C CO_2 extinguisher eliminates the fire while keeping you safe from electrical current—never use water!
	**HEAVY METALS** These fires usually occur in laboratories, where combustible metals like magnesium, lithium, or titanium may explode. Beware the noxious fumes, which can be fatal, as well as the intense heat.	Use a class D extinguisher to extinguish these flames. Sodium chloride or sodium carbonate can also help, as can copper or graphite powders.
	**COOKING OILS** Kitchen fires involving grease, oils, or fats burn hot and fast. Unless extinguished quickly, they can spread to other surfaces. Never use water on these.	The sodium bicarbonate in a class K extinguisher will put out a kitchen fire. You can also throw baking soda on it.

270 Stock Fire Safety Gear

Want to protect your family, pets, and vital documents? Go beyond extinguishers and smoke alarms to outfit your home with fire-safety extras.

COLLAPSIBLE FIRE-ESCAPE LADDER Home fires often fill stairwells and hallways, making the obvious escape routes unsafe. A number of manufacturers sell emergency ladders that roll and fold to a very small size for easy storage. When you need the ladder, you can quickly unfurl it, hook it over a windowsill, and climb to safety. Ideally, you should have a ladder in every upstairs bedroom.

FIREFIGHTER ALERT SIGNS You may be overcome by smoke or otherwise unable to communicate. Or firefighters may be rushing into your home so quickly that there's no time to get their attention. That's when stickers or signs alerting rescuers to the presence of children and pets can be lifesavers. Many fire departments give out these stickers. Or you can make your own—be sure to laminate them so they're sturdy.

FIRE SAFE Stow important documents and back-ups of electronic files in a fireproof, waterproof safe, along with any irreplaceable sentimental items. These range in size from tiny to enormous.

271 Smother a Fire

Fires need three things to thrive: heat, air, and fuel. Take away any one of these and the fire goes out. An effective way to extinguish a small fire is to deny it air. Use a heavy blanket or coat to completely cover the fire, and press down forcefully. Don't toss it lightly on the flames, or it will feed the fire. If a pan on the stove ignites, smother it with a metal lid.

272

STEP-BY-STEP

Use a Fire Extinguisher

Looking for something to read on a quiet evening? Check out the instructions for your fire extinguisher. It's good to know how to use that thing before you're faced with an inferno, and you can call the rules to mind by remembering PASS: Pull, aim, squeeze, and sweep.

STEP ONE Pull the pin from the handle.

STEP TWO Aim the nozzle at the base of the flames, not at the flames themselves.

STEP THREE Squeeze the handle to release short bursts of spray to knock down the flames and longer pulls to fully extinguish them.

STEP FOUR Sweep side to side until the fire is out. You typically have about ten seconds of operating time before the extinguisher is empty.

273

Escape a Burning House

The key to surviving a fire in your home is having an effective plan in place before the smoldering starts.

KNOW WHERE TO GO Visibility is nearly zero in smoky conditions, so you need to know your escape route by heart. Rooms may have more than one exit, so consider which one would work best in different situations.

STAY LOW Heat rises. So does smoke and flame. When trying to escape a burning building, get on your hands and knees and crawl toward an exit. If possible, cover your mouth and nose with a damp cloth to fight smoke inhalation.

ANTICIPATE Before you open a door, feel for heat on the flat surface rather than the doorknob, which could be dangerously hot. Look under the door, too, for visible flames. If there's any doubt, head to a secondary exit.

SHUN STAIRS If you're trapped in an upper level of a burning house, get out through a window. All exits above the first story should have escape ladders at the ready for just such an emergency. Don't use a stairway, because it can act like a chimney, funneling heat and smoke upward.

DON'T BE A HERO Under no circumstances should you remain inside to fight a blaze. If an initial flare-up, like a kitchen fire, is not immediately contained, evacuate right away. Run to a neighbor's, call 911, and let the professionals put out the flames.

274 Steer with Blown Tires

BLAM! When a tire blows out, it pulls the vehicle in the direction of the flat. Fight the urge to overcorrect or to slam on the brakes, which will cause a skid. Instead, hold the steering wheel firmly, ease off the accelerator, switch on your turn signal, and start moving toward the shoulder of the road. Once there, switch on the emergency flasher to warn approaching vehicles.

275 Deal with Brake Failure

You press on the brake pedal and it goes to the floor without slowing the vehicle. Now what? Don't turn off the ignition and remove the key: The steering column will lock. Leave your foot off the accelerator to slow down and negotiate traffic and turns as best you can. If you're going downhill and picking up speed, shift to a lower gear (even automatic transmissions give you this ability) and gradually apply the emergency brake. If there's an uphill escape route, take it.

276 STEP-BY-STEP Get Out of a Skid

The first sign of a skid may not come until you suddenly lose control and end up heading sideways down the highway. To regain control, try this:

STEP ONE Resist the temptation to hit the brakes. To steer out of the skid, you need to have the tires rolling, not locked up.

STEP TWO It may be counterintuitive, but turn the steering wheel in the direction of the skid. Do this gently, without overreacting. If your wheels start to skid in the other direction, turn the steering wheel in that direction. Be prepared to straighten the wheel as the vehicle returns to its normal trajectory.

STEP THREE Apply very light pressure on the gas pedal to help bring the vehicle back into position.

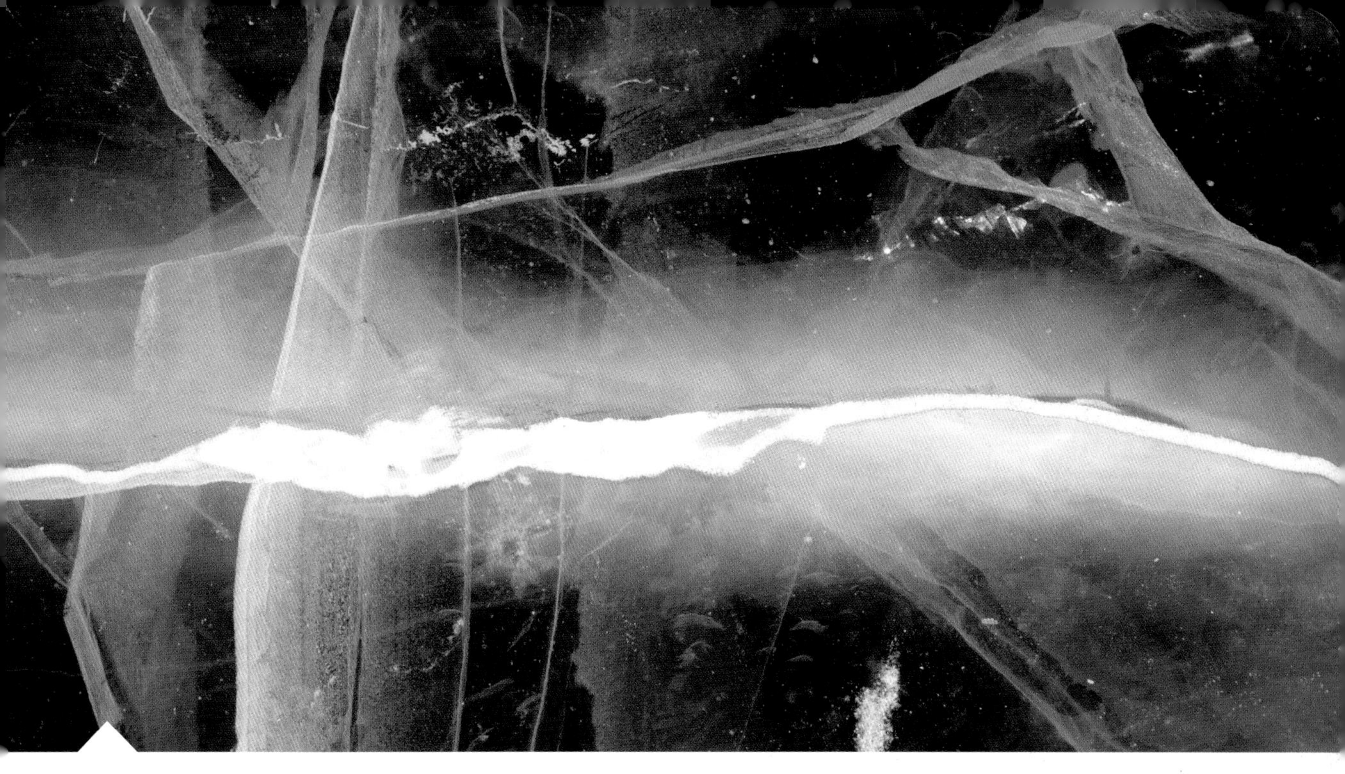

277 Drive on Black Ice

Black ice is invisible and slick as slug snot. You'll know you're driving on it because your vehicle will be totally unresponsive to steering, braking, or acceleration.

STAY HOME If you hear reports of black ice in your area, do yourself a favor and don't venture outside.

GO WITH THE FLOW Black ice basically transforms your vehicle into a sled, so all you can do is keep your foot off the brake and steer in the direction of the skid.

BUCKLE UP Wear a seatbelt—you'll likely need it.

278 Stop Hydroplaning

When tires encounter more water than the tread grooves can dissipate, the tire essentially floats on a layer of water. That's hydroplaning—and it ain't good.

READ THE CLUES When hydroplaning, the engine's revolutions per minute (RPM) sharply rises and the wheels have no traction.

EASE UP Don't turn the wheel or hit the brakes, since both will cause a skid. Instead, hold your course and ease off the accelerator, allowing your vehicle to slow down and the tires to penetrate the water layer.

279 Live Through a Cliff-Hanger

A car veers toward a cliff, then stops, leaving the front of the vehicle hanging in space. Way cool in a movie, supremely uncool in real life. What you do next can mean the difference between life and death.

CALL IN THE CAVALRY Call 911, explain your sticky situation, and give your location. If the car seems too unstable for you to safely get out of it, remain incredibly still while you wait for the rescue team.

RESCUE YOURSELF If waiting for rescue seems unwise, move very slowly to prevent unbalancing the car. Crawl into the back seat and exit through a rear door or window. If the car starts to teeter, stop and wait for someone to anchor it before you exit.

WORK TOGETHER But what if you're not alone in this car on a precipitous cliff? Those sitting in the front should move slowly to the back seat in order to keep the car's weight off the front axle. Everyone should then exit both sides of the car as quickly as is safe, turning to help others once outside the vehicle.

280

STEP-BY-STEP

Survive Crashing into the Water

Escaping a car that has gone underwater takes a cool head. If you panic, you probably won't survive.

STEP ONE Get your seatbelt off and try to open the door before the water level gets above a few inches.

STEP TWO If that doesn't work, open the window and climb out before the water level reaches the glass. If you can't open the window, use a blunt object to break the glass and crawl out.

STEP THREE No go? Stay calm—though of course that's easier said than done. Wait until the car fills with water, and then try the door again. It will probably open once the water pressure inside equals the pressure outside.

281 Put Out a Car Fire

Burning cars don't generally explode as spectacularly as they do in the movies—which is some comfort if you have to deal with one.

BE PREPARED Carry a small CO_2 extinguisher in your car. If fire breaks out, it'll likely be in the engine. As soon as you smell fire, exit the car immediately. Unlatch the hood but don't fully open it. Then insert the extinguisher's nozzle into the gap and empty the extinguisher.

BE A HERO If someone else's car is burning, call 911. Pulling someone from a car should be an absolute last resort, but if you must stage a rescue, move him or her at least 30 metres away.

282 Pack a Lifesaver in Your Car

After a wreck, you might have trouble escaping your vehicle. The seatbelt latch might not release, doors may be damaged, or power windows may no longer operate. What you need is a tool that gets you the heck out of there. Next time you're at an auto-supply store, look for a gizmo with a hooked blade on one end—perfect for cutting seatbelts—and a tip designed to break glass on the other end. Stow it in your center console so it's there if needed.

KNOW THE NUMBERS
Carjacking

1912 Year of the first known carjacking, which happened in Lyon, France.

1991 Year the term *carjacking* was coined. It was invented by investigative journalists at the *Detroit News*.

16,000 Average annual number of carjackings in South Africa, which is the most in the world.

49,000 Number of attempted carjackings in the United States each year.

205 Number of successful carjackings in Detroit in a one-day period in 1991.

93 Percentage of carjackings that happen in cities or suburbs.

74 Percentage of carjackings in which a weapon is used.

1 Percentage of carjackings in which three or more victims were in the car.

1.6 KILOMETRES Distance from home in which 44 percent of carjackings occur.

283 Avoid a Carjacking

Most carjackers are only after your car, but sometimes they want it so badly that they're willing to kill you for it. It's best to arm yourself with some preventative measures.

SIT TIGHT Keep your doors locked and your windows rolled up to deter carjackers.

LEAVE ROOM TO MANEUVER Don't box yourself in at intersections or in traffic jams.

GIVE IN FAST . . . If a carjacker confronts you, sacrifice your vehicle—it could save your life. Get out of the car and run away immediately.

. . . OR MAKE A GETAWAY Tromp on the accelerator and speed away. If you're caught in traffic, bend a few fenders if you must!

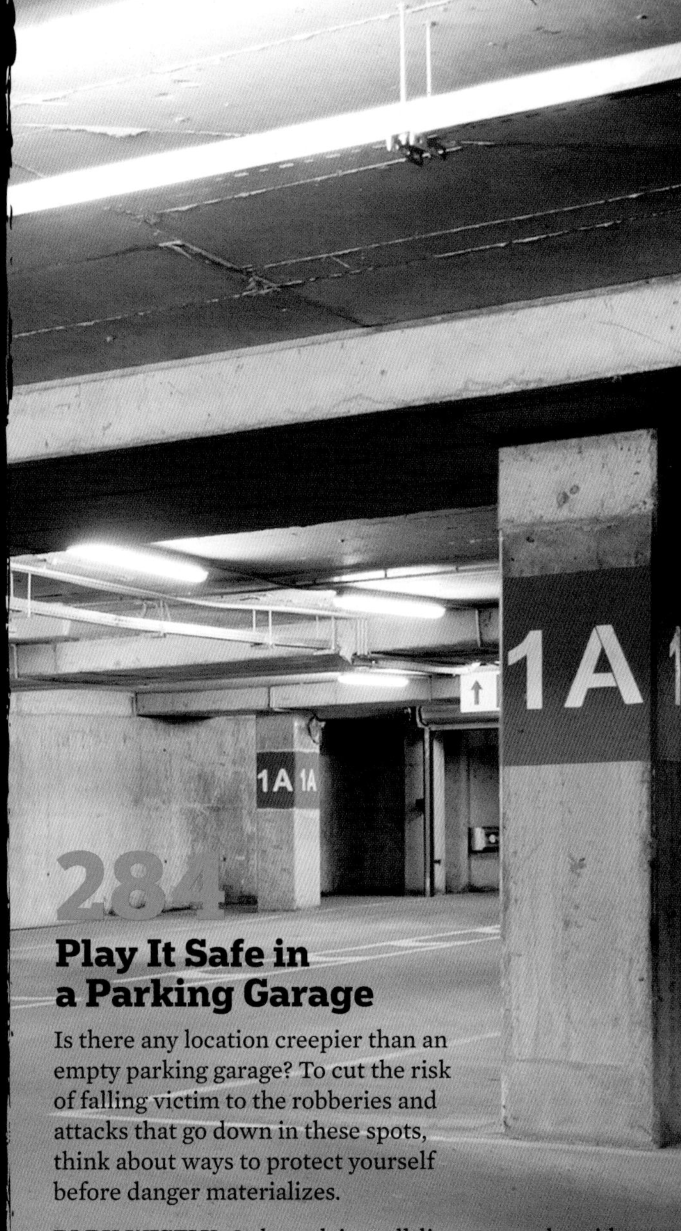

284 Play It Safe in a Parking Garage

Is there any location creepier than an empty parking garage? To cut the risk of falling victim to the robberies and attacks that go down in these spots, think about ways to protect yourself before danger materializes.

PARK WISELY Only park in well-lit areas, and avoid the top parking floor, which tends to be empty—leaving you more isolated. Park close to store entrances, exits, and security stations.

SCAN THE SCENE Be aware of your surroundings both as you look for a parking place and when you're returning to your car. Look for suspicious vehicles or people loitering near your parking space.

RAISE A RUCKUS If you sense trouble but don't see anyone, activate your car alarm, wait a minute, and then get into the car and lock the doors.

ERR ON THE SIDE OF CAUTION If you spot a suspicious character as you return to your car, go back inside the store and request that someone escort you.

285 Signal from a Car Trunk

You've been abducted and locked in a car's trunk in the dead of night. You're totally helpless, right? Wrong. You can use the taillights to draw attention to your plight. To gain access to them, you might have to remove or break through a lightweight panel covering the back of the lights. Pull the wiring to make the lights go out, which will attract police interest, or cut any of the wires in two and strip back the insulation. Then touch the ends of the wires together to create short and long flashes that spell out *SOS*.

286 Escape from a Car Trunk

Trapped in a trunk? Looks like you'll just have to rescue yourself.

PULL THE TRUNK RELEASE If you're lucky, there will be a glow-in-the-dark T-handle trunk release. If not, look for the cable leading to the trunk release in the driver's compartment and tug it toward the front of the car. This cable is usually along the floor on the driver's side.

USE SOME TOOLS Look for a screwdriver or tire iron you can use to pry the trunk latch open. Or use the tire jack to pry up a corner of the trunk lid, then signal other drivers for help.

KICK YOUR WAY OUT If the car's parked and empty, kick through the backseat and crawl out through the passenger compartment.

287 Outsmart Your Kidnappers

Being kidnapped is scary stuff for sure, and I hope it never happens to you (or me). But if you someday find yourself nabbed and stuffed in a dark closet, you should try to play your captors to your advantage.

KNOW YOUR ENEMIES Keep track of how many captors you have, noting their names, physical appearance, mannerisms, and where they fall in the hierarchy, if you detect one.

MAKE A CONNECTION Try to establish a rapport. Yes, they're kidnappers, but they probably have a human side (even Hitler liked animals). Try to get your captors to see your human side as well. You're better off if they view you as a person.

WATCH THE CLOCK Memorize your kidnappers' schedules and keep track of the passage of time. Don't have a room with a view? Pay attention to changes in temperature at dawn and dusk, bustle or quiet in the hallways, and your handlers' alertness. If it seems as if they need coffee, it just might be morning.

BE A GOOD "GUEST" This is one situation in which you have every reason to scream, shout, and kick anyone that comes near you. But don't. Follow all orders and instructions and, once you've achieved a basic rapport, try asking for any needed items, such as medicine, food, or water. Make requests in a reasonable, low-key manner.

ESTABLISH YOUR OWN ROUTINE Every day, try to do some mental as well as physical exercise—you want to be feeling clear-headed and fit when the chance for escape arises. If you can't move much, use isometric and flexing exercises to keep your muscles toned. Unless you think you're being drugged, eat what your captors give you—malnourishment makes you weak. And as for that very understandable stress, use meditation techniques to keep yourself from losing it.

REACH OUT Listen carefully for clues that there are other prisoners near you. If you detect the slightest sign that you're not alone, attempt communication. You may find a buddy who can help you bust out.

LOOK FOR OPPORTUNITIES Keep an eye out for patterns of behavior that you can use to your advantage. If your captors take regular smoke breaks or leave you unguarded to watch news coverage, you might have just enough time to make your escape.

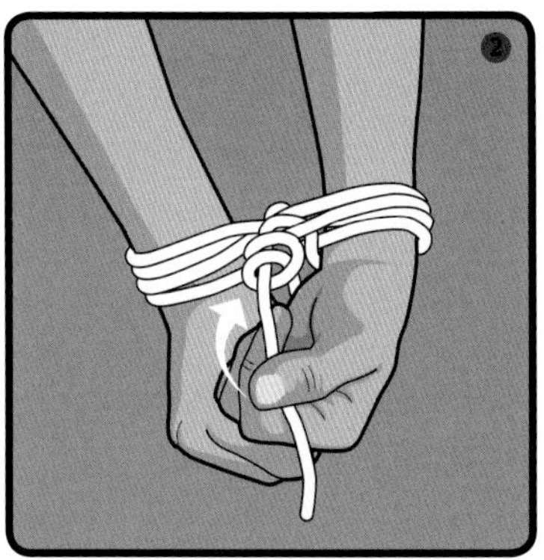

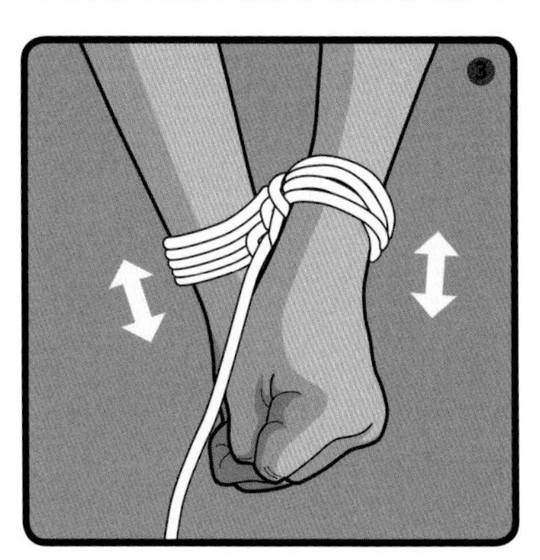

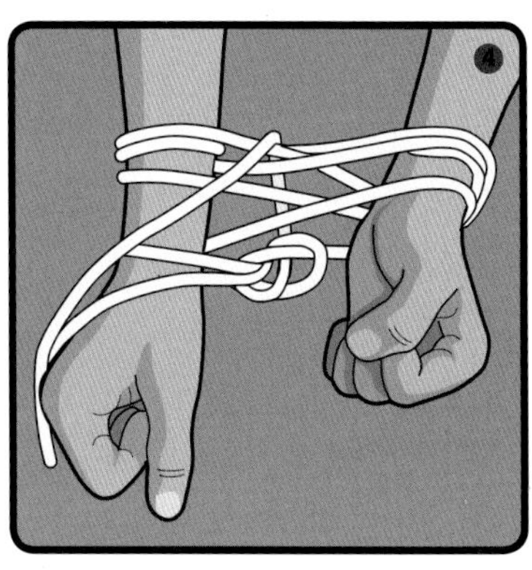

288 Deduce Where You're Being Held

A hood is thrown over your head and you're dragged into a vehicle. You're powerless at the moment, but if you can figure out where you're being taken, maybe later on you can get a message to rescuers so they know where to look.

Try to estimate the time between turns and stops. How many lefts, how many rights? How many stops at intersections? Does it suddenly get darker, then bright again, as if you're going through a tunnel? What do you smell: a farm, the docks, a bakery? What do you hear: children, a train, the splash of water? What do you feel: Is the road bumpy, hilly, or crisscrossed by railroad tracks? Memorize all of this and try to put the pieces together.

289 Avoid Stockholm Syndrome

If you begin to feel even the least bit positive toward a kidnapper, you're suffering from Stockholm syndrome, a psychological condition that leads hostages to identify with, and even defend, their captors. Weird, huh?

Sometimes these feelings emerge simply because your kidnapper isn't abusing you. But remember this: This criminal is denying you freedom. In short, this person is a jerk. So get your head in the game. Pretend to cooperate, but quietly maintain hatred of this person—when the time comes, it could save your life.

290 STEP-BY-STEP Free Yourself from Ropes

If your hands are tied and you don't have a knife (and what self-respecting kidnapper is going to let you have a knife?), you'll need to pull a Houdini to escape. Try these tactics:

STEP ONE Begin by pushing and twisting the rope or cord to see if you can create a release of tension.

STEP TWO Grab the lines on both sides of the knot and push them together to loosen the knot.

STEP THREE Move your arms up and down to loosen it more.

STEP FOUR With persistence and luck, the knot will unravel. Congratulate yourself. You're free!

291 CASE STUDY: NABBED BY THE CARTEL
Survive an Abduction

On November 15, 1992, fishing guide Kjell von Sneidern and an Italian friend drove the remote roads along the Orinoco River borderlands between Venezuela and Colombia. The two men were en route to survey a remote location for a fishing lodge specializing in trophy payara, also known as vampire fish. Visions of toothy monsters filled their heads, but when they rounded a bend, they faced a very different kind of danger.

Recently felled trees blocked their path, and they were pulled from the vehicle at gunpoint. Surrounding them was a group of twenty young men, drug dealers who had splintered off from the more disciplined cartels. They took the two men into the jungle and demanded a $500,000 ransom.

For 72 days, the men were held captive. They were forced to travel mostly at night to avoid detection. When resting, the captors would confine von Sneidern and his companion to hammocks, littering the ground beneath them with dry sticks and leaves that acted as an alarm system. One of the captors carried a human skull with a bullet hole in it as a warning against trying to escape.

Nature also worked to confound any attempt to escape. One spring they frequented was home to a 7-metre anaconda. And the jungle was full of other predators, including jaguars.

The two men endeavored to stay safe in their perilous captivity, safeguarding themselves against disease by taking steps like purifying drinking water. All the while, they tried to gain the good will of their captors. They were always cooperative, and gave their enemies their possessions as a means of winning them over.

Local officials were indecisive about the best way to respond, but von Sneidern's family sprang into action. They flew to the area, where they worked with officials and hired mercenaries to follow the kidnappers and rescue the two hostages.

Knowing they were being tracked, the kidnappers became desperate, and many deserted. One night, those that remained commandeered a boat and made for the Venezuelan side of the river. But the boat's motor gave out and they drifted to shore. Waiting for them were Venezuelan authorities, while von Sneidern's family and their hired guns stood guard on the Colombian side of the river. When shooting broke out, von Sneidern and his friend jumped ship, making a break for it. Moments later, a helicopter rescued the two men.

POST ASSESSMENT
Nabbed by the Cartel

Enterprising fishermen set out to find their fortune along the Orinoco River. Instead, they were kidnapped by vicious drug dealers armed to the teeth with AK-47s. Here's how they fared on our survival-o-meter.

✔

Worried about disease and out of water purification tablets, von Sneidern put two aspirin in every bottle of water they drank, which may have helped stave off dysentery.

At every opportunity, von Sneidern took off his shoes and socks to dry his feet and keep fungus from setting in—a real risk in a jungle climate.

He learned which of his captors would be most likely to be sympathetic, and he waited until they were on guard duty to ask for food or water.

He fought the urge to panic, instead remaining calm and having faith that help would come.

He gave his comb and other small personal items to some of his captors in return for kinder treatment and possible help escaping.

When von Sneidern finally got an opportunity to flee his captors, he did so decisively.

✖

The two men planned on setting up a tourist lodge in an area that was dangerous and too remote for immediate assistance.

They ignored the Colombian government, which was not supportive of the idea.

Neither man had a radio to call for help.

Von Sneidern's family hired mercenaries, which was successful in this case, but is generally considered a risky endeavor at best. It's better to try to work things out through your embassy.

The men were in unfamiliar territory, which made escaping their captors—who were intimately familiar with the terrain—nearly impossible.

292 Live Through a Hostage-Taking

If you're taken hostage, don't just sit there and quake. There are things you can do to improve your odds of coming out alive—and helping the authorities foil the bad guys.

SECRETLY REACH OUT Dial emergency services (if you can do so without being detected), and leave the line open so authorities can listen in. Some stores and banks even have an emergency button—if you know where it is, push it.

DON'T ROCK THE BOAT Hostage-takers want to maintain a position of power and control. If you threaten that role, you put yourself at risk. So don't try to fight or run away (unless you feel very confident of your chances of escape). Sit where and how the hostage-takers tell you, and do exactly as they say.

BE A GOOD WITNESS You're scared for sure, but that doesn't mean you shouldn't pay attention. Your insight into the situation will be invaluable to law-enforcement officials upon your release. Do your best to memorize detailed descriptions of the kidnappers (including how many there are). If you're released before other hostages, take mental notes so you can describe where the remaining hostages are being kept.

DO THIS, NOT THAT

Hostage Situation

DO give the hostage-takers anything specific they might request. Who knows? Maybe they'll take it and go away. Establishing a rapport may save your life if negotiations turn sour.

DON'T talk about religion, politics, or economics, unless you can do it in a way you're sure will be agreeable to the hostage-takers. In a sense, it's pretty close to Thanksgiving with the in-laws.

293 ASSESS AND RESPOND
Take a Blow

If you're being threatened, the best thing to do is get away. If that's not possible, fight back with all you've got. But the problem with fighting is that it's a two-way street: Sure, you'll get your licks in—but then again, you may have to take some as well. Here's how.

PUNCH

If you can't escape from a fist that's coming your way, brace yourself. For a blow to the head, clench your jaw and move toward the attacker to lessen the extension of his arm and the power gained by the momentum. Or duck to take the blow on your forehead instead of the more breakable parts of your face. For blows to the gut, flex abdominal muscles and exhale sharply to prevent the wind from being knocked out of you.

CLUB

Being struck by a pipe or club is similar to being punched, but with a much harder object. Your first defense is to close the distance between yourself and the assailant. Try to take the blow in soft spots like large muscle masses on the thigh, which will bruise, and not directly to bones, which could shatter.

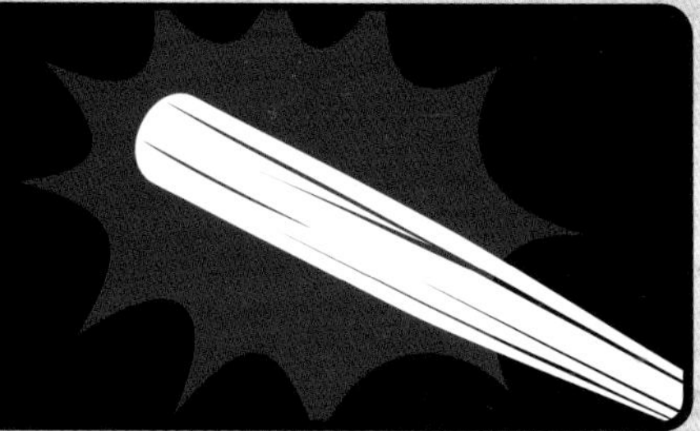

CAR IMPACT

If someone is running you down, try to get out of the direct path of the vehicle, putting heavy, stationary objects like telephone poles between you and the car. The most common car-versus-pedestrian injury is a leg break below the knee. So if you're about to be struck, roll into the impact, letting it take your weight off your feet—it's far preferable to being thrown into the car's path. Aim to land on the center of the hood and let your body roll through the impact up and over the windshield and roof.

KNIFE

Most lethal knife attacks take place inside a critical distance about two-thirds the length of the attacker's arm. The most common attack is a slash at the outer edge of this distance. Do not try to close the distance on a knife-wielding attacker. Instead, fight outside the critical distance. If you are being slashed, try to move your body in the same direction as the slash to minimize resistance. Immediately reestablish yourself outside critical distance to avoid being cut with a return slash.

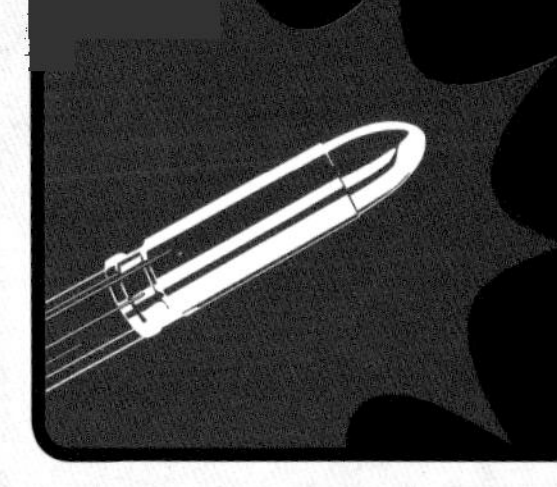

BULLET

When shooting starts, act fast. If you're against a wall, move away from it, since bullets tend to ricochet and travel along large, hard surfaces. Most lethal shots are to the head, neck, and back, so be sure to protect those sensitive zones. Turn your body to face your attacker, then drop to the floor with your legs together and your knees drawn up to protect your torso. Place your arms together in front of your head, resting your palms on top.

294 Know Basic Maritime Laws

One way to recognize when something's fishy at sea is by knowing maritime navigation and communication norms. A vessel that's ignoring these commonly understood conventions may be up to no good.

KNOW YOUR PLACE When two boats approach each other, one is considered privileged and the other is identified as burdened. The privileged boat has the right of way, and the burdened boat is responsible for moving out of its path. Generally, sailing vessels are privileged over motorboats. And a boat overtaking a slower vessel from the rear is burdened to that vessel.

PASS POLITELY If two vessels are coming toward each other head on, each boat should pass on the right, as they would on an American roadway. If two boats are approaching port-to-port or starboard-to-starboard, then each vessel should simply hold its course until they're safely past each other.

BE SIGNAL SAVVY Use your horn to indicate your direction. One short blast means you intend to pass on the starboard; two short blasts indicate a pass to port. Short, rapid blasts indicate imminent danger, so take evasive action if necessary when you hear these.

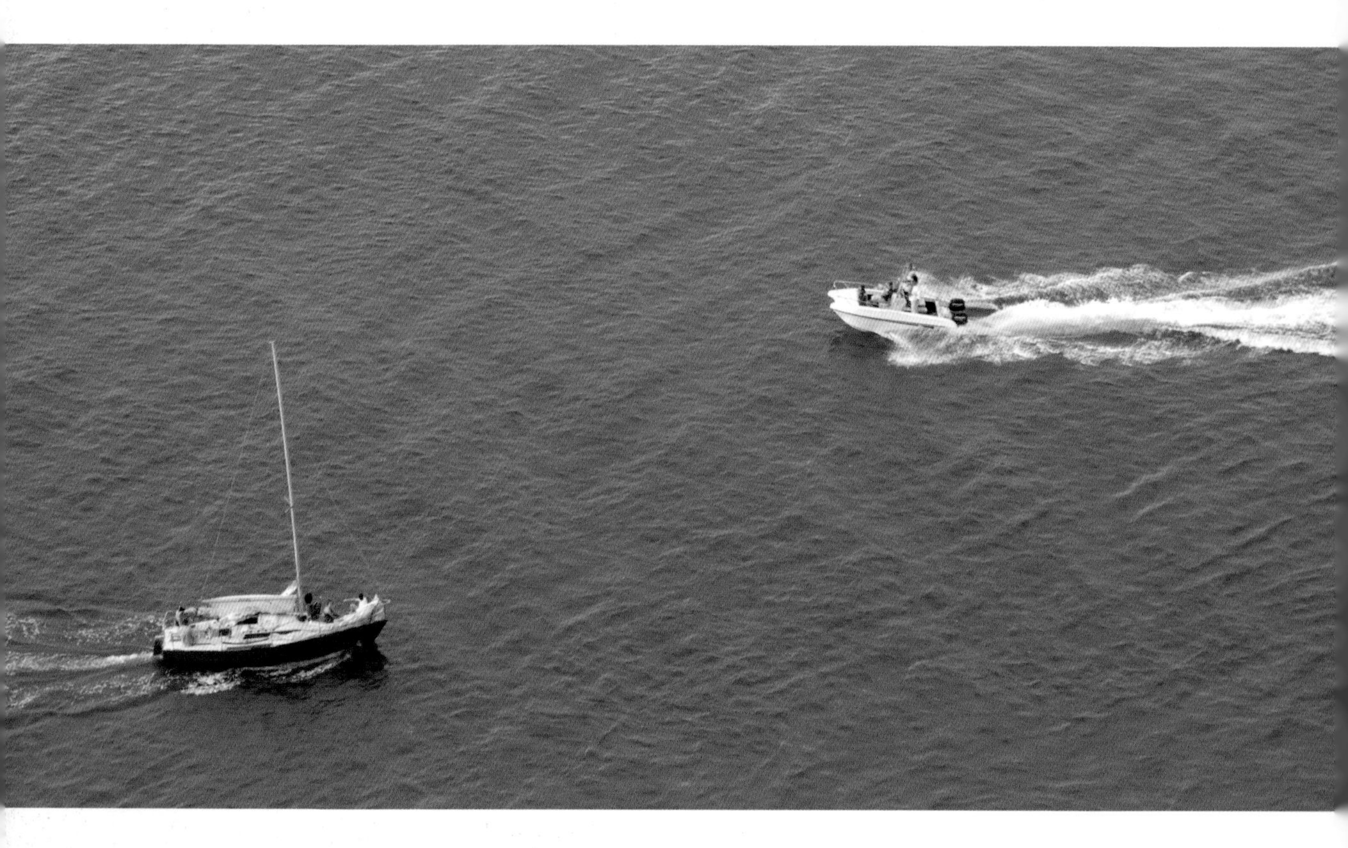

295 Safeguard Against Pirates

I'll be the first to admit, they're jolly good fun in the movies: all yo-ho-ho and a bottle of rum. But real-life pirates are a serious, and sometimes deadly, threat.

STEER AWAY FROM TROUBLE Consult one of the Web sites that help recreational and commercial boaters track—and avoid—piracy hot spots.

TAKE PRECAUTIONS AT SEA If you must travel in an area that's prone to piracy, go in a convoy. At night, run without lights. Avoid using the radio—pirates are listening. Use radar to track the boats around you.

STAY SAFE ON LAND At anchor, secure all hatches with iron bars, lockable from inside.

296 Call for Help During a Pirate Attack

If your boat is boarded by pirates, immediately lock yourself in the cabin and try to alert the authorities and other boats in the area to your plight. Use lights, foghorns, a loud-hailer, a siren, and whatever else you have at hand, and place a call for help on your radio. In case the pirates manage to swipe or disable the main radio, always conceal a small handheld Very High Frequency (VHF) marine-band or ham radio below deck or in the cabin where the bad guys aren't likely to find it. Other good ways to attract attention include sending up aerial flares and putting dye markers in the water. Good luck and godspeed.

297 Repel Boarders from Your Boat

Be sure before taking extreme measures: You don't want to mistake an innocent fisherman who is approaching your boat seeking water for a blood-thirsty pirate with foul intent. If you're positive that you're dealing with bona fide scourges of the sea, choose your weapon wisely. Many countries prohibit firearms aboard vessels, but there are no restrictions on flare guns. And at close range, a flare gun can deliver a belly full of fire to a would-be invader. Adapters are available to allow a standard flare gun to fire .38-calibre or 12-gauge shotshell ammunition, but tests suggest these guns don't hold up well when delivering multiple rounds, so make your first shot count.

Before you decide to come out with guns blazing, you might want to consider that these guys might be armed with automatic rifles. Preserving your life and those of others on board should be your priority, even if it costs you your boat.

THIS HAPPENED TO ME!
One Mean Machete

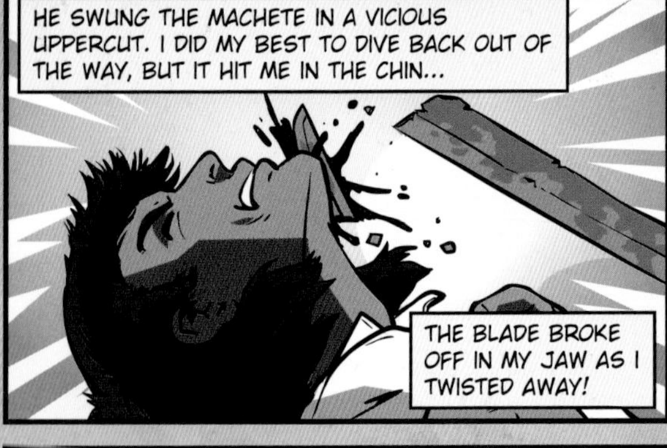

I WANTED A GENUINE SOUVENIR OF MY AFRICAN TRIP. I DIDN'T REALIZE JUST HOW AUTHENTIC A SCAR WOULD BE.

DO THIS, NOT THAT
Bribes

DO be honest and direct in dealing with any person in authority. Giving respect and being courteous is more likely to get you out of a situation than aggressive confrontation.

DON'T pay bribes, even if they're demanded. You're only trading one problem for another, because if they turn the tables and charge you with offering a bribe, you've got a new problem that's worse than your original one.

298 Get to Know the Customs

Knowing a culture's traditions will help you maintain a lower profile while visiting or working there.

DO RESEARCH It's your job to know the dangers and sensitivities of your host nation. For example, certain hand gestures common in your own country might be rude, and some countries have gender-specific dress codes.

PICK A GOOD DAY For instance, recent protests in the Middle East have been most intense after Friday prayers. So keep a lower profile at particularly fraught times.

WATCH THE CLOCK Violence often leads to curfews. Know what they are—and adhere to them.

299 Avoid Counterfeit Cops

While doing what a police officer asks is often wise, it can make you susceptible to travel scams.

CHECK CREDENTIALS When you're in a foreign country, know who the authorities are and what uniforms they wear. Be especially wary of individuals claiming that they need to inspect your belongings.

GO TO THE STATION If a police officer asks to search your purse or wallet, politely comply—at a police station. There's no crime in asking an officer to escort you to a proper station house, so don't be bashful about asking.

300 CHECKLIST Be a Smart Traveler

I don't want to be a buzzkill, but vacations don't mean a holiday from vigilance. Follow these guidelines for happy, crime-free travels.

- ▢ Check with appropriate government agencies for international travel advisories. If a place is deemed unsafe, don't go there.
- ▢ Be aware of the host country's entry requirements prior to travel. For instance, some require a passport be valid at least six months prior to entry. Know customs laws for both entry and reentry.
- ▢ Before your departure, make copies of all important documents and keep them in multiple locations in case of emergency.
- ▢ Have an itinerary and share it with a trusted friend. Set check-in times. And if your itinerary changes, alert him or her immediately.
- ▢ Know the contact information for embassies in any country on your itinerary. Program local emergency numbers into your phone.
- ▢ No matter where you're staying, don't open the hotel door without using the peephole to see who's there—just as you would at home. Don't allow strangers into your room.
- ▢ Don't display your room keys in public—you don't want strangers knowing your room number or even where you're staying.
- ▢ Don't carry large quantities of cash or expensive jewelry, and don't keep all your valuables or currency together in one place. Any valuables you absolutely have to bring along should be stored in the hotel or room safe-deposit box, if possible.
- ▢ Report any suspicious persons or activities to hotel management.
- ▢ If you're traveling off the grid, invest in a trustworthy travel guide.

RICH SAYS
"Carry whatever emergency gear your mode of travel will permit. Always keep escape routes in mind. To minimize the target on your back, leave your bling at home."

301 Blend In for Safety

Tourists are crime targets because they often carry valuables such as passports, credit cards, and lots of cash—and they're easy to spot. While you may not conform completely with the locals, you certainly can apply some cultural camouflage to blend in.

CLOTHES Don't wear things that are easily identifiable with your own culture. For instance, if you're American, avoid wearing fanny packs, baseball caps, tennis shoes, and casual clothing with prominent brand names. Instead, dress a little nicer than you might usually, and wear colors that correspond to those worn by the majority of the host population, like bright colors in the Caribbean and muted tones in London.

FOOD You're visiting for a reason, so don't seek out your usual comfort foods while you're traveling. Unless you have to worry about food-borne illnesses, eat what the locals are eating, and try to use your utensils the way they do. Also avoid asking for common Western condiments, such as ketchup. Go with whatever ones you are given, and eat your food in the order in which it arrives. You'll not only blend in—you'll have a culinary adventure.

HABITS Most locals don't walk around reading a map, so try to figure out where you're going ahead of time. And while you're bound to take pictures in a foreign country, stow your camera in a pocket or bag rather than on a strap around your neck. Keep your voice low to avoid drawing attention to yourself.

302 Hide Money in Your Clothes

To protect your cash while traveling, conceal it on your person in places a mugger won't think of.

GET CREATIVE Money belts and hiding currency inside shoes or bras are old and expected tricks. Leg pouches concealed beneath pants or skirts are better.

HIDE A POCKET Create secret pockets inside your clothing by slitting open the hem or waist seam of your pants or the collar of your shirt. Then slip bills inside.

TRAVEL LIGHT Don't stuff secret hiding places so full that they become obvious.

303 Use the Buddy System

When traveling in unknown or unfriendly territory, there is indeed safety in numbers. The buddy system works great—but only if you have the right buddy. A sound travel companion provides a voice of reason when in doubt. Two heads are often better than one, especially in a foreign country.

Divide up responsibilities. In airport terminals, hotel lobbies, or taxi stands, make sure one person is always with your luggage. If a stranger approaches, only one person should engage, allowing the other to keep an eye out for petty thieves or pickpockets.

304

STEP-BY-STEP

Exit a Tunnel Safely

Getting stuck on the subway is not only a drag—it can also be dangerous, especially if you need to make your own way out of the tunnel.

STEP ONE Avoid the two most dangerous things in a subway tunnel: moving trains and the electricity that keeps them going. Don't walk on the tracks, because a train can come without warning. And stay away from the third rail—which is usually elevated and to the side of the tracks—since it can electrocute you. Instead, walk along the ledge adjacent to the tracks.

STEP TWO Find the emergency exits, which are positioned along the wall and well marked.

STEP THREE Follow the signs up the stairs—you'll likely find a dead-end metal hatch. If you push hard against the iron bar, the hatch will open and you can climb out onto the sidewalk above the subway.

KNOW THE NUMBERS

Mass Transit

13 Number of people killed in the 1995 sarin gas attacks on the Tokyo subway.

201 METRES Plunge of the worst cable-car disaster in history, in Italy in 1976.

4 Number of suicide bombers who carried out the London attacks in 2005, which killed 52 people and injured more than 700.

1 in 94,242 Odds of dying in a bus accident.

10.2 BILLION Number of public transportation trips taken in the United States in 2010.

355 Number of people killed in the United States each year at railway crossings.

13 Number of improvised explosive devices placed on trains in the 2004 Madrid attack.

1 Person killed on the New York subway system by a lunatic wielding a power saw.

305 Stay Safe on Mass Transit

In general, public transit is a good thing: It gets people around fast and cheaply. But its egalitarian appeal can sometimes be a problem, since practically anyone can ride the bus, tram, or subway—and with practically any motive.

CHECK THE SCHEDULE Know when your train or bus is scheduled to come. Arrive close to departure, cutting down on the time you spend lingering around stops or stations (beside people who may be lingering for different reasons). This goes triple for night rides.

AVOID DODGY STOPS Sometimes the closest station isn't the safest one. If it's poorly lit, poorly staffed, or a gathering spot for thugs, walk farther to a safer transit hub. Again, this is very important at night.

SIT UP FRONT The closer you are to the driver, the more likely you are to benefit from his or her protection. Taking a seat in the back will put you out of the driver's line of vision and make you more vulnerable to mischief.

STASH GADGETS Most robberies today involve smartphones or MP3 players. Keep yours out of sight.

306 Survive a Human Stampede

People react differently to panic. Some stand still and make their undies wet (or worse). Others take off running and hollering as if their hair is on fire. If you find yourself in a panicked crowd, you're at risk of getting trampled. So act fast.

FIND SOME PROTECTION Look for something substantial and immovable to hide behind: a large tree, a utility pole, a structural pillar, a wall, or a vehicle. Unless the mob is in full car-rollover-and-burn mode, you might want to try taking refuge inside a vehicle until the masses have passed.

GO WITH THE FLOW If you get trapped inside the stampede, stay on your feet and conserve your energy (don't resist the movement). Keep your arms and hands near your chest so you can create a little space around you. Try to work your way diagonally toward the edge of the crowd. You'll be out of the worst of it and more likely to find a refuge or an escape route.

307

Be Alert to the Risk of Terrorism

You're waiting in the airport security line and you spot an unattended bag, or a person in street clothes ducking into an area marked "Authorized personnel only." Are those danger signs? You bet—and in today's tense times, we all need to watch out for them. Report anything that strikes you as strange to authorities so they can check it out.

GET PARANOID As you enter a space, look for things that don't belong. Such things might include a cake box sitting on a park bench, a car that's been parked outside the mall for three days straight, or someone wearing clothing that's inappropriate for the location or time of year. (Ski masks are fine on the slopes, but creepy anywhere else.)

BEWARE PHOTOGRAPHERS Mostly people you see photographing or videotaping in a train station or airport are just tourists—but sometimes they're terrorists surveying an area so they can later commit an atrocity. Even someone sketching a metro stop may be cause for concern.

WATCH FOR LINGERERS There's a big difference between waiting for a friend and waiting to activate a bomb, though the two activities may look alike. If someone has been hanging out in an area for a long time, he or she may be up to no good—likewise if someone keeps driving or walking by an area.

CHECK THE TIME Most terrorist activity goes down during periods of high traffic. (Sadly, that's to maximize casualties.) It's easy to miss things in all the bustle, but try to keep your eyes wide open during rush hour.

GET THE DETAILS When you're reporting a dubious character or a disconcerting oddity to security personnel or the police, be as specific as you can. Relay what the person involved looked like, how he or she was dressed and behaving, and when and exactly where you spotted them. If a vehicle is involved, note the make, color, and if possible, the license plate number.

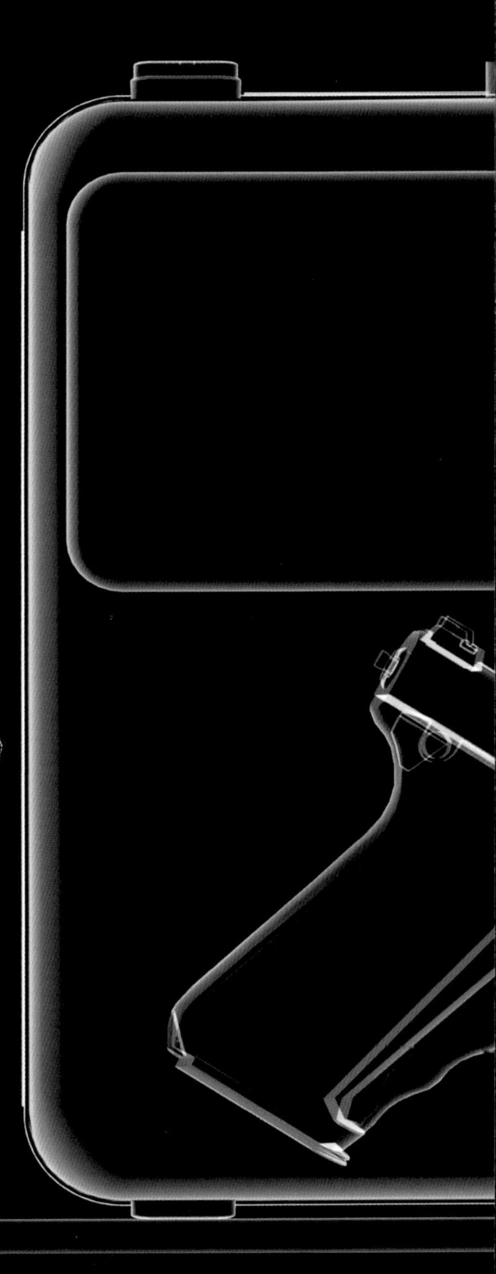

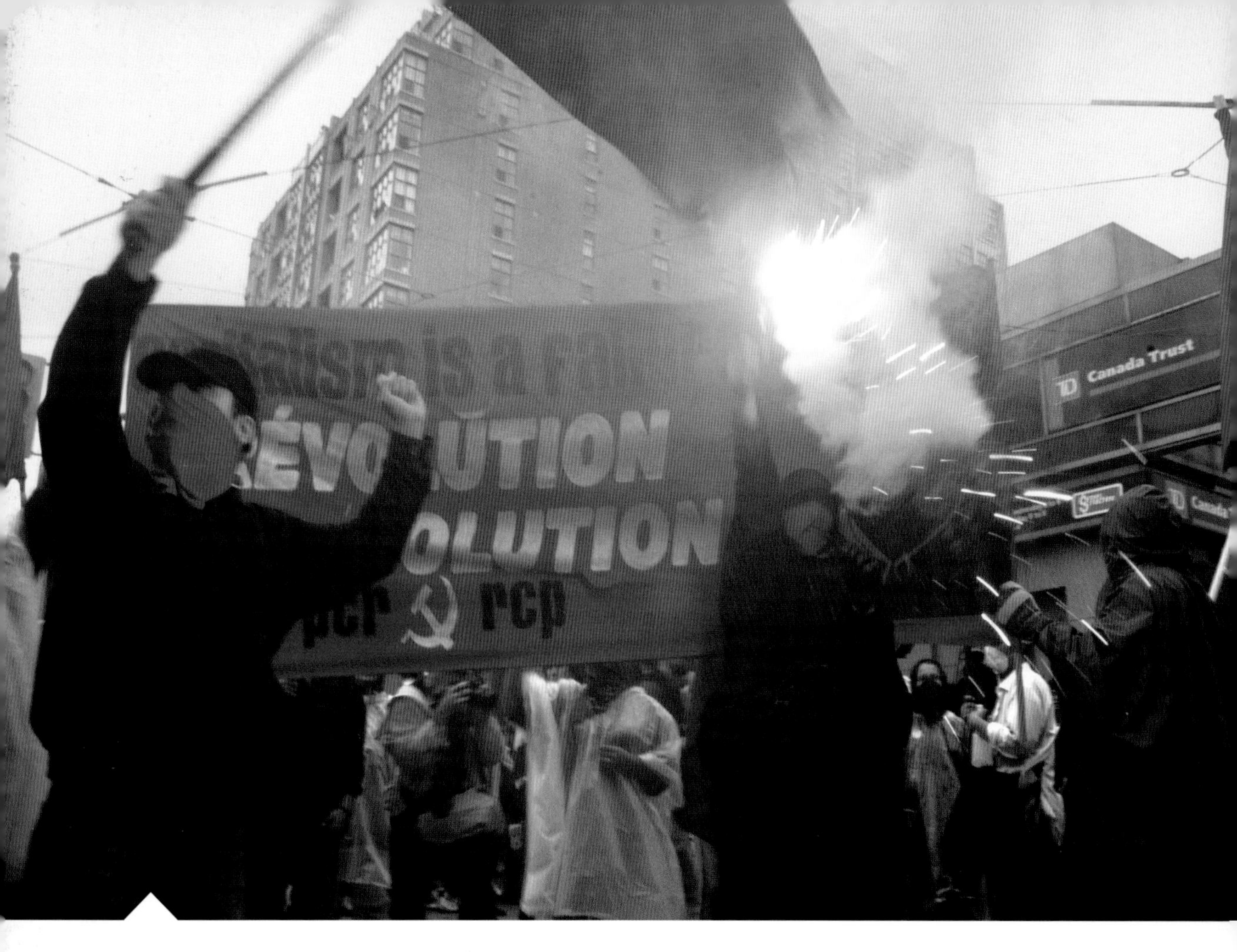

308 Prevail in a Riot

Be it political unrest or violence over a soccer match, rioting is bad news. It doesn't matter if you're home or abroad—it's wise to plan for the possibility of things getting rough. Here are some tips that'll keep you safe even if the crowd turns ugly.

KNOW WHERE YOU ARE Understand the political climate and perils in any region in which you're traveling, and pay attention to the local news every day. Similarly, keep big sporting events on your radar, as fan frenzy mixed with alcohol tends to create volatility—even for nonfans.

GET OUT OF THE CROWD Riots typically occur in streets, parking lots, and town centers. So if trouble is brewing, avoid those hot spots. Find shelter and don't go back out to watch the riot. As the bricks, bottles, rubber bullets, and tear-gas canisters begin to fly, spectators may be injured—either by a rampaging mob or by those trying to restore order.

MOVE OUT If you do find yourself at the hub of it all, try to look inconspicuous and move steadily and deliberately out of the center of activity, staying close to walls to minimize exposure. The more time spent in the center of a riot, the greater the chance for injury. Your best bet is finding a place where you can hole up safely until the danger has ended.

KEEP YOUR COOL Being caught up in an unsettled mob can get you riled up, but don't let yourself be ruled by an adrenaline rush. Think rationally, pursue safety, and act as an individual, not as a member of the crowd. During riots, both authorities and rioters tend to act en masse, so chances are you'll have to rescue yourself instead of relying on others to assist you.

STEER CLEAR OF COPS The police might use riot-control agents like tear gas and pepper spray. Also bear in mind that running toward police, even when you're seeking security, can be seen as threatening.

309 Know the Weapons of a Raging Mob

Suppose the worst happens, and you find yourself in the middle of an unruly riot. As you pick your way out of the center of the mob, it's a good idea to have an understanding of the kinds of crowd-control weapons law enforcement agencies might use—as well as the hazards you might face from rioters.

BATONS Keep your head down and your neck covered as you move low to the ground to get yourself out of the way.

SHIELDS When the police are using their shoulders and shields to shove rioters to the side, don't resist or push back. You can easily lose your balance, putting yourself at risk of being trampled.

CONCUSSION GRENADES These explosives are meant to scare people, and they work! You'll be stunned, so hunker in place and cover your head. Use the mayhem to your advantage by darting through breaks in the crowds to safety.

WATER CANNONS Don't stand up, as you'll easily be knocked off your feet. Instead, hunch down to protect vital organs, and keep your back to the cannon as much as possible.

RUBBER BULLETS They may be less than lethal, but they sure do smart. Crouch in a ball and cover your face with your arms. Don't turn your back to the shooter, as hits to the spine can temporarily paralyze.

ROCKS AND BRICKS Being hit in the back of the head is the biggest threat from the go-to missiles of the angry masses. Duck and cover yourself as you scramble to safety.

BOTTLES A missile that shatters is especially dangerous. If bottles start flying, keep your head low with your hands shielding your eyes. Don't run through broken glass—if you trip and fall, it could cut you up.

MOLOTOV COCKTAILS The worst hazard is burning fuel splashing off pavements and onto you. Run perpendicular to the cocktail's trajectory to evade it.

TEAR-GAS CANISTERS Yes, the cops may have lobbed them in, but the rioters may lob them back, even if they are already discharging their nasty, harmful contents.

310 Deal with Tear Gas

Don't let the movies fool you: Wearing a wet bandanna over your face is not going to protect you from tear gas. This stuff doesn't just affect your breathing—it also coats the skin and irritates the eyes. If you get sprayed, leave the area as quickly as possible, and breathe in short bursts through your nose. Avoid rubbing your skin or eyes, which can cause chemical burns. Once out of the fray, wash the tear gas off and pour milk in your eyes if they're still irritated.

311 Evade IEDs

Civilians have no business in combat zones, but in some countries, it's quite possible that you'll unwittingly wind up in the thick of things. Modern battlefields don't always rely on modern weaponry. In fact, most rebellions rely on low-tech weapons like improvised explosive devices (IEDs).

LOOK FOR TROUBLE If you must travel down a road where IEDs may be hidden, keep a sharp eye out for things that seem out of place. Piles of rubble close to the road's edge could indicate a concealed explosive. Watch for people loitering, since most IEDs require line-of-sight triggering. Don't drive a vehicle that stands out as foreign and, if you can, hire local drivers.

DON'T LINGER Make your way through a suspicious area deliberately yet quickly—and don't stop unless you absolutely must.

312 Escape a Dirty Bomb

Perhaps the scariest terrorist threat of all is the dirty bomb: an explosive device containing radioactive material. Dirty bombs do damage not through their blast, but through the radiation that spreads afterward. Lethality depends on many factors, so authorities will broadcast the risks and let you know if you're within the evacuation zone.

If authorities warn of the presence of radiation, immediately cover your nose and mouth with your hand or a cloth, and take shelter in an undamaged building. Close all windows and doors, and turn off heaters, air conditioners, or any other ventilation systems. If you suspect exposure to radiation, remove your clothing and, if possible, wash it or find something else to wear. Monitor emergency broadcasts for instructions on how and where you should proceed.

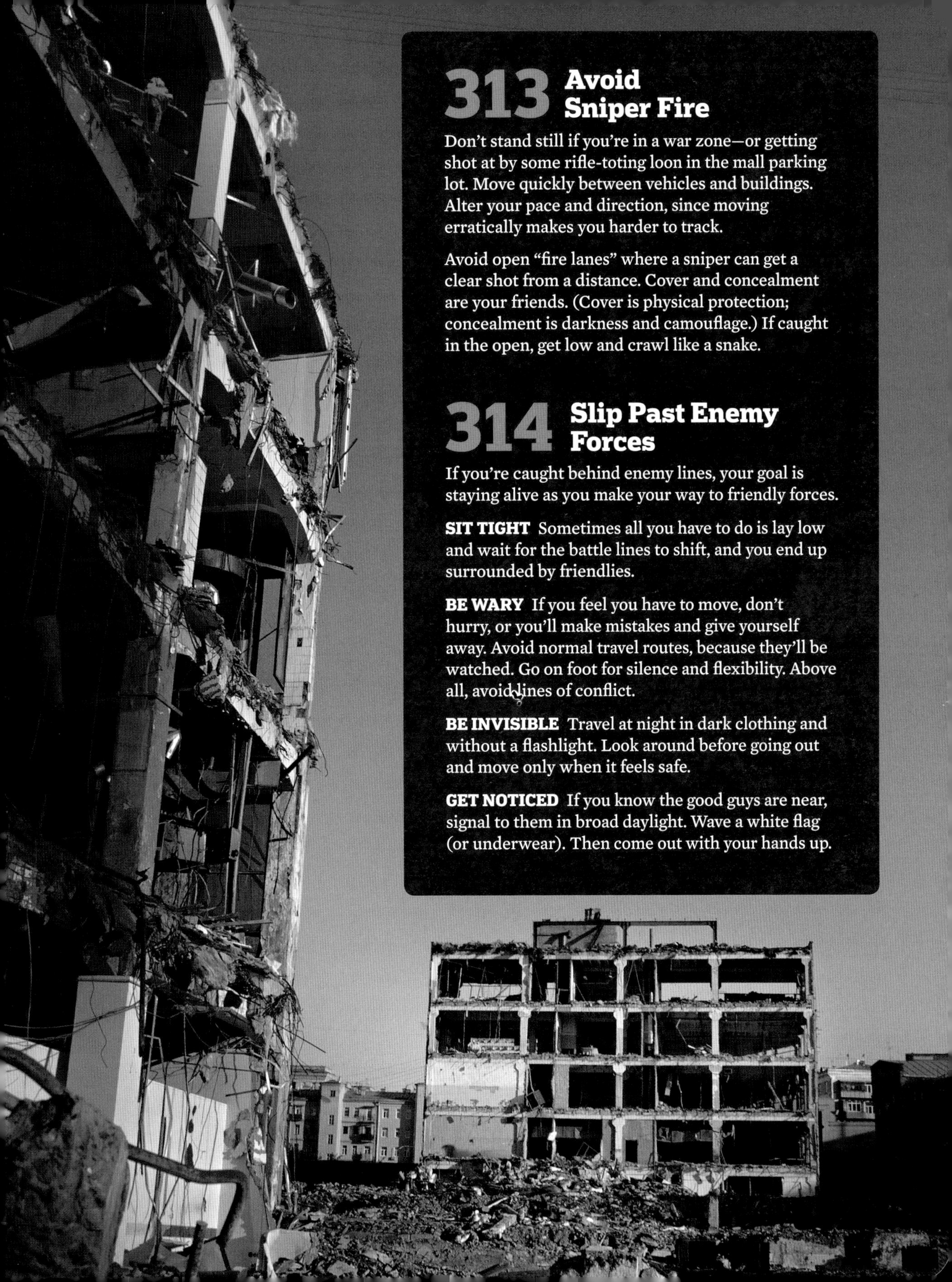

313 Avoid Sniper Fire

Don't stand still if you're in a war zone—or getting shot at by some rifle-toting loon in the mall parking lot. Move quickly between vehicles and buildings. Alter your pace and direction, since moving erratically makes you harder to track.

Avoid open "fire lanes" where a sniper can get a clear shot from a distance. Cover and concealment are your friends. (Cover is physical protection; concealment is darkness and camouflage.) If caught in the open, get low and crawl like a snake.

314 Slip Past Enemy Forces

If you're caught behind enemy lines, your goal is staying alive as you make your way to friendly forces.

SIT TIGHT Sometimes all you have to do is lay low and wait for the battle lines to shift, and you end up surrounded by friendlies.

BE WARY If you feel you have to move, don't hurry, or you'll make mistakes and give yourself away. Avoid normal travel routes, because they'll be watched. Go on foot for silence and flexibility. Above all, avoid lines of conflict.

BE INVISIBLE Travel at night in dark clothing and without a flashlight. Look around before going out and move only when it feels safe.

GET NOTICED If you know the good guys are near, signal to them in broad daylight. Wave a white flag (or underwear). Then come out with your hands up.

315 CASE STUDY: GONE POSTAL
Live Through a Workplace Shooting

Standing outside on his break, Dave Ciarlante saw a coworker, Yvonne Hiller, walk purposefully into the Kraft Foods factory in Philadelphia, Pennsylvania. All he knew about her was her first name and the fact that she worked on the second floor. When he went back inside, a panicked security guard told him that Hiller had a gun. Ciarlante made a decision to help if he could.

As he ran upstairs after Hiller, he had no idea she had already claimed her first victim and was on her way to find others. When he came face to face with her, she told him to get out of her way. He moved aside, saying only that she didn't have to do what she was doing.

After she brushed past him, Ciarlante followed her. He took advantage of any cover he could find, ducking behind pillars or into alcoves and relaying details of Hiller's mission to supervisors and security personnel on his walkie-talkie. That communication allowed Kraft management to clear out employees in Hiller's path.

Hiller was aware that he was following her, and she stopped frequently to confront him. His response was simply to remind her that he wasn't trying to stop her.

That tense standoff was shattered when one of Hiller's terrified coworkers rushed around the corner. Ciarlante yelled for the woman to get away, warning her that Hiller had a gun. Hiller turned and fired at Ciarlante, who turned sidewise and ducked into a doorway, sure he'd been shot. The bullet, however, missed, and Ciarlante was able to continue relaying vital information to authorities. Hiller fired at others, but no one else was killed once Ciarlante chose to step in.

When Hiller locked herself into an office, Ciarlante directed police to the room and the deranged woman was taken into custody. Given the enormous size of the plant, Ciarlante's courage, knowledge of the factory layout, and use of his trusty walkie-talkie saved lives and helped law-enforcement officials end the rampage.

POST ASSESSMENT
Gone Postal

When Dave Ciarlante saw an armed coworker enter his workplace, he chose to put himself at risk to save others. But by radioing intel to his supervisors and security personnel, he helped dozens of workers make their way to safety. Here's how his survival know-how measures up.

Ciarlante knew his coworkers. His knowledge of Yvonne Hiller and of her workstation location tipped him off to where she was headed.

When Hiller confronted him, he moved out of her way. Instead of trying to overpower her, he shielded his face with his arms, and told her she didn't have to carry out her plan.

When the shooter passed by, Ciarlante understood that she was not firing indiscriminately: She was looking for specific individuals. So he opted to follow her.

He didn't confront the shooter, instead shadowing her from a safe distance.

He used his walkie-talkie to relay Hiller's position to security guards and police officials, allowing them to warn other workers of the danger.

He warned any coworkers he saw about the situation, gave them instructions on where to go, and continued to follow Hiller.

When she turned her gun on him, he turned away quickly. The distance between the two—and the fact that he turned to the side and ducked into a doorway—made her miss her shot.

When police arrived, Ciarlante knew which office the shooter had hidden in after her rampage. He quickly identified the location for the officers, saving vital time that otherwise would have been spent searching the enormous complex—and possibly allowing Hiller to escape.

Despite the fact that he was unarmed, Ciarlante chose to follow someone that he knew was homicidal and packing a gun. That seldom turns out well, and I can't recommend it.

316 Be Gun Smart and Safe

With our longstanding history of hunting and outdoor sports, guns have been an integral part of Canadian culture since before we were a nation (and, until the 1870s, the government encouraged citizens to be trained in the use of firearms in case of an invasion from the U.S.).

While the odds of jackbooted thugs storming across the border from Michigan seem rather low these days, that doesn't mean that law-abiding folks don't still think about self-defence.

In general, that means considering whether your target-shooting or hunting guns would be useful in a zombie apocalypse (or other serious survival situation), rather than arming up with the latest tactical firearms.

If you want to buy a handgun in Canada the only two reasons normally allowed are collecting and target shooting. There actually are provisions for self-defence and concealed carry in Canadian law but only about two dozen permits are ever valid in any given year. Normally only Crown prosecutors, judges, or cops get them.

There are also permits issued for animal protection to prospectors, timber cruisers and people whose profession takes them outdoors in bear country. Hunters or hikers never get them. And trappers are only allowed .22s for dispatching animals caught in their traps, nothing for protection.

However, it's not illegal to use a handgun for defence even if you own it for target shooting. Just don't be stupid about it.

ARs are similarly restricted. They must be registered with the RCMP and can be fired only at designated ranges.

That means that when stocking your gun safe, whether for hunting, target shooting, or insurance against the fall of civilization, you'll want to look to a few basic rifles and shotguns. The models listed on the facing page are a good place to start.

LONG GUNS

- ☐ A .308 (7.62 x 51mm) rifle with 3-to-9-power variable scope is mainly used for hunting, especially targeting large game.
- ☐ A great option for hunting small game, a .22 or .223 rifle won't destroy the meat or pelt.
- ☐ A 12-gauge shotgun provides versatility for taking down large game, such as deer, and smaller targets, such as geese.
- ☐ A 20-gauge shotgun is great for small-game hunting in thick brush or branches that might deflect a rifle bullet.
- ☐ A combination gun has a rifle barrel on top and a shotgun barrel on the bottom, giving the benefits of both a small-game rifle round and a shotshell capable of knocking down small game and fowl.

317

Clean a Firearm

Start by removing any ammunition from the gun. Soak a rag with a gun-specific solvent, then run it down the inside of the gun's barrel, or bore. Allow three to five minutes for the solvent to loosen deposits. Next, run a solvent-soaked brush down the barrel, working it back and forth. Follow with dry patches until they come out clean. To finish, moisten a patch with three or four drops of gun oil and run it down the barrel.

318 Lock Up Your Weapons

Nothing's more dangerous than a gun that can fall into the wrong hands. The most secure method for storing guns and ammunition is to use a locked gun safe. Gun safes are too heavy to carry off, and most thieves won't take the time to try breaking into them. For extra security, all safes need a combination lock.

Also, consider locking your firearm in a small safe mounted to your bed frame, which will give you immediate access in an emergency. A bed safe can hold a handgun, a tactical flashlight, and ammunition, so it's small enough to go unnoticed.

319 Clear a Jam

When you're firing a semiautomatic weapon, sometimes a spent cartridge jams in the chamber without fully ejecting. To clear the jam, make sure the muzzle is pointed in a safe direction, then smack the bottom of the magazine to ensure it's properly seated. Pull the slide back and flip the gun smartly to the side to help the cartridge fall out, then let the slide slam forward to chamber the next round.

Set your sight and fire.

Angle your body toward the target.

Place one foot forward.

320 Shoot with the Proper Stance

If you find yourself in a situation where you need to use a handgun, it's important to fire from a good stance.

STAND LIKE A FIGHTER Stand sideways with your shoulder pointed toward your target. Move one foot slightly forward and lean toward your aim point.

GET A GRIP For extra stability, use a two-handed grip, wrapping your weaker hand over your stronger one. Grip the handle firmly but not as if you're trying to choke it, leaving your trigger finger relaxed. Position your trigger finger so that the crease of the first joint makes contact with the trigger.

TAKE AIM AND FIRE Line up the front and rear sights with the target, then squeeze the trigger smoothly (rather than jerking it). The instant of discharge should be unanticipated, keeping your shot true to the target.

321

STEP-BY-STEP

Treat a Powder Burn

If you've discharged a weapon improperly by holding it too close to your body, or if you've been standing too close to a shooter, you could find yourself with a nasty powder burn. Here's what to do.

STEP ONE Start by flushing the burn with cool water or, better yet, cool saline solution, like what you would use for contact lenses.

STEP TWO To prevent infection, lightly cover the injury with a nonadhesive dressing and get to a doctor. Stitches or even grafting might be required.

STEP THREE If you can't immediately get to a doctor, at least apply some aloe vera gel, for crying out loud.

322 Deal with a Gunshot Wound

Gunshot wounds come in all levels of severity. Unless you're a doctor (and no, it doesn't count if you play one on TV), this is not the time to try your hand at surgery. Get help—but if you can't get it soon, you might have to take some steps.

If the bullet has passed through the gunshot victim, your job is to plug the holes to stop the bleeding and stabilize him or her. If the bullet is still in the body, leave it alone. If you're dealing with a shotgun injury, there will be numerous individual wounds to treat. There is really nothing to be gained by plucking out the shot, since disturbing the projectiles might cause more-serious bleeding or other damage. And if your tools aren't sterile, you might inadvertently introduce infection. So keep it simple: Stop the bleeding, dress the wound, and leave it to the doctors to remove the bullets and shot.

323

STEP-BY-STEP

Help Someone Who Has Been Impaled

One of your buddies got himself shot with an arrow or stuck with a spear. Now you're dealing with a victim who has been impaled by a sharp object. This sucks for you—but bear in mind that it's even worse for him.

STEP ONE Do not try to remove the sharp object. You could end up with a sucking chest wound or rapid bleeding out, in addition to internal tissue damage. The best you can do is try to stabilize the object so that it doesn't move while the victim is transported.

STEP TWO If the impaling object is a long arrow or spear, carefully cut the length to make it easier to move the victim, leaving a bit protruding.

STEP THREE Pack the wound to stop the bleeding, then call an ambulance or drive the victim to an emergency room.

324 Silence Your Gun

The sound of gunfire can make you a target in a dangerous situation. If you want to cut those risks, make a quick and easy silencer and flash suppressor from an empty 2-litre soda bottle and a newspaper.

You'll want to start by cutting a hole in the bottom of the bottle that's about twice the diameter of the neck. Next, fit the bottle over the barrel of your rifle and secure it with electrical tape. Gather several sheets of newspaper and roll them up, then stuff the bottle with them. When you can't fit any more paper into the bottle, your sound and flash suppressor is ready to go.

325 Modify Your Shotgun

Note—this is totally illegal in Canada and most places around the world. It's the kind of thing you do in a drop-dead survival situation where your life is more important than the law. Why do it at all? You might choose to resize a shotgun to fit a specific purpose (if, for instance, you have a small space to defend where a longer gun would be more difficult to maneuver). Or you might saw off a shotgun so that a smaller person can wield it without discomfort. Sawing off the damaged barrel of a gun might even make that weapon work again. (Just be aware that the lighter weight means a heavier recoil.)

Amputate the barrel with a hacksaw or other suitable blade. Be sure to clean up the cut with a file to make sure you haven't left the barrel at a weird angle and that there are no splinters or shards sticking up into the barrel. It's also a good idea to smooth away any imperfections in the cut surface with an emery cloth. Clean often to prevent corrosion.

326 STEP-BY-STEP Make the Most of a Shotgun Shell

Sometimes what's inside a shotgun shell might be more useful to you than the shell as a whole. There's wadding inside that you can use as tinder. There's the shot, which you can melt down and form into another type of ammunition (shot is easier to work with than a slug, mind you). And, of course, there's gunpowder, which you can use to reload other shells—and it can also be useful in starting a fire.

STEP ONE Hold the shell by the brass end and use a knife to cut through the crimped end. Or pry the shell open with needle-nose pliers.

STEP TWO Once the crimp is open, turn the shell over and empty out the shot.

STEP THREE Use your fingertips or a pair of needle-nose pliers to pull out the wadding.

STEP FOUR Turn the shell over again and dump out the gunpowder.

327 STEP-BY-STEP Shoot a Crossbow

The crossbow is a medieval weapon that remains useful today. It has several advantages over firearms, two of which are stealth (it's much quieter than a gun) and reusable ammo (you can't fire a bullet more than once). Here's how to use one:

STEP ONE Place the crossbow stirrup on the ground and step on it.

STEP TWO Using steady tension, draw the bowstring back to its cocking mechanism. When it's secure, you'll hear a click.

STEP THREE Place your arrow into the barrel and bring the crossbow up to aim. Hold it as you would a rifle, and use the bow's mechanical sights to find your target. The optimum distance is 20 to 30 yards (18–27 m) away.

STEP FOUR Pull the trigger back smoothly to release the arrow. The crossbow will recoil, so brace yourself.

328 STEP-BY-STEP Sharpen a Knife

Some lessons learned in the kitchen can also prove useful in self-defense. And when it comes to survival, a sharp knife is crucial, so sharpen your knives regularly.

STEP ONE Use sharpening stones ranging from 300 to 1,200 grit. The lower the number, the coarser the stone and the rougher the finished edge. Applying a little knife lubricant to the stone will help the process.

STEP TWO Place the blade edge on the stone at a 45-degree angle, and position the pad of your thumb as a spacer under the blade's spine, opposite the cutting edge.

STEP THREE Move the length of the blade across the stone as if you're trying to shave a thin piece off it.

STEP FOUR Turn the blade over and repeat on the other edge, holding the knife at a 45-degree angle.

329 Pick Your Blade

In choosing the right knife for the task at hand, you first need to decide between fixed-blade and folding-blade knives. A folding blade collapses into the handle for easier carrying, while a fixed blade requires a sheath.

When deciding on a blade, look at two key areas: the knife point and the shape of the cutting edge. One of the most common types is the clip-point knife; the spine of the blade curves into a concave tip, making it ideal for piercing as well as cutting.

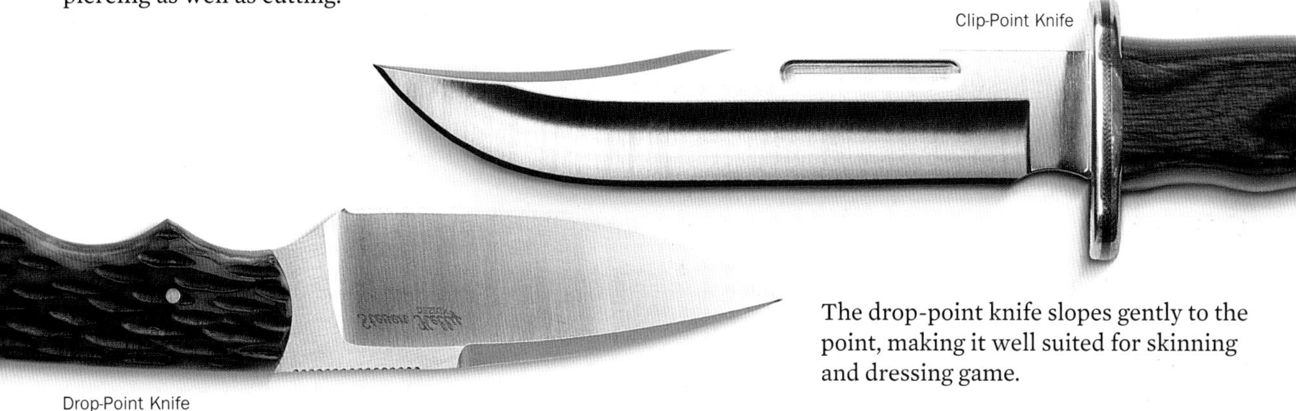

Clip-Point Knife

Drop-Point Knife

The drop-point knife slopes gently to the point, making it well suited for skinning and dressing game.

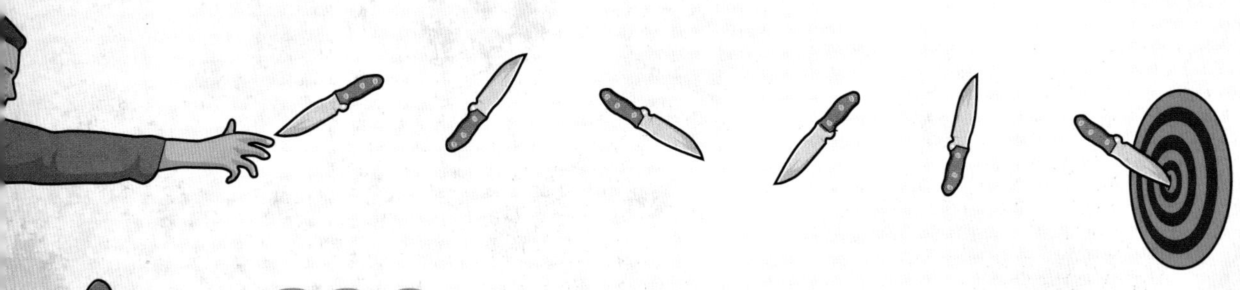

330 Throw a Knife

If you're being threatened and you have a knife, throwing it keeps a healthy distance between yourself and your attacker; otherwise, you'll have to get cozy and fight hand to hand. But you'd better be damned good at slinging that blade, because if you're not, all you've done is irritate—and arm—your assailant. Practice is imperative.

Grasp the knife by the unsharpened spine of the blade. Make sure you maintain a rigid wrist during the throw, as a floppy wrist results in uncontrolled rotation of the blade. Draw back the knife as your body rocks back slightly and your throwing arm reaches the cocked position. Then lunge forward and release the knife as if you were pitching a baseball. Learn to adjust your distance to accommodate the rotation speed so that the point penetrates the target.

Like I said, practice is key. Lots of practice.

331 STEP-BY-STEP Build a Better Bola

A bola (Spanish for *ball*) is a throwing weapon with three weights tied to the ends of three ropes. These ropes are then tied together on the unweighted end, forming a handle that allows you to (hopefully with some skill) throw the bola at an animal's—or a bad guy's—legs, binding and tripping in one motion. Here's a cheap and easy approach to making this effective short-range weapon.

STEP ONE Start with three tennis balls. Using a pocket knife or razor blade, cut two X-shaped holes on opposite sides of the ball.

STEP TWO Run the ends of a 1-to-1.25-metre section of rope through both holes, tying an overhand knot at the exit point to keep the ball from falling off. (To guide your rope through the holes, try taping it to a straightened clothes hanger.)

STEP THREE Shove anything weighted into the hole. You can try using rocks, sand, or even spare coins.

STEP FOUR Overhand knot the other end of the rope, so that the ball is anchored at the rope's very end. Then wrap each ball in duct tape to keep the whole strand together.

STEP FIVE Knot the three unweighted ends together, and wrap in twine or more duct tape. To use your bola, just twirl it over your head and throw it as you would a lasso. After some practice, you'll be able to trip any bad guy that's dim-witted enough to come your way.

332 Make a Shank

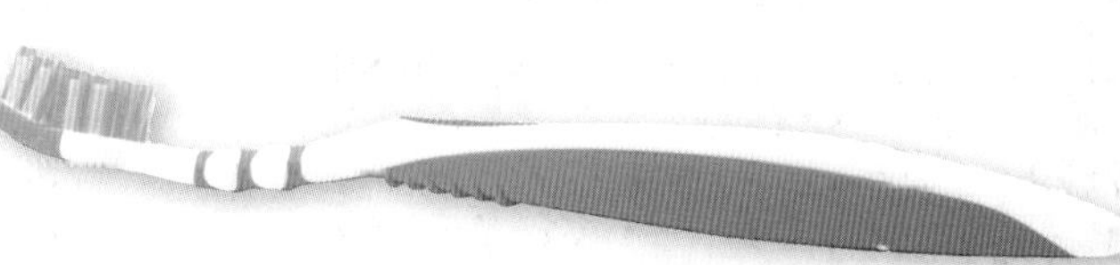

You know the terms *shank* and *shiv* from prison movies. But until now, you probably didn't know how to make these do-it-yourself knives.

Shiv is slang for *knife*, and it includes anything that's already sharp or has a cutting edge, such as a razor blade. An old saw or a lawn mower blade makes for a perfect shiv. If it's dull, sharpen it against concrete, or use a metal file if you have one handy.

If you don't have a shiv at the ready, make yourself a shank, which repurposes a mundane item as an edged or pointed weapon. A toothbrush can be filed to a point, and various plastics can be melted down into a solid weapon. A crude shank can even be made by folding a tin can lid in half. To make a handle, wrap a cord or cloth strip around the shank's end.

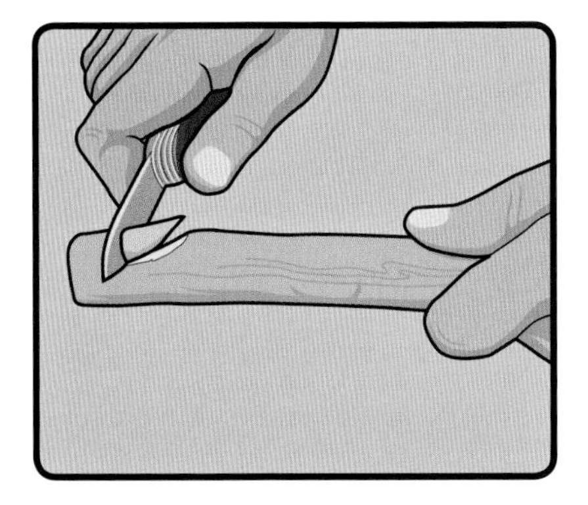

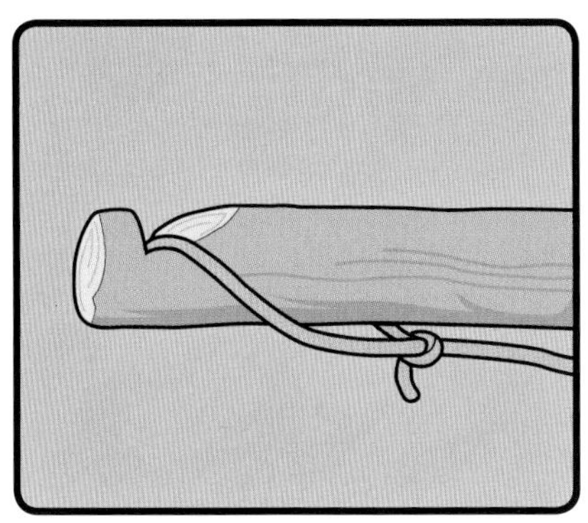

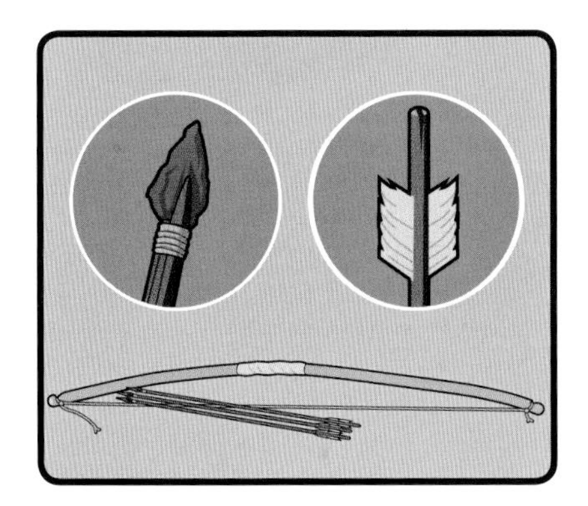

RICH SAYS
"Learn to view everything as a potential weapon, right down to the toothpick on your dinner table. I'm serious."

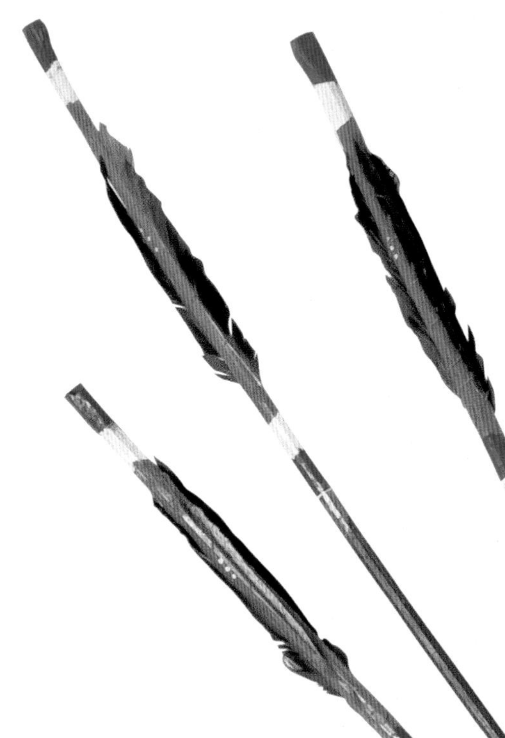

333 STEP-BY-STEP
Make a Bow and Some Arrows

The bow and arrow was once the weapon of choice, and in a survival situation it will still serve you well. You'll need a piece of dry, dead wood about 1 yard (1 m) in length and free of knots or branches. The ideal wood should be fairly flexible, so choose mulberry or juniper, if possible. You'll also need some sort of material to use as a bowstring. This string can be hemp, rawhide, sinew, or rope. It's the wood that gives the bow its power, not the string.

STEP ONE Cut notches at the top and bottom of the bow to hold your bowstring.

STEP TWO Tie off the ends of the rope in the notches. Your bow should have a slight bend to prevent it from snapping all the way back into a relaxed position.

STEP THREE For arrow shafts, select thin, straight rods of dry wood about half the length of the bow. Use any pointed object as an arrowhead.

STEP FOUR Use feathers for fletchings to balance the arrow in flight. Cut the feather down its center, then glue it (if possible) to the shaft, or tie it in place with twine or light string.

Index

C-GSFJ

U

V

W

About Rich Johnson

When it comes to survival, Rich Johnson has decades of experience. In the military, he was a paratrooper and demolition sergeant for the US Army Special Forces. In civilian life, he served as a Coast Guard Auxiliary instructor, and was an EMT and a firefighter for a volunteer fire and ambulance department. In his off hours, he has excelled as an advanced SCUBA diver, a sailor, and a backcountry skier. He specializes in urban survival, emergency preparedness, and primitive living techniques, and spent a year surviving in the desert wilderness with his wife and small children—part of which involved living in a cave and eating bugs (or anything else that moved). He's written extensively on survival topics for *Outdoor Life* and is the author of *Rich Johnson's Guide to Wilderness Survival*.

About *Outdoor Life*

Since it was founded in 1898, *Outdoor Life* magazine has provided survival tips, wilderness skills, gear reports, and other essential information for hands-on outdoor enthusiasts. Each issue delivers the best advice to nearly 1 million outdoorsmen. And with the recent launch of its survival-themed Web site, disaster preparedness and urban skills are now also covered in depth.

Disclaimer

Credits

Photography courtesy of *Shutterstock Images* except where otherwise noted: *Alamy:* 81, 179 *arindambanerjee / Shutterstock.com:* 230 *Atomazul / Shutterstock.com:* 125 *Back Country Access:* 188 *Eddie Berman:* 31 *Brad Fenson:* 50-51, 189 (coins), 224, 251, 253, 256 *Getty Images:* 71, 79 *iStock:* 69 (poison oak), 115, 117, 123, 141, 154, 202, 222, 233, 248, 249 *Alexander Ivanov:* 329 *Knives R Us:* 282 *Richard A. McGuirk / Shutterstock.com:* 157 (parachute) *Dan Saelinger:* 316 (.308 rifle, 12-gauge shotgun, 20-gauge shotgun, AR rifle) *Taurus US:* 316 (.410/.45 pistol) *Windigo Images:* 317, 318

Illustrations courtesy of *Conor Buckley:* 29, 33, 37, 53, 54, 57, 59, 64, 100, 103, 105, 111, 133, 140, 168, 169, 170, 172, 207, 212, 227, 242, 269 (icons) *Hayden Foell:* 13, 14, 35, 56, 58, 78, 149, 217, 228, 290, 320, 330, 333 *Joshua Kemble:* 11, 15, 16 *Raymond Larrett:* 62, 151 *Liberum Donum:* Back cover, When Grizzlies Attack, 48, Trapped in a Canyon, 87, 104, 130, 145, 162, Tsunami Race, 185, 186, Panic in the Air, 235, 245, 251, Home Invasion, One Mean Machete, 331 *William Mack:* icons unless otherwise noted *Christine Meighan:* 112 *Paula Rogers:* 224, 258, 271 *Shutterstock Images:* 26 (map), 169 (map), 214, 255, 276, 293 (icons) *Jamie Spinello:* 61 *Bryon Thompson:* 25, 28, 52, 83, 101 *Wil Tirion:* 113 *Lauren Towner:* 65, 66, 96, 226 *Gabhor Utomo:* 144, 260

Acknowledgments

Weldon Owen would like to thank Jacqueline Aaron, Maria Behan, Ian Cannon, Bridget Fitzgerald, Marianna Monaco, Gail Nelson-Bonebrake, and Mary Zhang for their editorial expertise and assistance and Meghan Hildebrand and Daniel Triassi for their design assistance.

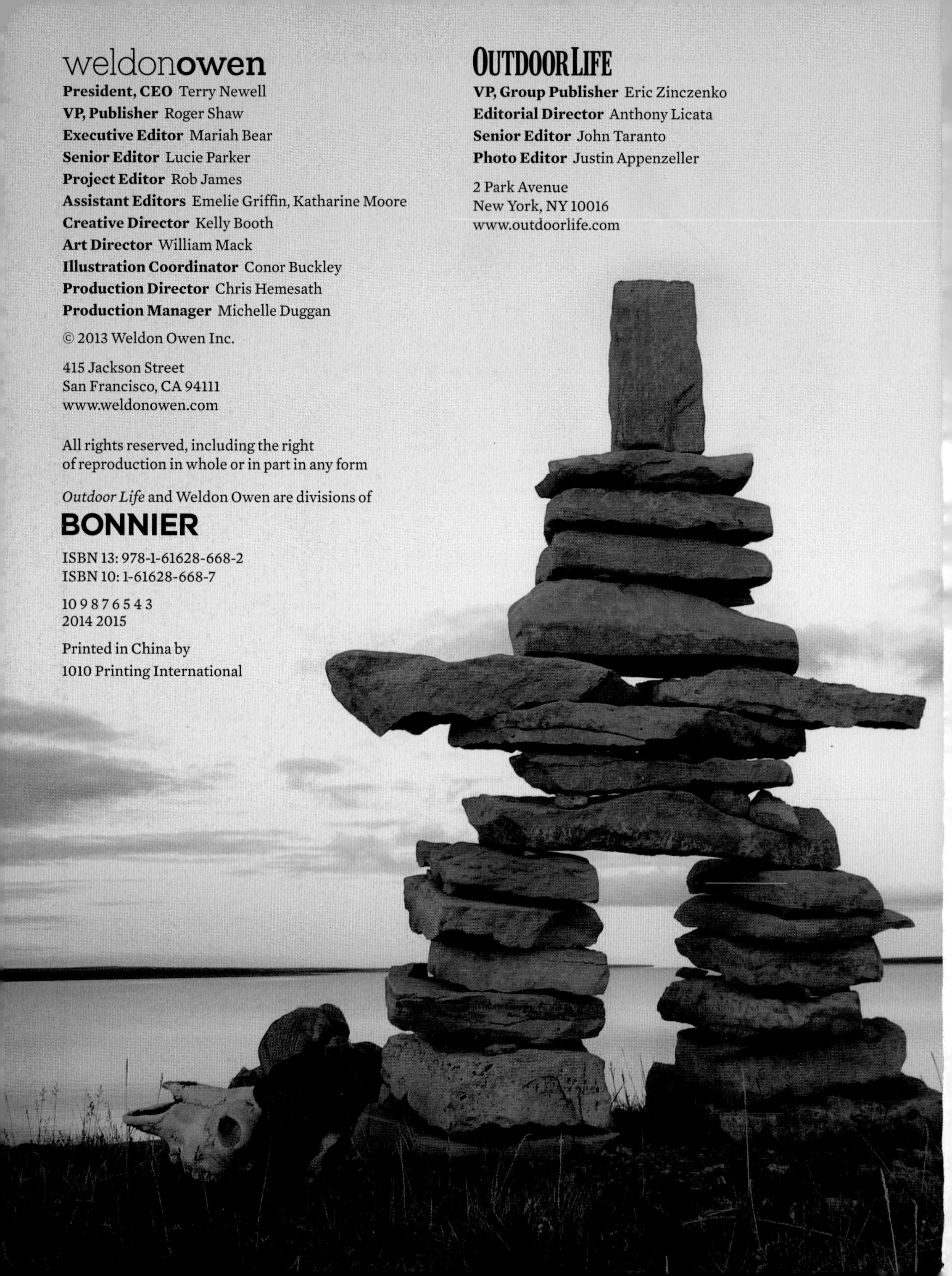

weldonowen

President, CEO Terry Newell
VP, Publisher Roger Shaw
Executive Editor Mariah Bear
Senior Editor Lucie Parker
Project Editor Rob James
Assistant Editors Emelie Griffin, Katharine Moore
Creative Director Kelly Booth
Art Director William Mack
Illustration Coordinator Conor Buckley
Production Director Chris Hemesath
Production Manager Michelle Duggan

415 Jackson Street
San Francisco, CA 94111
www.weldonowen.com

Outdoor Life and Weldon Owen are divisions of

BONNIER

ISBN 13: 978-1-61628-668-2
ISBN 10: 1-61628-668-7

10 9 8 7 6 5 4 3
2014 2015

Printed in China by
1010 Printing International

OUTDOOR LIFE

VP, Group Publisher Eric Zinczenko
Editorial Director Anthony Licata
Senior Editor John Taranto
Photo Editor Justin Appenzeller

2 Park Avenue
New York, NY 10016
www.outdoorlife.com